A Border Dispute

A Border Dispute

The Place of Logic in Psychology

John Macnamara

A Bradford Book
The MIT Press
Cambridge, Massachusetts
London, England

This book was set in Palatino by The MIT Press Computergraphics Department and printed and bound by Halliday Lithograph in the United States of America.

Library of Congress Cataloging-in-Publication Data

Macnamara, John.
  A border dispute.

  "A Bradford book"
  Bibliography: p.
  Includes index.
  1. Psychology—Philosophy. 2. Logic.
BF44.M32   1986   153   86-58
ISBN 0-262-13216-8

563 71784

For Joyce

Contents

Preface

What is logic to psychologists? A quarry from which to wrest hypotheses for experiments or an essential ingredient in the theory of the mind? In this century psychologists have mostly adopted the quarry view, whereas in the last century the essential-ingredient one held sway. Why the change in attitude, and was it well motivated? Is it simply that logic was taken as the preserve of philosophers and in the divorce between philosophy and psychology it went to philosophy? Or is there something deep-rootedly wrong about the nineteenth-century view of logic? If so, how do we go about describing the mind in its logical aspects? It seems possible for us a century after the divorce to survey the scene calmly and to try to understand why things went the way they did. It also seems reasonable to ask what the relation between logic and psychology ought to be.

I first began to reflect on this topic eighteen years ago in a conversation with Noam Chomsky. It seemed to me that something similar to his distinction between competence and performance in linguistics might be applied in the area of human reasoning. Logic, as formulated by logicians, I felt, might be taken to serve the function of competence, and logical aberrations might be attributed to performance factors. It soon became evident that for the purposes of everyday reasoning, with which psychology is most concerned, competence had to be confined to a basic logic, simple enough to be related to everyday thought yet rich enough to support the towering logical structures that abound today. It also became evident that we could learn more about basic logic through the study of natural-language expressions, rather than of formal-language ones and through the study of kinds rather than of sets.

Continued reflection made the idea more attractive, but it also revealed a number of problems. Among the attractions, at least for me, was that the idea made room in psychology for ideals, which seemed not to exist in the psychology that I learned in Edinburgh in the 1950s. Among the difficulties was the danger that I would be forced into making logic a subbranch of psychology. (After all, Chomsky has presented linguistics as a subbranch of psychology.) That position, known as *psychologism*, was branded as rank heresy by Frege—and for good reason, as his *Grundlagen* made abundantly clear. How could I posit logic as psychological competence and not fall into psychologism? First, I had to understand psychologism by studying its principal proponents and then, through a study of its antagonists, gain a clear grasp of the reasons for its rejection. Only then did I feel confident in tackling my problem, but when I did, the solution seemed to fall into my hands. I saw that even if we take the most extreme antipsychologistic position, even if we take the Platonist view that logical structures exist outside the mind in a realm beyond time and space, these structures must be realized in our minds somehow if we are to apply them in our thinking.

The first chapter of the book tells of all this. I present psychologism mainly through the wonderfully clear writings of John Stuart Mill and the less clear but more rewarding ones of Immanuel Kant. The rejection I present through the writings of Frege and the even more trenchant ones of Edmund Husserl, whom Frege converted from psychologism. In chapter 2 I work out the general thesis that logic ideally presents a competence theory for part of human reasoning. The aim is to lay down general principles that explain the mind in its logical aspect, including its aspiration to logical soundness. I also attempt to explain how logical intuition is grounded in properties of the mind. It is important to realize that the principles presented are psychological; they are not meant to justify the claims of logic.

Broad theses may be of the greatest importance for psychology, but they are unlikely to receive the attention of psychologists unless their import is shown in detail. Chapters 3 through 8 are worked examples. Each chapter illustrates the impact of the general thesis on a psychological problem. These chapters betray my background in developmental psychology, particularly in child language. My interest in child language has always been mainly for the light it throws on cognition. Child language is not, as many suppose, a specialty in cognition. It embraces all of cognition, but from the standpoint of the developing mind. Each of the main problems in the philosophy of science has its reflex in the study of child language. The problems I select to illustrate the relevance of logic to psychology are all in the semantics of child language: the learning of proper names, personal pronouns, sortals (common nouns), quantifiers, and the truth-functional connectives.

In these worked examples I press the theory hard. The problem in each is threefold: (1) to specify the logic of the element in question, (2) to specify the logical resources required to learn the element, and (3) to account for the availability of those resources to children and for their ability to deploy them. In these chapters I have preferred precision and completeness to caution. They should be read with that understanding.

Chapter 9 is a portmanteau in which I place a number of technical problems that would have encumbered the main part of the text. Readers who are not worried about these problems may well ignore them— until they begin to pinch.

In the last chapter I attempt to describe the type of science that can be hoped for in the area of cognitive psychology by those who accept the thesis of the book.

Acknowledgments

I owe a special debt to two dear friends. Some years ago I simply helped myself to an incomparable tutor in the person of Anil Gupta, attending his classes, submitting my papers to him, and discussing my projects with him. He read the first and third versions of the manuscript (there were at least three and a half) and did his utmost to save me. I have also been fortunate in having Steve Davis as friend and advisor. It cost him two readings of the manuscript and sheaves of notes, each pulling me off a reef or a sandbar. It is a joy to acknowledge their assistance.

Other friends who read and commented on an entire version were Melissa Bowerman, Peter Denny, Ray Jackendoff, Michael Makkai, Ray McCall, and Nini Warman (with an assist from her husband Nat). Their backgrounds are varied, but they share a deep interest in the topic of this book and I owe them much for their encouragement and advice.

While I was working on the book, many people asked me to give talks on my ideas, thus affording me opportunities to discuss them in ways that invariably helped. Rich Thomason had me give my first talk on the general topic, a joint talk to the Linguistics Department and the Logic Colloquium of the University of Pittsburgh, where I had fruitful discussions with Thomason himself and with Nuel Belnap. Peter Bryant twice had me address groups in Oxford, enabling me to have profitable discussions with L. Jonathan Cohen and Dan Isaacson as well as with Bryant himself. At MIT I gave a talk which was attended by Susan Carey, Jerry Fodor, Sylvan Bromberger, Steve Pinker, and Lance Rips—all of whom provided me with valuable comments, criticism, and advice. The following also had me address groups at their universities: George Madaus at Boston College; Ray Jackendoff at Brandeis; Keith Humphrey at Lethbridge, Alberta; Catherine Snow at Harvard; Brian Doan and Peter Jusczyk at Dalhousie; Michael Morgan at University College, London; Margaret Donaldson at Edinburgh University (a special joy since it is my alma mater); Elaine Neuman at Concordia; Patrick Masterson at University College, Dublin; John Morton at the MRC Cognitive

Development Unit, London; Nollaigh Byrne at the Family Psychiatry Centre of the Mater Misericordiae Hospital, Dublin; and Merrill Swain at the Ontario Institute for Studies in Education, University of Toronto. I am indebted to them all.

A special occasion for me was when, at the invitation of my friend Ida Kurcz, I read a paper on logic and psychology in Warsaw at the International Conference on Cognition and Language, organized by the University of Warsaw and the Polish Academy of Sciences, June 1984. The chairman when I spoke was Tadeusz Tomaszewski, who was a student of Kazimierz Twardowski, to whom the Polish school of logic owes its existence. Apart from the honor thus conferred on me, I had a chance to discuss my work with many Polish friends and also with Jim Jenkins, Norman Freeman, and Sam Glucksberg, who, like myself, were participants at the conference. In May 1985, at the invitation of Svenka Savić, I read at the Interuniversity in Dubrovnik three papers drawn from this book. The occasion was a conference entitled "Between Pragmatics and Semantics." I also had the honor of reading papers on logic and psychology to the Canadian Philosophical Association and the British Psychological Society, both in 1985.

To McGill University I owe more than to any other institution. The first complete draft of the book was completed while I was on sabbatical (1982–1983), with partial support in the form of a Leave Fellowship from the Social Sciences and Humanities Research Council of Canada. (The draft was mostly written while I was a guest of the psychology departments of MIT and Oxford, and I am deeply grateful to those departments for their hospitality.) The McGill Graduate Faculty gave me a grant to visit Anil Gupta in Chicago to discuss the book with him in January 1984. The McGill Graduate Faculty also gave me a further grant to have the manuscript set on a word processor. I have been a guest lecturer on the topic of this book for the McGill Mathematics Department (on the invitation of Jim Lambek), the McGill Electrical Engineering Department (on the invitation of Steve Zucker), and the McGill Psychology Department (on the invitation of David Ostry). My secretary at McGill, Susan Gregus, has patiently and cheerfully performed the innumerable corrections and produced the whole manuscript. I have lectured to several McGill undergraduate classes on the materials of the book and benefited from the discussions. Altogether, McGill has been generous in its support. I am deeply grateful to it and to the many persons at it who have helped me in so many ways.

To many individuals who helped me with particular problems I am also grateful: David Thompson (the problem of representation and that of the identity of kinds), Mike Hallett (quantum logic), Michel Seymour (reference), Zenon Pylyshyn (competence theory), Bill Demopoulos (proper names and quantum logic), Daniel Saumier (figures), and Bill Masicotte (Husserl). Michael Dummett allowed me to read to him my remarks on Frege and, fortunately, as I had beggged him, commented on them as if I were an undergraduate. One of my graduate students, Yuriko Oshima-Takane, was particularly helpful on the chapters on self-reference and proper names. Her own Ph.D. thesis on the learning of personal pronouns was completed this year, and I borrow heavily from it. I also borrow heavily from the Ph.D. thesis of a former student, Nancy Wargny, on the learning of proper names and sortals. My remarks on perception derive in large part from conversations with another of my graduate students, Keith Niall. The final chapter, on laws in psychology, draws equally heavily on joint work with a former graduate student of mine, Brian Doan. To our great joy and advantage we have recently been joined in this work by Vishwas Govitrikar. Three undergraduate students have carried out research under my direction on children's understanding of sortals and quantifiers: Paul Bloom, Robert di Meco, and Shelly Surkis. I appreciate their help but particularly that of Paul Bloom, who has labored longer with me than any undergraduate student in recent times. He helped me especially with the psychological literature referred to in chapters 7 and 8. I have always enjoyed and benefited from our wide-ranging conversations.

It has been a pleasure to write this book for Harry and Betty Stanton of Bradford Books, an imprint of The MIT Press. Harry's advice about the arrangement of materials and his encouragement with the project as a whole have been invaluable.

Authors usually accept responsibility for all views expressed in their book. Because I have been nudged, cajoled, and teased out of so many of my original positions, I cannot do that. But with such a long roster of coadjutors, blame for particular howlers and praise for particular insights is going to be difficult to apportion.

McGill University
October 1985

A Border Dispute

1

Preliminary Positions

Logicians and psychologists generally behave like the men and women in an orthodox synagogue. Each group knows about the other, but it is proper form that each should ignore the other. To a psychologist, logicians appear to be rather remote beings who are concerned about ideals of inference. To a logician, psychologists appear equally remote, grubbing around among the facts of actual attempts to draw inferences. Is this situation satisfactory? Have the two disciplines so little to do with one another? The thesis of this book is that the present situation is entirely unsatisfactory, that the disciplines ought to have a far more intimate relation.

At the same time it is possible to err on the opposite side and make logic a subbranch of psychology, deriving its fundamental principles from psychology. The theory that would so situate them, known as *psychologism*, is not popular today, though it was very much so in the last century. I wish to propose a moderate position midway between the present standoff and the psychologism of the last century.

I begin by describing the present-day attitudes of psychologists to logic. I then present a certain set of general intuitions that led me to my own position. In doing so, I make no attempt to formulate my position precisely—I leave that task to the next chapter. My purpose is to lead the reader to see that there is something deeply the matter with present-day attitudes. Lest my arguments prove too successful, I go on to discuss psychologism in its historical setting. The end of the last century saw a vigorous and altogether successful attack on psychologism by logicians and philosophers. The same period also saw the birth of empirical psychology as a discipline independent of philosophy. So, as Sober (1978) says, "While the psychologists were leaving, philosophers were slamming the door behind them." Ever since, their coexistence has been rather uneasy.

It is not just that the present orthodoxy squarely opposes that of the last century; the present one seems to result in part from the overthrow of psychologism. It seems that, if logic and psychology could not be as intimate as psychologism would have them, they would not talk to each other at all.

Psychologists' Attitudes toward Logic

Truth to tell, there is little in the psychological literature on the role of logic in the psychology of thinking. The general stance of psychologists is well put by Woodworth and Schlosberg (1954):

> The fascinating science of logic, though it is by no means a psychology of the reasoning process, is useful to the experimenter because it provides a check on the validity of conclusions. (p. 843)

This is to give logic no role in psychology other than what it plays in all sciences.

In keeping with this evaluation of the role of logic is the idea that logic is just a learned discipline, like Latin, calculus, or any other. Just as we do not expect or require any special status for Latin in a general theory of psychology, the idea goes, we do not expect it for logic either. George Miller (1951) put it this way:

> The fact is that logic is a formal system, just as arithmetic is a formal system, and to expect untrained subjects to think logically is much the same as to expect preschool children to know the multiplication table. (p. 806)

We frequently hear logic put on a par with mathematics, as if that could dismiss the notion that logic should figure in a general theory of cognition. Actually the parallel is quite instructive, but in a way that is not suspected by those who propose it. We might equally well ask: How do we come to know arithmetical truths? The truths of arithmetic, like those of logic, are not inductions over experience. How might a mind that has no arithmetical concepts and principles acquire them? Does it not seem likely that the mind is naturally arithmetical in some way that it is not naturally Latinate (or possessed of Latin)? Does it not seem likely, also, that the mind is in some sense naturally logical? How might a mind that is not logical become logical? It is enough to raise these questions to show that we cannot, by noting a parallel with arithmetic, dismiss the idea that logic should feature in a general theory of psychology. In fairness I should note that Miller made the general observation in the context of a rather technical point of propositional logic. Nonetheless, although there are problems relating formal logic to everyday reasoning, it simply is not the case that preschool children are alogical or nonlogical in the sense that the majority of them are illiterate.

Sometimes logic is taken to be a sort of quarry from which to extract hypotheses for psychological experiment, a standard against which to compare general performance. The following is taken from one of the best works of the genre (Wason and Johnson-Laird 1972):

> We were interested above all else in a number of apparently simple deductive problems which so many intelligent people almost invariably got wrong. The important point was not simply that they got them wrong, and departed from the canons of formal logic, but that they usually came to realise their mistakes. Moreover, these mistakes were nearly always of a particular kind rather than being random. Hence we were interested in their determinants, the factors which governed "performance," and made it fail to reflect logical "competence," to borrow a distinction drawn by Noam Chomsky. (p. 2)

The one really dominant figure in twentieth-century psychology who does not fit this pattern is Jean Piaget. He noted that few psychologists appeal to logic to explain intelligence and that few logicians see any relation between logic and psychology (1953, p. 2). He allowed that it is a fallacy to use logic in the causal explanation of psychological facts (1953, p. 1). At the same time, he saw logic as supplying "a precise method of specifying the structures that emerge in the analysis of the operational mechanisms of thought" (1953, p. xviii). Later, Piaget seemed to go further than this, claiming that some of the logicomathematical structures he sought to specify have a reality in the adult mind; they are descriptions of "the simple forms of equilibrium attained by thought activity" (1953, p. 40). Although there is some ambivalence (1953, p. 45) about this, the position he was most comfortable with allowed a close correspondence between logic and the information-processing devices of the adult mind. At the same time, Piaget was adamant that the logical structures he ascribed to adults had no place in children's minds. His whole life's work is a testimony to this. And because his impact has been most felt in developmental psychology, he has to some extent fostered the divorce between logic and psychology. The thinking seems to have been that, because logicians might be construed (from the Piagetean point of view) as building models of the adult mind, their work reveals little of children's minds. At best, logic provides models from which it is interesting to see how far children depart. Logic, on this reading, is a source of hypotheses for psychological research in cognitive development.

In the appendix to the next chapter I examine a claim made by the psychologist Johnson-Laird that there can be no such thing as a mental logic. We will have a look at what the claim means. At first glance it seems to contradict my whole position. We will see, however, that the arguments do not present a serious threat.

Among some psychologists the feeling is growing that the relation between logic and psychology is closer than traditional psychology realizes. Witness, in particular, Cohen (1981) and the large number of comments that accompany his paper. In the same spirit is Pylyshyn (1972), Braine (1978), Henle (1978), and Rips (1983). Nevertheless, to my knowledge there has not been a full-scale analysis of the whole matter.

General Orienting Intuitions

Logical Layman

The main problem with the traditional attitude toward logic among psychologists is that it places too large a gap between the layman and the logician, as though the logician's work were esoteric and quite different from everyday thought. In fact, most of the logician's ideals are quite familiar to the layman. The logician as a logician desires to work in a language that is clear, to present arguments that are irrefutable, granted the truth of the premises, and to steer clear of incoherent notions. The layman shares these ideals, as well as many others, such as to be amusing, interesting, or nontrivial. The layman values clarity of expression, as achieved by the avoidance of ambiguity, the definition of terms, and sticking to the point. The layman is normally embarrassed to learn that some notion he has been using in discussion is incoherent or that one of his arguments is invalid. If the layman is not, we consider him to be unscrupulous or too involved personally in imposing his point of view.

For example, if a man professes to be a stout supporter of women's liberation and yet opposes his daughter's going to college, we are inclined to charge him with inconsistency or worse. His stance on his daughter's education may be reasonable. Yet on the face of it, it is inconsistent with his principles, and we, his friends, may feel compelled to challenge him for an explanation. We must all, from the bank manager down, be on the alert for inconsistency.

If, then, the layman shares the logician's ideals, does it not follow that the layman has some representation of those ideals? Does it not follow that the description of the layman's mind should include these ideals? Psychology considers itself as having the task of describing what is actual in the mind. If we grant that an aspiration to a set of logical ideals is actual in the normal mind, must not psychological theory include a description of these ideals, which in turn requires a statement of the ideals themselves?

The role of logical ideals is even greater than the foregoing suggests. Because the ideals exercise some influence over everyday thought, must not their role be accounted for? Does not psychology have to account for how people come by those ideals, how they are realized in the mind, and how they function there?

If the normal mind shows sensitivity to those ideals in its everyday functioning, psychology cannot afford to treat logic as an unusual property or skill, such as Latin or a flawless knowledge of the history of the Hapsburg family. Miller (1951) is right: A training in formal logic is acquired in an academic setting. It does not follow, however, that the untutored mind is devoid of logical skills, intuitions, and ideals.

Student of Logic
Consider the layman who attends a class in introductory logic. What does he need in order to learn formal logic? Having mastered the formalisms, does he not need an ability to grasp the necessity of valid logical arguments? Suppose that the professor demonstrates the logical equivalence of $(p \lor q)$ and $\sim(\sim p \;\&\; \sim q)$, where p and q stand for propositions, $\lor$ means inclusive *or*, and $\&$ means *and*. What does the student need in order to follow the demonstration? The answer would appear to be basic logical ability. He has to be able to work with symbols, grasp their logical structure, appreciate what it is for two strings to be logically equivalent, and see that the two strings in question are logically equivalent. If the layman does not understand the expression "logically equivalent," for example, it must be explained to him in words that can be understood; it must be brought home to him that he has long grasped the notion that it expresses. Put another way, how can we explain failure to follow the demonstration in a student who has been taught the meanings of the symbols? We would probably say that he was unable to grasp the precise meaning of formal symbols or the essential nature of a formal proof or that he could not handle so much information all at once. We would not say that he was unable to grasp the logical form of any sentence, appreciate its truth conditions, or draw any inference whatsoever. And we would try to help him to relate the task in formal logic to his informal skills.

Again, consider what happens when a logic student hands in to the professor a "proof" of some theorem in which there is a logical mistake. When all goes well, the professor reveals the mistake to the student. The professor's is not a role like that of an umpire in tennis. The umpire calls a fault, and that is how the players must play it, no matter what the facts are. A good professer succeeds in showing the student that he has made an error by the standards of the student's own mind. Ultimately, this means that the student must bring to the formal study of logic a set of fundamental logical notions and principles. These notions and principles must guide logical intuitions. These intuitions need to be tested and sifted, always in the light of other logical intuitions; logic class does not bestow basic logical intuition on neophytes who lack it totally.

Some cynics take a different view of what goes on in logic classes; they regard most of it as indoctrination. And indeed there are many critics of classical logic, which is almost certainly what students learn in introductory courses. Such critics claim that a formation in classical logic is a deformation. Take, for example, relevance logicians who claim that classical logic misrepresents logical implication. They show people examples of the so-called paradoxes of implication (see the example in what follows) and hope that they will be shocked. Implicit in the debate is the assumption that, although classical logic is a deformation, it is possible to appeal to something more basic, more permanent, and more logically wholesome than the effects of an education in classical logic. This in turn implies that students bring to an education in formal logic a basic set of logical notions and principles.

To get a better grasp of what is going on, it is important to appreciate that relevance logicians do not accuse classical logicians of downright illogicality. Consider the schema

$$A \supset .B \supset A,$$

which is a theorem in classical logic. It can be read as saying that, if any proposition is true, it is implied ($\supset$) by any proposition whatsoever. So let *seven is a prime number* be a substitute for A and *snow is puce* for B. On ordinary interpretation, then, the schema would seem to warrant: On the assumption that seven is a prime number, it follows that snow is puce implies that seven is a prime number. (This example is adapted from Anderson and Belnap 1968.) The example does seem to shock logical intuition, not because we have "proved" a falsehood on true assumptions; we have not. What is shocking is that the color of snow seems utterly irrelevant to whether seven is prime. Relevance logicians claim that what is wrong with all this is that it violates certain basic assumptions we all have, or should have, about valid logical implications. It is not my purpose to decide between relevance and classical logicians. All that interests us at present is the assumption that there are certain logical notions and principles that students bring to the study of logic. In fact, Anderson and Belnap (1968) appeal to "untutored intuitions" and to the experience of "anyone who has ever taught elementary logic." This underlines the point. The only answer classical logicians can give is that, despite appearances, their logic does not violate untutored intuitions; it actually captures them correctly.

It seems, then, that a person can become a professional logician only by starting out as a competent nonprofessional one. With Fodor (1980) I agree that it is difficult to understand how people can by intellectual means increase their basic logical abilities. Of course, the newly formed human embryo does not actually have any logical skills, and there is physiological development that results in the emergence of basic logical skills. But this is not an intellectual development in the sense that it represents conclusions based on evidence—at least so I shall argue. It is rather a physiological process that has nothing immediate to do with evidence and conclusions. In any event, it would seem that a person becomes a professional logician by systematically applying basic logical skills and principles, by building logical structures with them, and by proving theorems with them, including such interesting theorems as the (in)completeness and (un)decidability of systems. All this leads to the conclusion that cognitive psychology cannot afford to neglect the basic logic that is common to all adults whether or not they ever study logic—a basic logic that is sturdy enough to support all the valid logical structures that professional logicians build on it.

Professional Logician

Logicians, tradition has it, study ideal reasonings; psychologists study actual reasoning. That suggests, faintly, that ideal reasonings are not actual or, perhaps, that psychologists do not need to distinguish in their theories valid from invalid inferences. It is worth noting that inferences carried out by logicians in conformity with the rules of the ideal logic are still actual. And, of course, cognitive psychologists need to distinguish in their theory valid from invalid inferences, just as they need to distinguish correct from incorrect computations in children's arithmetic. In the long run, errors have to be explained in a different way from nonerrors.

One significant aspect of professional logicians' work is worth reflecting on. Logicians, unlike all the empirical scientists, need no laboratory. They do their work by consulting their own logical intuition. They cannot ignore the work of other logicians or others' critiques of their work, but they test what others say against their own intuition. Only when what others say passes that test can logicians accept it and use it to advance their own original work. Of course, logicians may be working from established theorems at a level far beyond basic intuition, but again they must satisfy themselves that those theorems are derived from principles and inference rules that do satisfy basic intuition. Nowadays, logicians might employ a computer to perform some of the more routine, programmable work, but again they must satisfy themselves that the computer program satisfies their logical intuition. The effect of this observation is to underline something I have already said. Logicians build on a basis that they bring to the study of logic, a basis that is common to all adults at least. The basic notions and principles of physics have to be learned. To be sure, in the last analysis they are learned on the basis of unlearned mental abilities, but there is considerable empirical content in physics. There is none in classical logic. (In chapter 9 I examine the thesis that some of the foundations of classical logic should be revised in the light of certain findings of quantum physics.) It does not matter for present purposes how we answer the great metaphysical question about logic. Even if we are as Platonistic as can be imagined and posit abstract entities to explain the truth of logical propositions, we would still have to endow the mind with something that explains knowledge of these entities. Because Platonistic entities are causally inert, knowledge of them presupposes essential properties of the mind. It follows, then, that a general theory of cognition should explain what those properties are and how they come to yield knowledge of logical truths.

Unless it rejects the idea of logical truths altogether, psychology cannot escape this duty. To discharge it, psychology must have access to logical truths, for without them it would not know what to look for as the psychological source of such truths.

With some reason, psychologists are interested mainly in everyday thought and everyday reasoning. They are less interested in the developments in mathematical logic or in logical studies of computer languages. I am not suggesting that all logical studies are useful to cognitive psychologists. Although ultimately these studies must rest on the foundation of basic logical intuition, many are special-purpose studies and remote from everyday thought.

Perhaps the most telling argument for the position I am taking rests on the observation that professional logicians and laymen share the same basic concepts, notably reference, predication, and truth. This can be brought out by looking at the philosophy of language. On most people's views, one of the main undertakings of a philosopher of language is to specify the contribution of certain classes of words to the truth conditions of sentences in which they occur. These classes of words include proper names, indexicals (such as *I, this*), predicates (such as *red, loves*) and sortals (such as *dog, adult*). In large measure, this is specifying part of the logic of everyday thinking. The notion of reference for the formal logician is the same as that for the philosopher of language. Both have isolated part of what ordinary language means by such expressions as "name" and "referring to." True, the ordinary-language expression "referring to," for example, has uses other than those of the logician—literary reference and allusion, to name just two.

But it also has in ordinary speech the meaning it has for logicians: It signifies the function of designating objects about which one wants to predicate something or that one wants to include under a sortal. It is not as if there is an erudite and a primitive concept of the reference of proper names and indexical pronouns. A single concept covers both. Formal logicians, however, tidy things up in their language so as to avoid such logical inconveniences as ambiguity. But formal logicians do not develop a distinct concept of reference.

The same can obviously be said of predicates and sortals (though formal logic for the most part does not distinguish them). The notion of truth, however, is so central to logic that it merits a few remarks on its own. It might at first seem that the layman's notion of truth is rather different from the logician's. For example, the layman is apt to say such things as "How very true!" Problems of vagueness apart, with few exceptions logicians take truth to be bivalent and therefore not coming in degrees, as heat does. It seems likely, however, that what the layman means is something like "How very important that truth is." The layman's notion of truth in the application of sortals, such as *dog* and *horse*, seems to be bivalent, as is the logician's. And if it could be shown that the layman's notion in such cases is not bivalent, that would be a great support for many-valued logics; then it could be claimed that many-valued logics, not classical logic, reflect a basic logical intuition. We must not allow ourselves to be puzzled by the towering mathematical structures that, for example, Tarski (1956) and Gupta (1982) erected in providing a model for the truth predicate. Gupta does not imply that such structures exist in the minds of users of the word *true*; he claims that such structures lay the specter that the notion of truth is paradoxical. The notion of truth he thus seeks to secure is the same for layman, logician and philosopher of language. It is the notion a child invokes when he says, "I'm telling the truth, Daddy." Notice that in so doing, the child is embracing what he said earlier to his father and also what he is saying in uttering the sentence. The remark is self-referential, and self-reference, remember, is the principal source of paradox for the truth predicate. The child's concept has attached to it all the problem-making resources of the logician's notion of truth. Little wonder, since there is only a single notion between them. The intuition I am working on seems to have been shared by Montague (1970), who goes even further in the same direction than I do, saying, "I reject the contention that an important theoretical difference exists between formal and natural languages."

We should also resist any temptation to regard the layman's idea of a valid argument as equivalent to a plausible or convincing one. The layman is well aware that plausible arguments are sometimes fallacious, that conviction sometimes rests on spurious arguments. True, he is more likely to evince such an argument when faced with an opponent than with a friend. But the fact that he shows varying degrees of alertness does not take from the general point, which is that the layman does not, in principle, take the plausible or the convincing for the valid.

The burden of these remarks is this: If logician and layman share the same basic logical notions and if, as we noticed earlier, they share the same ideals (or principles), then the logic of the logician and the thought of the layman cannot be so utterly distinct as psychological tradition has portrayed them. It follows that a psychological theory of the layman's thinking will have to make more room for logic than tradition allows.

Psychologism: Claiming Too Much

There is a temptation, if we have been impressed with the arguments just given, to rush in the opposite direction. The foregoing arguments depend on the naturalness of logic, and we may, if unwary, tend to see logic as a natural property of the mind. To achieve a balanced position, we must examine that theory, called *psychologism*. In doing so we have an opportunity to gain a deeper understanding of the issues and of how they constrain theorizing in the area.

Because my purpose is to expose the main lines of the psychologism debate rather than to record its history, I do not explore the considerable literature on the subject. Instead I concentrate on four major figures: Kant and John Stuart Mill on the pro side, Frege and Husserl on the contra side. In keeping with my purpose, I do not even attempt a complete analysis of any of these four authors' thinking on the relation between logic and psychology. Nor do I follow the development of any of the authors' views. Instead, I concentrate on those writings that have had the strongest influence on one or the other side of the debate.

Psychologism is the name given to the doctrine that philosophy is a study of the mind, though I confine it to the doctrine that logic is a study of the mind. Authors vary on how to interpret this. Some, such as John Stuart Mill, take it to mean that logic is an introspective science generalizing over inferences that are judged satisfactory. That is also the sense in which Frege took and rejected it. Kant, however, saw transcendental logic as expressing a set of a priori conditions on all judgment. These conditions, he believed, hold for all thinking beings, though we know them in the first instance by studying the exercise of our own judgments. Psychologism is opposed by the view that logic is not in any sense a psychological study, that it has to do with the truth conditions of sentences and with inferences from sentences to sentences, all conceived of as independent of any psychological state or act. This captures a core element in the thought of Frege and Husserl.

Psychologistic logicians make a number of distinctions that help to define their position. The first is that, although psychology studies all the inferences that are actually drawn, logic studies only those that necessarily lead from true premises to true conclusions. In other words, the concern of logic is valid inferences. The second distinction is between the form and the content of an inference. Most actual inferences have a particular content, such as whether the government's economic policy bears unduly hard on the poor. Logic, they note, is not interested in any particular content, but rather in a form, which can be applied to any content whatsoever. In addition, psychologistic logicians do not study a whole range of mental events that are of great concern to psychologists: perception, memory, imagination, and the like. Instead, they study the drawing of inferences and the semantic function of certain sorts of words.

Immanuel Kant: Forerunner of Psychologism

Although Kant rejected any attempt to ground philosophical positions in their "vulgar origins in human experience" (*Critique of Pure Reason*, p. A.ix), he nevertheless revealed himself in some measure as a psychologistic logician in his central thesis about the nature of logic. Kant defined logic as an "a priori science of the necessary laws of thinking . . . a science of the right use of the understanding and of reason . . . " (*Logic*, p. 18). Although the definition contains a number of technical Kantian expressions that would have to be touched on in a thorough study of its meaning, a cursory glance is sufficient to set Kant's idea of logic apart from that of contemporary logicians who place the emphasis on valid inference conceived in total abstraction from mental events.

There is a certain tension in Kant's use of the word *law*, which, incidentally, helps us to grasp the psychologistic element in Kant's thought. On the one hand, Kant argued that the laws of thought are such that "without them no use of the understanding would be possible at all" (*Logic*, p. 14). That is reminiscent of the laws of physics, for physical events necessarily conform to physical laws. On the other hand, Kant was well aware that reasoners make logical errors, that their thinking does not always conform to the supposed laws of thought. That fact Kant found difficult to comprehend, for it is "contrary to the understanding" (*Logic*, p. 59). The understanding, in falling into logical error, he noted, resembles a "force which should deviate from its own essential laws" (*Logic*, p. 59).

This observation reveals how literally we are to construe "necessary laws of thinking." The point of interest is not just the extent of the psychologism revealed in Kant; it is the ensuing problem of explaining logical error. If the laws of logic relate to thinking as (say) the laws of motion relate to the movement of physical objects, logical error would seem to be ruled out. On the other hand, we also have the meaning of *law* as what the mind ought to follow in its operations. Kant intended the word in that sense, too, but clearly not just in that sense; the sense of law as norm creates no difficulty in relation to logical error. Kant sought to explain such error by laying the blame for it on factors extraneous to reason itself—on factors such as lack of reflection and prejudice (*Logic*, p. 84) and on the sensory basis of knowledge (*Logic*, pp. 59, 60). It is only fair to say, however, that the reader comes away feeling that, on the Kantian view of mind, logical error has not been adequately explained. We need to bear the point in mind when we explore a position that is in many ways similar to Kant's but that endeavors to make more adequate provision for logical error.

At the same time we must underline strong antipsychologistic elements in Kant's overall theory. Kant clearly warned us not to base the rules of logic on actual reasonings, for that would be "as absurd as taking morality from life" (*Logic*, p. 16).

Kant was also quite explicit on the point that logic owes nothing to "empirical (psychological) principles" (*Logic*, p. 18). The word "psychological" is particularly interesting. To understand Kant's attitude toward psychology and its relation to logic, we must appreciate that he saw psychology as aimed exclusively at the actual, not at all at the ideal. The following makes that clear (*Logic*):

> If we took the principles from psychology, i.e., from observations about our understanding, we would merely see *how* thinking occurs and how it is under manifold hindrances and conditions; this would therefore lead to the cognition of merely *contingent* laws. In logic, however, the question is not one of *contingent* but of *necessary* rules, not how we think, but how we ought to think. (p. 16)

Kant saw clearly that the central problem is to account for the necessity of logical laws. Many of these points are well made by Notturno (1982).

John Stuart Mill: Full-Blown Psychologism
Mill is regarded with affection as a not-too-remote ancestor by many contemporary psychologists. His full-blooded empiricism is still endorsed by many, and his associationism lives on in cognitive psychology, often thinly disguised. It is particularly important, then, for psychologists to understand Mill's psychologism, for it has numerous points of contact

with their own position. It seems fair to say, in fact, that Mill worked out the implications of contemporary empiricism in psychology more thoroughly than almost any contemporary psychological empiricist. We begin with his squarely psychologistic position on the metaphysical question as to what logic is all about (1874):

> Logic is not a Science distinct from, and coordinate with, Psychology. So far as it is a Science at all, it is a part or branch of Psychology; differing from it, on the one hand, as a part differs from a whole, and on the other, as an Art differs from a Science. Its theoretic grounds are wholly borrowed from Psychology, and include as much of that science as is required to justify the rules of an art. Logic has no need to know more of the Science of thinking, than the difference between good thinking and bad. (p. 359)

Mill, of course, made the usual distinctions between logic and psychology. What is central to his thought, however, is logic's debt to psychology. It borrows all its theoretical grounds from psychology, but at what cost?

Logic, as Mill saw it, does not yield necessary truths, only propositions whose negation we take as *inconceivable* (1843, bk. 2, chap. 5, sec. 6). Why does their negation strike us as inconceivable? The answer is found in Mill's whole theory of knowledge, which consists of a tissue of associations. Among associations some are older, more familiar, and more confirmed by experience; their negation is practically inconceivable. Those deep-rooted qualities of certain associations ground a "fundamental law of the human mind" (1843, bk. 2, chap. 5, sec. 6). All this is compatible with the view that experience differs from individual to individual, so what passes with some as inconceivable does not do so with others, particularly if they are young.

According to Mill, we have no logical intuition of the type that Kant claimed. All depends on experience and the basic laws of psychology, which determine how experience will be construed. This applies to the laws of number and of geometry. It applies even to the principle of contradiction, logic's most basic rule (1843):

> I consider it to be, like other axioms, one of the first and most familiar generalizations from experience. The original foundation of it I take to be, that Belief and Disbelief are two different mental states, excluding one another. (bk. 2, chap. 7, sec. 5)

The law of excluded middle (either p or $\sim p$ must be true) receives a similar treatment. Mill cited Bain's *Logic* with approval (1843):

The law on Excluded Middle, then, is simply a generalization of the universal experience that some mental states are destructive of other states. It formulates a certain absolutely constant law, that the appearance of any positive mode of consciousness cannot occur without excluding a correlative negative mode; and that the negative mode cannot occur without excluding the correlative positive mode. . . . Hence it follows that if consciousness is not in one of the two modes it must be in the other. (bk. 2, chap. 7, sec. 5)

Mill thus succeeded in solving a problem that is pressing for psychologistic philosophers of logic, but at enormous expense. The problem is this: If logic expresses the fundamental laws of the mind, how is logical error possible? Mill's solution was to deny an intuition of necessity that is not based on psychological experience. This, in effect, denies logical principles both the type of necessity that is commonly attributed to them and their fundamental position in theorizing. Whatever about Bain, this removed for Mill the necessity that the mind should invariably function in accordance with any set of laws. Further, if the laws of logic are not universally valid, then there is no reason to be upset if on occasion we find an inference form in good standing that leads from true premises to a false conclusion. This can happen even if the reasoner applies the logic perfectly. To explain error, Mill did not have to call on factors (such as inattention and misperception) extrinsic to the purely logical functioning of the mind, though those factors, too, were available to him if he needed them.

Gottlob Frege: Antipsychologism
The person most identified with antipsychologism and the most influential, perhaps, in discrediting nineteenth-century psychologism is Gottlob Frege. He is also the principal person we must confront today if we are to reinterpret the impact of the psychologism debate on the relations between logic and psychology. In many of Frege's writings, notably his 1884 work, he had Mill in mind, though in the remarks addressed specifically to logic rather than arithmetic the main antagonists were German logicians.

For Frege the crux of the dispute was the conception of what makes a sentence true—which is quite appropriate, for truth is the central concept in logic. Frege was a realist in his views about truth (see Dummett 1981, chap. 13). That is, he believed that what establishes the truth of a sentence is something objective, something independent of the mind. To make this concrete, Frege believed that what establishes a sentence such as "The earth is a planet of the sun" as true or false is something about the earth, the sun, and being a planet (Frege 1968

[1918]). Most emphatically, what gives the sentence its truth value is not any idea or representation or theory in our minds about the earth, sun, or planets (1964 [1893]):

> Survey the whole question, it seems to me that the source of the dispute lies in a difference in our conceptions of what is true. For me, what is true is something objective and independent of the judging subject; for psychological logicians it is not. What Herr B. Erdman [a logician] calls "objective certainty" is merely a general acknowledgement on the part of the subjects who judge, which is thus not independent of them but susceptible to alteration with the constitution of their minds. (p. 15)

The last sentence in this passage shows us what Frege was opposing. Frege accused Erdman of interpreting logical validity, which depends on truth, in terms of *certainty*, construed as a psychological condition, and of grounding certainty on general agreement, itself dependent on states of mind. Frege insisted that what makes the sentence about the earth and the sun true or false is not what we feel or what most people say but something independent of both.

Frege's views about such empirical matters as the planetary status of the earth also apply to arithmetic and logic. What makes arithmetical and logical sentences true or false is likewise something objective and independent. A law of logic holds "no matter where, or when, or by whom the judgement is made" (1964 [1893], p. 15). It is a law that states how all thinkers *ought* to judge.

Frege had a powerful sense of the objectivity of logical truths, of their independence of us, and of their eternity (1959 [1884], p. 37; 1964 [1893], p. 14; 1968 [1918]; 1979, pp. 4, 186). They do not become true when we discover them; they were true before we did and merely continue to be true when we do. In Frege's mind, one of the most unfortunate consequences of psychologism is closely related to this: It is the confusion of the manner in which a truth is discovered and the truth itself (1959 [1884]):

> We suppose, it would seem, that concepts sprout in the individual mind like leaves on a tree, and we think to discover their nature by studying their birth; we seek to define them psychologically, in terms of the human mind. But this account makes everything subjective, and if we follow it through to the end, does away with truth. (p. vii)

The temptation is particularly strong for people like Mill, and his descendants in contemporary psychology, who work from a strong conviction that all knowledge must be derived from sensory experience and who allow this conviction to limit the nature of knowledge. Against them Frege pitted his, and our, sense of the nature of logical and mathematical truths and their objective status. The quotation expresses another important admonition, as valuable today as it was dear to Frege (1959 [1884], pp. vi, vii, 3; 1968 [1918]; 1979, pp. 2, 147, 176): not to take the account of how a belief originates in the mind either as expressing the content of that belief or as proving its truth.

The pivotal notion in the debate is the necessity that attaches to logical laws. Frege was always sensitive to the ambiguity of the word "law" (1964 [1893], p. 12; 1968 [1918]; 1979, pp. 4, 186). What he most feared was that "law" would be taken to mean what it means in the physical sciences, an induction based on empirical observation. To take "law" in logic as an induction over successful inferences would, of course, be to succumb to the psychologism he wished to eradicate. Frege, like Kant and unlike Mill, intended "law" in a normative sense. True logical laws for Frege are presupposed in the establishment of all empirical laws. They cannot, then, he argued against Mill, themselves be empirical laws. Instead, like Kant, Frege held logical laws to be necessary in the sense of holding in all possible circumstances.

The final lesson that Frege sought to teach psychologistic logicians is that they had the intentionality wrong. The point, which relates to the objectivity of truth, is of fundamental importance to us and can be put simply. Suppose that someone says, "Grass is green." The psychologistic logician takes green to be a psychological entity, perhaps an image (idea), that is predicated of another psychologicl entity, the concept of grass in the speaker's mind. This way of construing the event is still current in psychology under various guises. Frege observed, and surely he was fully justified, that that account must be wrong, for it turns an utterance that is patently true into a falsehood (1964 [1893], p. 19). If the grass involved is something in the speaker's brain or even mind, it is certainly not green. By the same token, neither can the actual image of green itself be green. The speaker who claims that grass is green claims that the grass in the world outside the mind is green— that it, not something in the mind, has the property of being green. The same mistake is even easier to make in relation to logical and mathematical expressions. The following quotation, which captures Frege at his most vivid, makes the point about the intentionality of mathematical expressions (1964 [1893]):

> While the mathematician defines objects, concepts and relations, the psychological logician is spying on the origin and evolution of ideas, and to him at bottom, the mathematician's defining can only appear foolish because it does not reproduce the essence of

ideation imagery. He looks into his psychological peep-show and tells the mathematician: "I see nothing at all of what you are defining." No wonder, for it is not where you are looking for it. (pp. 24–25)

Edmund Husserl: Convert to Antipsychologism

One of the earliest converts to Frege's point of view was Edmund Husserl, who began life as a psychologistic logician. One of his earliest works was his *Philosophy of Arithmetic* (1894), written in a psychologistic frame of mind. Frege (1952 [1894]), then at the height of his intellectual development, reviewed it and, among other things, trounced its psychologism. Husserl learned the lesson well and subsequently applied it to logic in the 200-page prolegomenon to his *Logical Investigations* (1970 [1900]). Frege's attention in the writings cited was mainly on arithmetic, whereas in *Logical Investigations* Husserl's was, naturally, on logic. Husserl's is the most thorough treatment of the issues that I have come across.

The most obvious point in psychologism's favor, one that I take quite superficially for the moment, is the fact that all the logical inferences that are ever made are psychological events. This establishes right off a solid contact with psychology. The opponents of psychologism tend to respond, as if by reflex, that there is a big difference: Whereas psychology in its approach to such events is factual, logic is normative. Husserl (1970 [1900], p. 92) points out, however, that the response just won't do. Even if we allow that logic is normative and specifies how we ought to think, it might be that the norms are based on the nature of mind and of mental activity.

Take the physiology of walking, and consider the set of laws that might be discovered for it. Such laws might well be advanced as a set of norms for walking: If in our perambulations, we wish to make progress and avoid falling, we abide by a given set of laws. Yet those laws would have been based on the study of human physiology. Might not logical laws, likewise, be based on human psychology? It would follow that thinking as it should be would be just a special case of thinking as it is; thinking as it should be would be thinking in conformity with the nature of mind and its laws (Husserl 1970 [1900], p. 91).

At this point Husserl brought out the ambiguity in the word "law," made familiar to us by Frege, but conceded that it does not clinch the issue. The response is still open; we are aware of the distinction, but the "ought" must be grounded in an "is," and the grounding we need is psychological (Husserl 1970 [1900], pp. 93–94).

Here Husserl made an interesting move. He goes so far as to concede that logic is basically not a normative science at all (1970 [1900], pp. 88,

96, 170). Logical norms, he claimed, presuppose logical truths. The law of contradiction (p and $\sim p$ cannot both be true) is to be obeyed in reasoning not because it is a rule but because it is true. Moreover, the law in its basic form makes no mention of reasoning or of the mind (1970 [1900], p. 169). The psychologistic logician, then, needs a strong argument to establish that the truth of these laws rests on psychological foundations. That argument is not forthcoming (1970 [1900], p. 96).

Husserl pressed the advantage in a number of telling points. One is an important distinction between content and act. We reason and judge, and both are psychological acts. But the content of our acts is not normally psychology. If I judge a rock to be igneous, my judgment is a psychological act, but the content is not; it is geological. If I judge that a logical principle is true, my judgment is psychological, but its content is logical. This line of thinking strongly suggests that logic and psychology may be as distinct as geology and psychology (1970 [1900], pp. 102, 184, 186).

Husserl felt that Mill and the psychologistic logicians generally did not see the objectivity of logic because they failed to distinguish clearly the content of mental acts, in the sense of what the acts were about, from the acts themselves. Had they done so, they might have seen that the content presented itself as objective, whereas the acts presented themselves as subjective. But they failed to discriminate between mind and what the mind knows. Mind, Husserl concluded, is the study of psychology: What the mind knows (except, of course, when it is studying mind itself) is the study of some other discipline, be it economics, physics, geology, or logic.

Perhaps the deepest point that the antipsychologistic logicians made related to the modal status of logical laws; the most telling one was the act/content distinction. I have not in the foregoing discussion done justice to any of the writers looked at; I had to be content with giving only a flavor of their thought. Still, the overview of the debate enables us to reflect on at least the principal issues and to glimpse the strength of the case against psychologism. So strong is that case, in my view, that it blocks any tendency to reinstate psychologism. The position toward which I am working is not psychologistic.

The true relevance of the psychologism debate was not well understood by psychologists for quite a simple reason. Few psychologists seem to have known anything about it or, if they did, to have thought it of any consequence for psychology. Although Boring's (1957) history of psychology, the standard work on the subject, contains many references to Husserl, they all have to do with phenomenology. None has to do with the psychologism debate, and there is no mention of psychologism in the index. I have made a rapid survey of some of the best textbooks on psychology, "ancient and modern" (Osgood 1953, Woodworth and Schlosberg 1954, Hebb 1958, and Gleitman 1981) and found no mention of psychologism and extremely little on logic. In the small number of textbooks on cognitive psychology that come readily to hand (Johnson 1955, Harper et al. 1964, Anderson and Ausubel 1965, Reeves 1965, Reitman 1965, Lindsay and Norman 1972, Kintsch 1977, and Bransford (1979), there is no mention of the subject. The same holds for a number of the better-known monographs on the psychology of thinking that I have examined (Wertheimer 1945, Mandler and Mandler 1964, Berlyne 1965, Bruner et al. 1956, and Neisser 1976). One important psychological monograph in which I do find explicit reference to psychologism is George Humphrey's (1951), and to my mind he construes the relevance of the debate wrongly. Although he describes Husserl's attack on psychologism as "extraordinarily able" (p. 77), he claims that one of its effects is to "free psychology from the shackles of logic" (p. 78). Humphrey is not clear about what those shackles are, but whatever they might be, he has no grounds for so interpreting Husserl's *Logical Investigations*. It is a simple error to conclude that, if Husserl freed logic from psychology, he thereby freed psychology from logic—at least if "freed" is intended to mean "shown the irrelevance of." We might as well conclude that the irrelevance of biology to physics establishes the irrelevance of physics to biology.

The section has been long, so it may help to summarize the main points. Frege and Husserl's most telling points have to do with the objectivity of logical truths—that they, like the truths of geology, seem to depend on the state of objective reality. In particular, because logical truths make no special claims about the mind, mental states and properties have no special role in making them true. To think otherwise is to get the intentionality wrong—it is to confuse the content of what is expressed with the means used to express it; it is to confuse objective content with psychological states and actions. Both Frege and Husserl deny that there is empirical content in logical truths, as there is in statements of the laws of physics. The point is more open to dispute today than it was ninety years ago, before the coming of quantum mechanics. I believe, however, that Frege and Husserl are right—though I defer discussion of the matter to chapter 9. Frege and Husserl base their argument on the intuition that logical truths are of a higher level of necessity than empirical laws and on the fact that all empirical science presupposes logic. Frege especially insisted that we distinguish accounts of how beliefs and notions arise in the mind from accounts of what the beliefs and notions are. The admonition is valuable because in later chapters we take up accounts of how children come by certain basic logical resources. I might at this stage observe that, although a specification of such resources is independent of their psychological origin, a theory of their psychological origin is essentially dependent on their specification. To account for the presence of a logical resource in the mind, we must know what it is whose presence we seek to explain. Finally, our glance at Kant brought home to us that, if we take the basic laws of logic to be laws of mental functioning, we raise problems for the explanation of logical error.

Conclusion

We have seen something of the marriage between logic and psychology in the last century, of the divorce proceedings, and of the present-day studied neglect of each by the other. Although I do not wish a re-marriage, there seem to be solid grounds for exploring a new business relation based on mutual benefit and friendship. As a psychologist, I emphasize the benefits of such an arrangement to psychology. I also believe that the benefits to at least the philosophers of logic will be substantial. In the next chapter I present my position in some detail but always at the level of a general theory. In subsequent chapters the benefits are spelled out by applying the general theory to a small number of particular cases.

2
Logic as Psychological Competence

Main Thesis

Constraints on Theory
We have come to the conclusion that logic and psychology are of their nature intimately related, though we have not yet attempted to say *how*. In particular, we have stressed that cognitive psychology needs logic, not only as all sciences do to ensure coherence but as an essential part of a general theory of cognition. In itself this is a substantive claim, but it needs to be made far more specific. We must study the precise way in which logic enters the theory of cognition; we are looking for a theory of how it does. The work so far, especially in the review of the psychologism debate, has alerted us to a number of important constraints on such a theory. It would be wise to rehearse them before proceeding.

Room must be left for the possibility of logical error. This constraint rules out theories, such as Kant's, that equate the laws of logic with the laws of thought. We can go further and use the constraint to rule out the theory that the laws of logic govern the production of a sequence of related thoughts, for it is in such sequences that error frequently occurs. Moreover, we sometimes indulge in fantasy, which is usually a sequence of thoughts in which the passage from one to another is not governed by the laws of logic.

Yet logic is itself errorless. We must then formulate a theory of how logic and psychology are related that embraces both error and errorlessness. In making room for logical error in human thought, we must not allow such error to invade logic. We are under the constraint to keep logic error free.

Another constraint arises from the fact that, unlike physics, chemistry, and biology, there is no empirical content in logic. Moreover, all empirical science presupposes the principles of logic, whereas those principles presuppose no other deeper discipline. It follows that access to logical principles is different from access to the principles of the empirical sciences, and the psychology that accounts for the access has to vary accordingly. Psychological theory must make provisions for logic's fundamental status. Psychology is under no obligation to justify the principles of logic. It seems that access to logical principles is through logical intuition, so our theory must show how logic can guide and illuminate intuitions of a certain sort.

Finally, we have agreed to accept the main conclusion of the psychologism debate, that is, that logic is not a branch of psychology receiving its basic principles from psychology. Psychologism is one attempt to state the relation between logic and psychology, but it is wrong. We must avoid that error and yet discover a theory that brings logic and psychology into a relationship close enough to explain how we can know the laws of logic and employ them in our reasoning without our attaining them by generalizing over empirical data.

General Statement of Thesis

My thesis, baldly, is this: A logic that is true to intuition in a certain area constitutes a competence theory for the corresponding area of cognitive psychology. By *competence theory* I mean something quite close to what Chomsky (1965, 1980, 1984) means by it, though he is concerned almost exclusively with language. It is from him that I borrow the notion, though it will be necessary to modify it to make it suit my purpose.

As I see it, the idea that a logic constitutes a competence theory for a part of cognitive psychology comes to this: The mind in part of its functioning applies the principles of that logic. It is this that entitles us to say that to each ideal logic (true to intuition) there corresponds a mental logic. By *mental logic* I mean (1) linguistic resources in the mind sufficient to express propositions, (2) the ability to understand sentences formed with those linguistic resources, and (3) the ability to grasp inferences among such sentences. For Chomsky, at least in his earlier writings, linguistic competence is a set of grammatical rules that are applied in linguistic intuition and guide the use of language. Chomsky attributed ungrammatical utterances to factors other than linguistic competence, such as slips of attention, limitations on short-term memory, and complexity. Similarly, I can attribute logical errors to performance factors, that is, to factors other than the mental logic whose principles are violated by the errors. The distinction between competence and performance gives us a glimpse of how we might account for logic's errorless ideals and the reality of logical blunders in a single theory of the mind.

The position I am taking has affinities with Kant's. Kant, remember, thought that logical laws are laws of mind, and he attributed logical error to factors other than logical capacity, such as perception and imitation. But there is a crucial difference between Chomsky's position and Kant's. Chomsky does not construe grammatical rules as laws to which the mind must conform in its linguistic functioning as, say, moving bodies must conform to the laws of motion. Kant does seem to take the laws of logic as governing the functioning of the mind.

In the spirit of Chomsky, I take the laws of logic as governing only part of our logical functioning, only part of our interpretation of linguistic expressions and our inferences among them. It will be necessary to specify the division; error is possible in both. I will be looking for mental logics that guide intuition and reproach deviations. That I am correct in doing so is brought home by, among other things, Husserl's observation that it is possible for the fully conscious, fully reflecting mind to deny or doubt any law of logic. For example, when confronted with a contradiction in our views, it is possible for us to wonder about contradictions—whether they really scuttle a position, whether fear of them is a peculiarly Western phenomenon resisted in the East, and so on. I am not implying that we ought to give up our abhorrence of contradictions; only that we can scrutinize it. Such deliberations are not precluded by the very nature of the mind, as they would be if the law of contradiction were a fundamental condition on thinking in the way that the laws of motion are fundamental conditions on the movement of physical objects. Logical errors, then, need not be attributed, as Kant thought they should be, solely to factors outside the mind's reasoning capacity. They can arise from factors both within and without. The whole notion of competence, however, is an obscure one, and I had better pin it down before discussing the theory of logic as competence further. I begin by considering how Chomsky describes it.

Competence

Chomsky on Competence
The notion of competence in Chomsky's (1965, 1980, 1984) writings is a complex one that, on his own admission, has given rise to numerous misunderstandings. I attempt to achieve clarity by listing what I take to be the main elements in the notion and by commenting on each one.

1. Competence Is an Abstraction   To describe linguistic competence, we must abstract from performance in several different ways. We must abstract from grammatical errors in performance as revealed by intuition reflecting on strings of words that have actually been produced. We must also abstract from the many dimensions of performance that are extraneous to questions of strict grammaticality, such as the style, rhetorical force, and emotional appropriateness of a string of words. Finally, we must abstract from the particulars of the device that seeks to apply the competence. There are infinitely many ways in which any set of rules, any competence, can be instantiated in a device that produces strings of words in accordance with those rules. The way that the rules of English are instantiated in my head, for example, is one of this infinite set. A theory of competence for English aims to characterize the set as a whole without specifying how English rules are realized in my head.

2. Linguistic Competence Is an Idealization   "Linguistic theory," writes Chomsky (1965, p. 3), "is concerned primarily with an ideal speaker-listener, in a completely homogeneous speech community, who knows its language perfectly." Idealizations are familiar in mathematics and in science. We have all experienced smooth tabletops, and we can easily idealize such experiences and achieve what a geometer calls *planes*. We have little trouble thinking about ideal measurements to which our actual attempts at measurement only approximate, ideal measurements that are free from all slippage and inaccuracy. It follows from Chomsky's position, then, that only to the extent that individuals have mastered their native language does a competence theory for the relevant language characterize the mental grammar that informs their linguistic intuitions. (I should add that, although this is still broadly true of Chomsky's position, in an unpublished paper of his (1984) there seems to be an idealization for each competent speaker of a language rather than a single idealization for all.)

Matters are complicated for Chomsky by a distinction he makes between two sorts of mental grammars, a distinction that will prove interesting to us. The first is the mental grammar that we have recourse to, albeit tacitly for the most part, in forming judgments of grammaticality about strings in a natural language, such as English, that we happen to know. Another is a "universal grammar" that guides our learning of such languages. Because Chomsky (1980, p. 28) sees the universal grammar as supplied by nature, rather than as learned, the relevant idealization is that universal grammar is uniform across individuals and complete in each one.

3. Linguistic Competence Consists of Knowledge—at least Chomsky's early writings strongly suggest this. The competence that is universal grammar is mainly knowledge of the possibilities for natural language. Competence in a language such as English is knowledge of the grammar of English. Chomsky (1965, p. 8; 1984) is quite explicit that the knowledge in question is not a habit or set of habits. In language that I find convenient, he seems to deny that it is knowledge-how, saying instead that it is knowledge-that. This is how Chomsky is interpreted by his friend and lifetime colleague Fodor (1983, pp. 7ff). And for Chomsky the step a learner takes from universal grammar to competence in a particular language seems to be inference based on evidence. Chomsky (1984) speaks of "parameter fixing," which is relatively simple and automatic. Nevertheless, the learner responds to "evidence" and makes "conjectures." There is a puzzle in all this inasmuch as the successful learner, Chomsky is well aware, is rarely able to state what he is held to have learned. In recognition of this Chomsky (1965, p. 27; 1984) speaks of tacit or implicit knowledge of grammar. There is also some suggestion (Chomsky 1984 and even more so in his paper to be published) that Chomsky is uneasy with the idea that competence is knowledge-that. It is fair to say, however, that he has not been explicit enough in his recent writing to reverse the impression that universal grammar consists of knowledge-that.

4. *Linguistic Competence Is the Key Element in the Psychology of Language*   Chomsky (1980) insisted again and again that it is senseless to make a division of labor that assigns the theory of linguistic competence to linguists and the theory of linguistic performance to psychologists, as many writers have done. He claimed that a psychology of language must account in the first instance for the ability of people to judge the grammaticality and appropriateness of strings in a language such as English. To do this, he argued, psychologists need to know the grammar of English precisely, because that grammar describes the relevant properties of what is to be explained. He argued further that the only reasonable explanation for that ability is the individual's knowledge of the grammar of English. This point is hammered home by the obviously justified claim that no individual can learn by heart the set of grammatical sentences of English, because the set is infinite. Nor can individuals learn the finite set of sentences that they themselves will produce or that they will encounter in the sentence production of others with whom they will communicate, because that set is both too large and too random a selection from the infinite set to permit prior memorization. Chomsky (1980, pp. 201ff) concluded that linguistic competence, as described by linguists, must, if correct, be "psychologically real," a common expression today but one with which he is not happy. He sees linguists, psychologists, and others as all contributing to competence theory. All have to set out from linguistic performance, which includes linguistic intuitions as a subset, for that is all there is to go on. The main task for linguists and psychologists of language alike is to establish the true theory of linguistic competence.

5. Linguistic Competence Informs Linguistic Intuition   Linguistic intuition is a reflective judgment on the grammatical status of a string of words. Because grammaticality is not definable on the perceptually given properties of strings and because we cannot memorize the set of strings that we can judge grammatical, our judgments of grammaticality must be guided by a set of rules. The relevant set is linguistic competence.

The objects of linguistic intuition are strings of words in a language. The form of intuition is a judgment about the grammar of the string: that it is or is not grammatical, that it is or is not structurally ambiguous, and the like. To say that the judgment is intuitive is to emphasize that it is not based on any conscious inference, that the judgment presents itself as immediately known. This does not rule out the possibility that in certain cases the process of intuition may need careful priming. It does mean that the priming will not be conscious inference from consciously given premises. By way of a footnote, Chomsky considered the possibility that we have intuitions of degree of grammaticality, that is, of the extent that a string departs from well formedness. We will not concern ourselves with this claim.

Even further, linguistic intuition often needs conscious attention if it is to be a safe guide to tacit competence. Chomsky (1965, p. 21) pointed out that many people do not at first notice that the sentence "Flying planes can be dangerous" is not only ambiguous but also that the meanings are associated with different grammatical analyses of the sentence. With a little help, intuition recognizes the grammaticality of the two parsings: (i) to fly planes can be dangerous, (ii) planes that are flying can be dangerous. In fact it may take generations on generations of linguists to sift intuition so that it leads to a correct characterization of competence.

We must not forget, however, that Chomsky sees competence as twofold: There is the learned competence that guides intuition about the natural language we speak, and there is the deeper, unlearned competence that guides the learning of that language. The deeper competence is universal grammar. Its rules determine "the form of language as such" (Chomsky 1965, p. 27); they define *natural language*. They would supply us, if we could state them, with fundamental principles for the construction of a grammar for any particular natural language, such as English. I noted earlier that Chomsky is quite vague about how universal grammar plays a role in the learning of a natural language. His recent talk of parameter fixing reminds us less of the exercise of an intuition than of the operation of a procedurelike device.

6. The Object of Linguistics Is to Describe Linguistic Competence   A grammar for a particular language, Chomsky tells us, is "descriptively adequate" if it "correctly describes its object, namely the linguistic intuition—the tacit competence of the native speaker" (1965, p. 27). A grammar attains the level of "explanatory adequacy" if it is based on universal grammar, that is, on the "specific innate abilities that make the learning of language possible" (1965, p. 27). This marks Chomsky's position squarely as psychologism. But we do not have to *infer* this from his statements because he has been quite explicit: "I would like to think of linguistics as that part of psychology that focuses its attention on one specific cognitive domain and one faculty of mind, the language faculty" (1980, p. 4). Of course, his psychologism is confined to linguistics.

This aspect of Chomsky's theory is attacked by Katz (1981, chap. 5), who proposes a Platonistic view of language. Whatever the value of Katz's Platonistic alternative, I agree with him that Chomsky's position is psychologistic and, for reasons similar to those advanced in the psychologism debate, that it is in this respect unsatisfactory. I believe, however, that the observation is largely irrelevant. Even if language with its grammar is an abstract Platonic entity that does not reside in the mind, it needs to be represented in the mind in some form that will guide both the learning of natural languages and intuitions about the grammaticality of strings. In other words, Katz is still going to need psychologically real linguistic competence along the lines indicated by Chomsky.

Logic as Competence

Now that we have a sketch of linguistic competence as Chomsky sees it, we can go on to ask how much carries over to logical competence. It would seem that a great deal does, but to be systematic, I go through the six points. We must realize, however, that after going through the six, the work will only have just begun, for we must attempt to be quite explicit about the form and functioning of the logical competence being posited.

1. Logical Competence Is an Abstraction   In all the three ways I discussed, logical competence is an abstraction: It abstracts from logical error, from other psychological functioning that accompanies logical thought, and from the specifics of the many devices that could apply the competence.

2. Logical Competence Is an Ideal   It is not, however, the same sort of idealization that linguistic competence is. Linguistic competence, according to Chomsky, demands the idealization of a homogeneous speech community in which each individual has mastered the grammar perfectly. One source of difference is that, although people must learn their native language in its entirety, they do not learn the foundations of logic. Those foundations, as we considered them in chapter 1, are closely akin to Chomsky's universal grammar. On those foundations people can build elaborate structures and prove theorems. The foundations must be solid enough to sustain any logic that the human mind can construct and powerful enough to yield any logical theorem that the mind can prove. It is nonsense to think that basic logical skills can be learned. But this is a matter that I try to show in later chapters. In particular, I endeavor to show that we do not somehow acquire basic logic in the same way as we acquire our mother tongue.

The second form of idealization to which Chomsky points is unproblematic in relation to logic: the idealization that linguistic competence is uniform in a speech community. Few would raise any difficulties with this idealization as it relates to universal grammar. Pathological factors apart, all children succeed in mastering the grammar of their dialect, and there is no reason even to suspect that they employ different general principles and constraints in doing so, no matter the differences among natural languages. Still, whatever hesitations we might have about the uniformity of universal grammar, we can have none about the uniformity of logic. Logics do not vary geographically as natural languages do. People differ in their ability to think logically, but we do not attribute the differences to differences among the logical systems that they are seeking to apply. Instead we attribute them to individual differences in the ability to work with a common, uniform logic or set of logics. A person with little ability in logic we simply call a logical dunce, not a deviant logician. Certainly, there are differences among logics, such as that between the propositional and predicate calculus, but it seems that they all might be subsumed in a single comprehensive logic. Even if that turns out to be illusory, the hope is that on mature reflection any sound logic should appear sound to persons whose logical penetration is deepest.

There is a sense in which logical competence is an ideal that may be a little different from the way linguistic competence is. Not only is logical competence error free, but it also gives rise to intuitions of absolute necessity. We have, for instance, an intuition that the principle of contradiction could never under any circumstances prove false. We have intuitions that certain forms of inference cannot under any circumstances lead from true premises to false conclusions. There is a sense, then, in which logical intuition prompts us to seek an ideal in our logical thinking, an ideal of absolute clarity and rigor. We certainly aspire to perfect grammaticality, and in that sense linguistic intuition also prompts us to seek an ideal. But we have no intuition that any particular structure in a natural language could not be other than it is. On the contrary, we have every reason to believe that, although there are constraints on the structures of natural languages, there is also considerable flexibility.

The existence of disputes about a supposed logical principle does not threaten the foregoing position on intuitions of necessity. For instance, in any many-valued logic the principle of excluded middle is rejected. But the dispute is precisely about the necessity that attaches to that principle. Once that matter is settled, the dispute is over.

3. Basic Logical Competence Does Not Consist of Beliefs   I reject the position that basic logical competence consists of beliefs. (Here I part company with Chomsky in at least some of his moments, though not perhaps in his more recent ones.) I am uneasy with the idea of propositional knowledge that we cannot state, unless we become professional linguists or logicians. Besides, at the deepest level of cognition we need devices that perform an operation, not inert sentences or propositions. There is no reason to believe that such devices draw inferences from propositions. Hence there is no need for basic beliefs of the sort that Chomsky often speaks about. Finally, I am uneasy with the position that we are forced by nature to believe anything.

On the other hand I am even more uncomfortable with the idea that we can derive logical resources from the performance of logic-free operations. There is a strain of influential modern writing stemming, I believe, from Wittgenstein's *Philosophical Investigations* (1953) and strongly evident in the writings of Piaget (for example, 1953) and Quine (especially 1973), that logical resources emerge from logic-free activities. I find this writing impossibly muddled. There are simply no grounds for believing that a frequently uttered noise can gradually become a proper name that can combine with other frequently uttered noises to form a logical structure with truth conditions, that is, an interpreted sentence.

I therefore adopt an intermediate position. I argue that basic logical competence consists of a set of devices that perform certain operations when certain conditions are satisfied. Part of the operations they perform is to invoke unlearned logical symbols. In effect, this is to say that basic logical resources are of two kinds: devices that perform certain operations and symbols that can be combined, perhaps with learned symbols, to form sentences having logical structure and truth conditions. The reader will grasp at once that this commits me deeply to there being a language of thought of the sort argued for by Fodor (1975). Such a language is the natural home for the unlearned logical resources of which I speak. Indeed, throughout this book I argue that patient psychological and logical study may reveal some basic elements in the language of thought.

In some ways the word "competence" is misleading. When contrasted with "performance," it suggests something static, such as a set of rules. The contrast might be more happily expressed as one between idealized performance and actual performance. The word "competence" is so deeply embedded in modern literature, however, that I continue to use it.

It sometimes seems to me that Chomsky's reluctance to abandon the notion that linguistic competence consists in knowledge-that comes from his sense that we cannot comprehend how logic-free activities can ever yield logical resources. In any case, I take it as a basic working assumption that we cannot. This is not to deny that unlearned logical resources are the output of logic-free biological processes in the developing organism, but only that we can account for their presence by means of some form of learning-how.

Because the distinction between learning-how and learning-that is a crucial one, we must be sure to grasp it. If we engage in learning-that, the item that we learn is an interpreted sentence. Thus we can learn-that: Benjamin Franklin invented bifocal spectacles. An event of learning-how, by contrast, need not involve an interpreted sentence. For example, one learns-how to type. That learning-how presupposes the ability to press the keys with one's fingers. Learning-how results in the ability to sequence key pressings smoothly, to press accurately without looking, and the like. Conditioning, either classical or operant, is on a par with learning-how; it presupposes basic abilities and channels their use. It is for this reason that I reject the notion that learning-how can yield a logical resource. A logical resource, like a demonstrative or a predicate, is not the channeling of preexisting nonlogical skills or capacities. I shall press this conclusion pretty hard.

4. Logical Competence Is the Key Element in the Psychology of Human Reasoning   This is the central tenet of this book. At the beginning we considered the standard positions in logic and psychology. Psychologists mostly feel that logicians are remote scholars who explore certain ideal forms of inference that have little to do with our everyday thought processes. Logicians generally find psychologists equally remote, busily studying the facts of actual reasoning without much concern for logical soundness. Every argument that Chomsky adduces for the relevance of linguistics to the psychology of language applies, mutatis mutandis, to the relevance of logic for psychology. To his arguments I can add those that we considered in the last chapter. The main task for the psychologist who is studying human reasoning is to account for both our ability to reason validly and our intuitions about logical validity. The set of valid inferences is infinite. The subset of those that any individual will formulate or encounter in the reasoning of others is too large and too random to permit its being memorized. It follows that we must have access to a set of rules that can be combined in various ways to yield an infinite set of inferences. Thus the foundations of the logic(s) at which logicians aim, the ideal logic(s), must be psychologically real in the sense of being instantiated in some form in the mind. Further, the best logics found in logic books today provide the best available guides to logical competence. It does not follow, of course, even if a logic characterizes an aspect of logical competence, that the competence is instantiated in any of its currently available forms, say, axiomatic or natural deduction.

All this is not to say that mathematical logic, the main concern of contemporary logicians, is the most substantial element in logical competence. Increasingly it is becoming apparent that the first-order predicate logic, with its model theory, is not a good guide to the logic of ordinary language and ordinary thinking. Indeed, our subsequent inquiries will lean more heavily on the logical analysis of ordinary-language expressions than on standard logical treatises. Perhaps the main difference is that the logic of ordinary-language expressions depends on the logic of kinds, not on that of sets. What this means will gradually become clear.

Psychologists might be tempted to agree with this general position about the role of logic in psychology and yet wonder if it entails any practical consequences for how they should go about their work. In most of the remaining chapters of this book I attempt to show in a few central cases the difference it makes. The difference is substantial.

5. Logical Competence Informs Logical Intuition   The object of logical intuition is interpreted sentences and inferences among such sentences. The form of logical intuition is a judgment about the logical role of the constituents of sentences or about the soundness of inferences— not that intuition yields immediately what logicians might be seeking, but it provides them with a check on their formulations. The check usually takes the form of submitting sentences to intuition to see if their interpretation is in keeping with theoretical prediction. Just as linguistic intuition is a judgment about grammaticality, logical intuition applied to ordinary language is a judgment about truth conditions and speakers' intentions.

By describing these judgments as intuitions, we emphasize their apparent immediacy, the lack of conscious inference. Because logic has so much to do with inference, this calls for comment. One set of logical intuitions has to do with the interpretation of sentences, with a comprehension of what the world has to be like for the sentence to be true. Take the sentence "Freddie is a dog," as asserted of a particular animal. We know that its truth depends on whether the object picked out by *Freddie* is in the kind called *dog*. Not everyone can state the truth conditions so, but every English speaker on hearing the sentence can tell what the individual in question is called and can say to which kind the sentence assigns it. If we had the suspicion that the phrase *a dog* similarly identified an individual, we could check it by considering the sentence *Freddie is not a cat*. It makes no sense at all to ask which cat is being identified as the one that Freddie is not. This would lead to the conclusion that the function of *a cat* is not that of identifying an individual cat and therefore, that *a dog* in "Freddie is a dog" does not identify an individual either. I borrow the point from Peter Geach, and it serves to illustrate how logical intuition serves as a check on theorizing.

Similar points can easily be made about the logical role of other types of words: sentential connectives (such as *not* and *and*), quantifiers (such as *all* and *some*), predicates (such as *hot* and *red*), sortals (such as *dog* and *bicycle*), and so on.

Inferences are often complex, and we sometimes claim an intuition that a certain conclusion follows. When challenged, we can sometimes spell out all the steps in the inference, and this might give the impression that intuitions about inferences can be buttressed by further inferences. Ultimately, however, we are pushed back to inferences that cannot be further analyzed, to the inferentially simple steps. A favorite candidate for that status is *modus ponens*. Take an example: If we have it that *it is raining* and if we also have it that *if it is raining, then the ground is wet*, then we are safe in concluding that *the ground is wet*. If logicians satisfy themselves that all inferences of this form are valid and that there cannot be an invalid one, then they are entitled to give the common form of such arguments in an abstract schema and state that it is a valid rule of inference. Their judgment rests ultimately on logical intuition, that is, presentations that do not depend on conscious inference. It is with these basic presentations that logic is most confident, and it is these presentations that are the surest guide to the form of logical competence.

By parity of reasoning with Chomsky, if we can trace particular inference forms that satisfy people to the mind's basic logical resources, then we are entitled to claim that we have achieved explanatory adequacy with regard to those inference forms. In other words, our explanation would then be based on the mind's natural resources—which, by the way, is not the same as a reason for judging those inference forms valid.

6. The Object of Logical Investigation Is Logic, Not Psychology   In this I also part company with Chomsky, who takes a psychologistic position about linguistics, and I stand closer to Frege and Husserl. But I do not move all the way to their side. With Barwise and Perry (1983), I hold that logic is sometimes obliged to characterize mental states in its task of specifying truth conditions and valid inferences. Even then, however, the specification is for logical, not psychological, purposes. Be all that as it may, the rift with Chomsky is far from serious, because I hold that as a side effect, so to speak, logical studies supply a characterization of psychological competence. For this reason, the work of logicians is essential to psychologists. Logical competence is, perhaps, easier to study than linguistic competence. The competence that Chomsky is most anxious to study is universal grammar, but it reveals itself only in the learning of grammatical competence for particular languages and in the ability to function in and exercise intuition with respect to particular languages. Universal grammar, then, is at two removes from the data: First, linguists must establish the grammars of particular languages; then they must divine the set of universal constraints on all such grammars. Cognitive psychologists seeking to characterize basic logical competence are at only one remove from the data. There is nothing in logic akin to natural languages in the linguistic case.

Basic Logical Competence
Throughout I have been using the expression "basic logical competence" to speak about the psychological capacity that informs logical intuition. The force of "basic" is to rule out all theorems that can be proved within a logic and all metalogical theorems about such matters as the completeness, soundness, or decidability of a particular logic. Clearly, there are large individual differences among people in knowledge of such matters. "Basic logical competence" means something that is common to all nonpathological human minds.

It does not seem possible to specify basic logical competence in its entirety. It is easier to specify some of its constituents and leave it to the development of logic to fill out the details. Basic competence probably includes certain fundamental principles, of which the principle of contradiction is the most basic. It must also include the logical resources that are deployed in natural-language sentences. These include some set of sentential connectives, possibly *not*, *and*, exclusive *or*, and *necessarily*. (I discuss these in detail in chapters 4 and 7, where I show that this choice is not completely arbitrary.) Logical resources also include the logic of sortals (common nouns), predicates (such as *red* and *loves*), and quantifiers (such as *all* and *some*). An important special case of predicates is the intentional ones, such as *believes* and *wants*. The logical resources deployed in natural language also include the logical role of proper names, function words (such as *parent of*) and individual variables (such as *someone*). Basic competence must also include a certain number of inference rules. For example, it might include the natural-deduction rule of *and*-elimination. To illustrate, suppose that we have conjoined sentences that do not contain any pronouns or indexicals: "Joe is tall and Joe is handsome." By the rule of *and*-elimination we have "Joe is tall." Matters are more complicated when the original sentence contains pronouns or indexicals (see Barwise and Perry 1983, chap. 8), but we need not delay here over the complications. In fact, the logic of the sentential connectives in its simplest aspects may be given to us in a form that is close to natural-deduction rules. There also seems to be a basic competence with respect to the presuppositions of sentences, questions, commands, and obligations. The elements so far mentioned are some of the resources of basic competence in deductive logic. There is also a basic competence in inductive logic that is not nearly so well understood.

The list might be continued, but as it is, it goes well beyond the scope of the logic that I will be discussing in detail in later chapters. I must limit myself severely, so I concentrate on those elements whose logic has been most thoroughly explored. The choice indicates no assumption about the relative importance to either psychology or logic of the elements chosen.

Putting Logical Competence to Work

In the list of elements of basic logical competence, the lion's share went to the logical form of sentences. A great part of basic competence has to do with the interpretation of sentences. There is a well-known and important fact about the interpretation of sentences: In the last analysis the interpretation cannot be done by sentences. The basic idea, which I draw from Ryle (1949, chap. 1), can be illuminated by considering translations of sentences. Take the Irish sentence

Tá ceithre chos faoi mhadra

and its English translation

A dog has four legs.

The meaning of the Irish sentence is thus conveyed to the Sassenach because he is able to interpret the English translation. The English sentence, however, is just as much in need of interpretation as the Irish one. Suppose, with Fodor (1975), that we posit a language of thought into which natural-language sentences are translated (or compiled); language-of-thought sentences corresponding to English sentences are themselves in need of interpretation. No matter how many such translations are performed, an interpretation would still not be achieved. The attempt to handle interpretation by means of sentences alone leads to an infinite and pernicious regress.

What is needed to perform the interpretation is some device that actually places the mind in intentional contact with the semantic values of a sentence's constituents and their combinations. Apart from the logical difficulty, sentences are too inert; they are not able to perform tasks. What should be put in their place? Today we almost automatically think of procedures of the sort used in computer work. Procedures in a computer are mechanisms that perform a certain task when certain conditions are satisfied. Their general form is

Under circumstances X, perform O,

where O is some operation. Although we must employ a sentence to state its form, a procedure itself is not a sentence but a device that performs a certain operation.

There is, however, a problem with adopting this attractive idea from the world of computers. A procedure is an electronic device that in the last analysis can be described completely in the language of physics. Existing computers, replete with acres of procedures, are notoriously inept in the matter of interpretation (see Fodor 1981, essay 8). To claim that the mind does the work of interpreting sentences by means of procedures is to invite the impression that the business of interpretation is, in principle, easy to understand. Nothing could be further from the case. My interpretation of the words that I utter and hear involves a large number of what are technically called "intentional states." For example, normally when I use the name *Freddie*, I refer to an object that is outside my mind; in fact I refer to our family dog, who spends much of the time curled up on the sofa. It is precisely this intentional contact between my mind and the objects picked out by my words that is difficult to explain in the nonintentional language of neurophysiology and computer science. The question of how intentional states can be explained is the most profound one facing cognitive psychology and the philosophy of mind today. In the interests of avoiding misunderstanding, then, I do not call the mind's interpretative devices *procedures* but simply *interpreters*. This is to give warning that what has to be explained is an intentional state. There exist at present no devices or arrangements that place a computer in an intentional state. Nevertheless, interpreters are like procedures in that they are not sentences or beliefs but devices that place the mind in intentional contact with the objects that form the semantic content of some linguistic expression.

Sometimes I appeal to an interpreter to perform the double task of setting up and interpreting a string of symbols. For example, I posit the existence of an interpreter to explain the learning of a proper name. The interpreter yields a sentence that expresses the meaning of the proper name and also interprets the expression. Its function, then, is composed of two parts: a syntactic function, which is when certain conditions are satisfied to print out a certain expression, and a semantic function, which is to interpret the expression. It is conceivable, at least in principle, that the syntactic function could be modeled using a computer. Despite serious efforts (see Dretske 1981 and Stalnaker 1984), it is fair to say that we are almost completely without insight into the semantic function. With Fodor (1975), Dennett (1978), Cummins (1983), and Churchland (1984), a varied set of bedfellows though they be, I do not expect that intentional states can be explained through the notion of physical causality. For this reason I am inclined to leave intentionality unanalyzed, and thus I use "interpreter" in its semantic function to speak of what I see largely as a mystery.

What about logic's rules of inference? How are they realized in the mind? Among such rules are probably several of the rules of natural-deduction systems, such as the rule of *and*-elimination, which we have already considered. Historically, the inference rule most deeply embedded in logic is the one called modus ponens, which, when p and q stand for propositions, has the general form: If p is true and p *implies* q is also true, then q is true. Here, the truth of p and of p *implies* q is sufficient grounds for concluding that q is true. The mental device that applies this inference rule—if indeed the mind does apply it—might be this: Recommend q for acceptance to judgment with no less confidence than one is prepared to accord jointly to q and p *implies* q. Again the inference rules have some similarity to procedures, but for the reason specified in connection with interpretation, I do not call the psychological devices that perform the task of drawing inferences *procedures*.

But are the mental devices that draw inferences different from interpreters? It would seem that there must be two distinct sets of devices, though it is not clear exactly where to draw the line. Clearly my interpreting *Freddie* to mean our family pet is not an inference. On the other hand, there are inferences that are not just a matter of interpretation. For example, take the following two sentences:

Mark Twain is the author of *Tom Sawyer*.
Samuel Clemens is the author of *Tom Sawyer*.

Together they warrant the inference

Mark Twain is Samuel Clemens,

though neither singly nor together do they directly *mean* that. The inference is warranted by reason of the transitivity of identity, here signaled by *is*. It is warranted, then, by the meaning of the *is* of identity, but the conclusion is not the interpretation of either sentence or of the pair in combination. It follows that besides interpreters we need a second set of devices to draw inferences. I call them *implicators*.

Part of the trouble in distinguishing interpreters from implicators is the close connection between meaning and inference. Husserl (1970 [1900], p. 323) actually said that logic is the "science of meanings." Meaning seems to ground inference; but for all that, meaning and inference are not identical.

Finally, there are the fundamental logical principles, the most fundamental of which is the principle of contradiction. This principle states that it can never be the case that both p and $\sim p$ are true at the same time. How are such principles realized in logical competence? In modern texts they are handled normally by the semantics of $\sim$, which specifies that, when p is true, $\sim p$ is false, and when $\sim p$ is true, p is false. This eliminates the possibility that both p and $\sim p$ could be true at the same time. Further, the principle of contradiction is handled nowadays by the natural-deduction rule of neg-introduction. This rule applies whenever under assumption q a contradiction (p and $\sim p$) is derived; it allows the inference to $\sim q$. All this means that the principle of contradiction can be realized in logical competence by the two types of entities that I have already posited, an interpreter to handle the semantics of $\sim$ and an implicator to operate the rule of neg-introduction.

If these proposals are correct, we need not base logic on any genetically given propositions. Neither interpreters nor implicators are sentences or propositions. They are devices that perform a task. The task may well be the production of a sentence that may then be interpreted by the set of interpreters, but sentences are produced by devices that are not themselves sentences. A fortiori, the position being explored attributes no genetically given beliefs to the mind. Even an interpreted sentence is not a belief, for we do not believe every sentence we understand. Besides, I have not attributed genetically given sentences to the mind.

General Remarks on the Functioning of Logical Competence
Interpreters seem to function automatically and to give content to the symbols they interpret. There is nowadays a good deal of psychological

evidence that the interpretation of individual lexical items is automatic and initially unconscious (see Tanenhaus et al. 1979, Swinney 1979, and Seidenberg et al. 1982). The evidence is that a person, on encountering an ambiguous word such as *tire*, accesses its two meanings—to grow fatigued and rubber tire—even though only one is appropriate to the semantic context and even though only one is allowed by the syntax. For example, when confronted with the phrase *the tire*, where the definite article specifies that the word is a noun, people still elicit the verb meaning, to grow fatigued. The contextually inappropriate meaning is deleted sometime in the first 200 msec after contact and does not normally enter consciousness. The technique that reveals this is known as *priming*. It has been established (by the researchers named above) that words that have recently been interpreted are interpreted more rapidly on renewed contact. The studies of processing ambiguous words make use of this fact. They show, for example, that on renewed contact with the word *tire* as a verb, after contact with it as a noun, the meaning *to grow tired* is elicited more rapidly than if there had been no contact with the word at all.

I should point out that the studies cited in the previous paragraph do not show that the mind is placed in intentional contact with the semantic values of *tire* in both of its senses every time the word is encountered. It could be that the process of lexical lookup is accomplished for each sense. My main reason for alluding to those studies is to underline how automatic, how recondite, how remote from consciousness most of the processes of sentence interpretation are.

At the level of phrases or sentences there is also some evidence that interpretation, as well as parsing, is normally automatic. Tyler and Marlsen-Wilson (1977), for example, have shown that ambiguities at the phrase level are reflected in longer processing times, though subjects are not normally aware of the ambiguity. For example, sentences such as "Flying planes can be dangerous" take longer to interpret than the unambiguous "Taking breaks can be dangerous." This evidence (that both interpretations of the ambiguous sentence are automatically elicited) is not nearly as solid as the evidence that the several meanings of an ambiguous word are automatically elicited. What does seem solid, however, is that in even the simplest cases, such as "Freddie is a dog," the process of interpretation is normally automatic and unconscious. What may not be unconscious is the product of that process. Native speakers of English can show you in some appropriate manner that they have understood the sentence. They cannot, if they hear so simple a sentence at all, fail to interpret it, but they have no awareness of the process of interpretation. They may not even be reliable about the precise form of the interpretation. We saw earlier that native speakers of English may imagine that the phrase *a dog* refers to a particular creature in the same way that *Freddie* does. Logic classes are often required to dispose of such impressions. Still, we would not want to say that the logically naive fail to understand such simple sentences.

I also claimed that interpreters assign content to sentences. That is, they turn an uninterpreted formula into an interpreted one. What differentiates the uninterpreted formula from the interpreted one, the meanings specified for the lexical items and syntactic structures, is often called *content*, so we can use the word for that purpose. In this way interpreters contribute content to thought; in some sense they contribute what is essential.

Not so the implicators that draw inferences. Inferences involve passing from one or several thoughts to another one. They have to do with the sequence of thoughts. If we were to propose that implicators generate the sequence of thoughts, that they are the laws of thought-sequence generation, then logical error and logic-free reverie would be impossible. Moreover, if the functioning of implicators were automatic, they could be turned off only by unconsciousness or death. For example, the implicator for *and*-elimination on encountering *p and q* would infer *p* and separately *q*. Then the implicator for *and*-introduction would uselessly infer (*p and q*) *and p* and separately (*p and q*) *and q*—and so *and*-introduction and *and*-elimination would go on indefinitely. For such reasons, it is wiser to regard implicators as devices whose functioning is available to the mind in assessing the soundness of inferences. Their functioning must be to some extent under voluntary control so that they do not go on aimlessly.

The picture that emerges is in some ways analogous to that which I at least have of capacities to deal with the prosodic features of words and strings of words. The stress and prosodic properties of individual words are assigned in the lexicon. The prosodic properties of strings of words are discovered after we string them together, in retrospect as it were. The poet or versifier must try out words for their prosodic contribution to the string. Of course, the experienced poet may have worked out the prosodic effect of many words in many contexts so that he finds the right word more quickly than the beginner. Nevertheless, the poet began by trying out individual words in individual contexts for particular effects. So interpreters would seem to function automatically in establishing the content of strings of words. Implicators would seem to apply in retrospect after certain sequences of propositions had already been produced. And, just as poets when attending to their business are more sensitive than most of us to prosody, so logicians when attending to theirs are more sensitive than most of us to logical soundness.

This picture fits well with the popular view of deductive logic of the sort we are considering. Hebb (1958), for instance, assigned a quite modest role to such logic in the scientific process. He saw deductive logic as playing no recognizable role in the processes of discovery or invention. He saw the role of deductive logic in *"verification, the process of testing, clarifying and systematizing new ideas"* (p. 213). This seems to be correct. It means that the role of interpreters and implicators that I am positing is a modest part of what we call *intelligence* or *genius*. The main business of intelligence appears to be the generation of a sequence of thoughts that is appropriate to some purpose. Of this I have little to say. The business of assessing the sequence for logical soundness is secondary. Of course, I am not suggesting that an argument must be completed before it is assessed for validity. We are able to assess the validity of each step as we go along.

My position also helps us to understand Husserl's statement that the laws of logic are not laws of thought but truths about how we *ought* to judge. Husserl was prepared to abandon the notion of law altogether in connection with logic for fear that it would be interpreted as a law of thought. As I construe them, implicators are not laws that have to do directly with the generation of a sequence of thoughts but devices that give us indirect access to necessary truths about inference, and in that sense implicators do give us laws of logic. Precisely because the laws of inference are not laws of the generation of thought but of the validation of thought, they do not rule out the possibility of logical error. They do not even rule out the possibility of error in the assessment of validity, for assessment is ultimately a matter of judgment. All that the operation of an interpreter or implicator guarantees is the presentation to the mind of an interpreted string. The picture I am sketching is that an implicator applied to certain simple inferences cannot fail to present a correct assessment of the inference.

None of this is intended to suggest that interpreters and implicators lead us to logical truths automatically. Many of us may not discover a single logical truth in a whole lifetime. But it is open to us to do so. We have all exercised logical intuition when we claimed to know that we understood a sentence or when we judged a certain inference to be valid. For instance, who has not said something such as "But the day had to have been cloudy, because you said the day was cold and cloudy"? Our conviction in making such a remark rests on the operation of the counterpart of an *and*-eliminator in logical competence. Presumably, the relevant logical truth about the soundness of *and*-elimination is occasioned by spotting the occurrence of several such particular intuitions, spotting their common logical structure, reflecting on the meaning of *and*, and concluding (at least when matters are not complicated by pronouns and demonstratives) that *and*-elimination is an undubitably sound inference form. I consider certain difficulties for this position when I discuss the propositional calculus in detail in chapter 6. These difficulties are easily disposed of, however, and so the conclusion just reached seems to be the correct one.

What I am claiming is that logical intuition is a sure guide to basic logical truths, provided that it is exercised on single applications of a single inference rule. It is possible for intuition to fail or even mislead if we attempt to apply several inference rules at once, especially to syntactically tortuous sentences (for example, those with several negatives or with numerous embeddings). Logicians have always sought to ground logic on intuitively clear and simple cases. They are right, because our processing powers are limited.

There is a problem with interpreters, already alluded to, and it is time I return to it. I have continually claimed that interpreters perform the operation of interpreting strings of symbols, that they contribute the content to thought; at the same time I have noted that we are not normally aware of the logical form of interpreted strings. We might suppose that, if the interpreters assign logical form, as they must, then we should be aware of that form. The reason we are not, most probably, is the intentional nature of all thought and all knowledge. For example, when someone uses *Freddie* to speak of my family pet, my mind goes at once to the pet. It does not dwell on the word or on its logical function. If someone says "Freddie is sick," my attention goes again to the pet and to the state of his health. It does not dwell on the words *is* and *sick* or on their logical functions. Because I grasp which individual is spoken about and something about the state of his health, I can translate the sentence into other languages that I know or paraphrase it in English: "Freddie is unwell"; "Our dog is in poor health"; "Freddie belongs to the class of things that are sick." The paraphrase comes out right if I grasp the state of affairs specified by the original sentence. I do not need to be conscious of the sentence's logical form, nor in fact am I usually. This explains why it is so difficult to establish the logical form of sentences. The same explanation, slightly adapted, reveals why it is so difficult to discover the forms of valid inference. A thinker's attention is on the matter he is thinking about, not on the form of the thought. So much is this the case that he cannot, by changing the focus of attention, discover the linguistic or inferential rules that yielded the thought or the logical form of the expression in which it is couched. For a different view of our unawareness of logical form, see Jackendoff (unpublished).

To sum up the message of this section. I am suggesting that basic logical competence consists of a set of procedurelike devices that perform the work of interpreting symbolic expressions and checking inferences among such expressions. To perform the work of interpretation, the mind has a set of automatically functioning devices that I call interpreters. These operate on expressions in the language of thought in the first instance. They are not beliefs. Much of the rest of the book is given over to the attempt to specify them and their manner of functioning. Distinct from interpreters is another set of devices that the mind has; I call these *implicators*, whose function is to check on inferences among interpreted sentences. The functioning of implicators is subject to voluntary control.

Competence and Foundations

In this final section I want to dispel any suspicion that my position is psychologistic. I hope to be more persuasive by showing how it agrees closely with the deepest theoretical roots in those arch-antipsychologistic logicians, Frege and Husserl. The exercise will bring to light a number of additional points about the relation between meaning and language that will prepare us for the succeeding chapters in which the general theory is applied to a small number of cases, always with meaning at the focus of attention.

It might at first appear that my position comes dangerously close to psychologism with its emphasis on psychological interpreters and implicators. It might appear that, although I escape Kantianism by locating the implicators in the evaluation of inferences, not in their generation, I am nonetheless grounding logic in psychological properties and events. To be clear of the charge of psychologism, however, it is enough to note that my claims have to do with access to logical principles, not with justifying them.

Frege repudiates the idea of justifying foundations for the whole logic (1964 [1893]):

> The question of why and with what right we acknowledge a law of logic to be true, logic can answer only by reducing it to another law of logic. Where that is not possible, logic can give no answer. If we step away from logic, we may say: we are compelled to make judgements by our own nature and by external circumstances; and if we do so, we cannot reject this law—of identity, for example; we must acknowledge it unless we wish to reduce our thought to confusion and finally renounce all judgement whatever. I shall neither dispute nor support this view; I shall merely remark that what we have here is not a logical consequence. What is given is not a reason for something's being true, but for our taking it to be true. (p. 15)

Frege certainly held that we have a "fundamental conviction" (1964 [1893], p. 25) about the truth of the basic principles: that their truth is "immediately obvious" (1979, p. 189); that they are "self-evident" (1964 [1893], p. 234); and that they are "known a priori (1959 [1884], p. 83; 1979, p. 277). But for Frege a truth is known a priori when "its proof can be derived exclusively from general laws, which themselves neither need nor admit of proof" (1959 [1884], p. 4). There is still the appeal to unjustified foundations.

The deepest that Frege was prepared to go was to base logic on language. He noted that language comes to us from empirical experience; we must use our ears to learn a natural language, like German. Yet Frege also recognized that language is not entirely an empirical matter. He observed that, although language is a human creation, mankind shapes language "in conformity with the logical disposition that is alive in [it]" (1979, p. 269). This position seems close to the one I have just outlined and to the one I develop in subsequent chapters about specific linguistic elements and types. Frege had nothing to say about the form of this linguistic disposition or about its provenance in the mind. In a way, I see myself as trying to supply some of the detail.

Husserl's position is similar to Frege's. He returned to the epistemological grounding of logic again and again. His most firmly held position is that logic's basic principles are not the conclusion of any "theoretical proof" (1970 [1900], p. 152). Like Frege, Husserl frequently spoke of a certain "inner evidence" for the truth of logical axioms (1970 [1900], p. 61), or of "apodeictic inner evidence" (1970 [1900], p. 99). Here *apodeictic* seems to be taken in the sense defined by Kant: "universally and objectively certain (valid for all)" (*Logic*, p. 73). Elsewhere, Husserl speaks of "insight into . . . the truth of the logical laws" (1970 [1900], pp. 100, 109). Again he tells us that such insight, such inner evidence is "the most perfect 'mark' of correctness. . . . It counts as an immediate intimation of truth itself" (1970 [1900], p. 61).

The bedrock of Husserl's thinking in *Logical Investigations* is, like Frege's, meaning. The ultimate support for logic's basic principles is the meaning of the expressions in which they are couched. In other words, logic's basic laws are analytic. At least, that is how I read the several remarks that appeal to sense as the ultimate ground for logic (Husserl 1970 [1900]):

> For me the pure truths of logic are all the ideal laws which have their whole foundation in the "sense", the "essence" or the "content" of the concepts of Truth, Proposition, Object, Relation, Combination, Law, Fact, etc. More generally stated they have their whole foundation in the sense of the concepts which make up the

heritage of *all* science, which represent the categories of constituents out of which science as such is essentially constituted. Laws of this sort should not be violated by any theoretical assertion, proof or theory, not because such a thing would render them false . . . but because it would render them inherently absurd. (p. 144; see also p. 159 and especially p. 323)

Husserl had an elaborate theory of sense and concepts. One feature to emphasize is his insistence on the objectivity, or better "intersubjectivity," of sense and concepts. This I take as agreeing with Wittgenstein: Language is essentially public, objective; it is not, normally, about mental states and acts. That is how logical truths present themselves to us, as objective. And logic is the "science of meanings" (Husserl 1970 [1900], p. 323). In that capacity it studies "the pure 'laws of thought', which express the *a priori* connection between the categorial forms of meanings and their objectivity or truth" (1970 [1900], p. 323). This seems to mean that without inference from experience we grasp the truth of logic's laws in grasping the meaning of the words in which the laws are expressed. Husserl was not of course committed to the doctrine that we grasp logical truths effortlessly; he was committed to the view that logical truth is revealed when "we take the trouble to detach the ideal essence of meanings from their psychological and transient and grammatical connections" (1970 [1900], pp. 322–323).

How might meaning play so central a role as Frege and Husserl envisage for it? To see how, we have to consider some broad principles relating to how we assign content to linguistic symbols, and, in addition, we have to reflect on the general conceptual framework within which interpretation takes place. There are constraints on both the assignment of content and on the metaphysical framework within which the content is dealt with. Presumably such constraints are the major explanation for the intertranslatability of natural languages and also for the (assumed) consistency of logical intuition across people. Our task in the next six chapters is to work out some of these constraints and to examine how they are realized and how they operate. There is a temptation to state the lot as a set of metaphysical presuppositions. But presuppositions suggest beliefs, and we have decided to eschew unlearned beliefs. We will, then, be seeking to locate the constraints in interpreters and implicators. Frege and Husserl warn us that even if we succeed, we will not have proved the truth of any logical principle; we will have explained why we tend to think in a certain way. That is precisely what saves the position from psychologism—it does not appeal to psychology to justify logical principles.

Appendix
Johnson-Laird on Mental Logic

In a recent book one prominent psychologist, Johnson-Laird (1983), opposed strongly the position I am working toward. An important aim of his book is to reject the notion of "mental logic." It is not clear what he means by that, so we must test some possible interpretations. On any interpretation, however, he makes a greater gap between logic and psychology than I consider reasonable.

Johnson-Laird set up the question of mental logic by asking how people can reason validly. The most tempting explanation, he suggested, is mental logic. The one clear interpretation that he suggested is that to explain, say, valid propositional reasoning, we posit the existence in the mind of "the proposition calculus itself." Even this suggestion, which he considers ludicrous, is not clear. Does it mean that the propositional calculus is in the mind in the way it is in a textbook? In a textbook we find uninterpreted symbols that we have to interpret. As we have already seen, grasping the logical notions and arguments presented by a teacher demands of the student a prior logical competence. What would interpret the inert symbols of the propositional calculus that we are imagining in the mind? If whatever interpreted them needed to grasp the propositional calculus to do so, we would be no nearer an explanation of valid reasoning than we were without the inert symbols. If that is what "mental logic" means, I could agree with Johnson-Laird in rejecting it.

Another possibility is that the mind acts in conformity with the propositional calculus, that it never violates any principles of that logic in its inner workings. This is much too weak because no device in its inner workings violates that logic. If that is all that is meant by the claim that the propositional calculus is in the mind, it would be trivially true, for on the same reading that calculus would be in my bicycle, my motorcar, and my watch. This is not what Johnson-Laird is considering and rejecting.

In order to obtain some grasp of what "mental logic" might mean, we must make a distinction between mental activity and its content, much like that between sentences and the content that they express. An interesting proposal for a mental version of the propositional calculus, so far as I can see, consists of a set of constraints that has to do with content, constraints that are characterized by the propositional calculus. The most plausible place for those constraints to operate is in the evaluation of content for logical soundness, not in the generation of a thought sequence in the first instance. The reason for this choice is the requirement, noted in the assessment of Kant, to leave room for logical error. If the production of a sequence of thought were constrained by logical laws, no such sequence could be produced in violation of those laws. This would debar not only logical error but also much of the fanciful thought of which we are all capable. It seems more natural to situate the constraints in the process of evaluating thought for logical soundness. That process can be turned off altogether, as when we indulge in fanciful reveries—which might help to explain why some logical errors slip through even when the process is meant to be turned on. The evaluation process seems completely secure only when the semantics of the language is clear and unambiguous and when the step to be evaluated is a small one, as in a single application of the rule modus ponens. Thus language could be another source of logical error and yet another could be attempts to evaluate too large a logical step all at once (see Henle 1962).

Johnson-Laird raises a weighty problem for the notion of mental logic by asking which one of the many modal logics that have been proposed to handle a certain set of intuitions is supposed to correspond to the mental one. This is not so much a problem in connection with, say, competing propositional calculi; for example, classical, relevance, and intuitionist logic. Because these logics are in competition, each claiming to be the sole correct representation of the relevant set of intuitions, we can say that the best one is the one that corresponds to the relevant mental logic. We could leave it to logical research to decide which is the best. The problem is much more acute in modal logic, in which we can see an infinity of distinct systems. Not every one of these systems can be psychologically real. Even if it turned out to be impossible to choose among several modal logics, we would still be uneasy if we ended up proposing several thousand mental modal logics. This problem is treated fully in chapter 9. To anticipate what will be said there, it seems we have a choice: (1) Dismiss the multitudes of modal logics as resulting from the uncertainty of modal intuitions, in which case we need not bother about the problem of mental modal logics; or (2) discover a principled way to cut down to a few the number of modal logics that represent modal intuition. While holding on to both possibilities, I favor the second.

Johnson-Laird's next objection to mental logics is not a serious one. He pointed out that there are many logically equivalent ways to axiomatize any logic. He asked how we could ever choose the one that was supposed to be realized in the mind. First, even if it were not possible to make a principled choice, mental logic could remain undisturbed. The mental-logic proposal is simply that a logic is realized in the mind in some form. Second, we have the usual empirical evidence to help us choose. One line of such evidence is ease in following logical arguments expressed in one way rather than another—witness the greater ease with which we can do proofs in natural-deduction form rather than on an axiomatic base, at least when working on problems in logic and not in metalogic. Other lines of evidence are speed of processing, number of errors, and age at which a certain inference form is manifested. I am not saying that it will ever be easy to decide.

Yet another of Johnson-Laird's objections is the observation that people's logical performance is greatly dependent on the content of thought, yet logic is content independent. That performance is affected by content is well attested. It is not clear, though, how this is supposed to undermine the idea of a mental logic. Part of the problem is Johnson-Laird's failure to specify what "mental logic" might mean. My own proposal has little trouble handling the data. I locate language as a source of error. If a person has not mastered a particular vocabulary, his attention may be so taken up with understanding the meaning of the sentences that the evaluation of logical soundness may be proportionately skimpier (see Kellaghan and Macnamara 1967 and Macnamara 1970). This would not mean that the proper statement of that person's principles for logical evaluation should be content sensitive.

A final argument that Johnson-Laird advanced against mental logic goes altogether wide of the mark. He pointed out that everyday reasoning often involves quantification over sets, for example, in reaching general conclusions about numbers. It follows that everyday reasoning sometimes involves higher-order predicate calculi (higher than first order, in which generalizations are over individuals only). Johnson-Laird noted that higher-order calculi are incomplete (1983):

> That is to say, there is no way to formalize the calculus so that all valid inferences are derivable from it. If there can be no formal logic that captures all the valid deductions, then *a fortiori* there can be no mental logic that does either. . . . This failure is a final and decisive blow to the doctrine of mental logic. (pp. 140–141)

This point has been put to me by several psychologists, but it rests on muddled thinking. Why should a logic be complete simply because it is mental? I see no good reason why it should; but even if it had to be complete to be mental, the result would not count against there being a mental propositional logic and a mental first-order predicate logic, because those logics are complete. To say a logic is incomplete is merely to say that there are some logical valid sentences in the relevant language that cannot be proved within the logic that employs that language. This means that truth in that language cannot be equated with provability. If the logic were a mental one, it would mean that the notion of a logically valid sentence in the language could not be identified with provability by means of the resources of the language and its inferential devices. This says nothing about whether or not that language and its inferential resources can be realized in a human mind. Johnson-Laird's case seems to be a non sequitur.

More generally, Johnson-Laird has not produced any telling, much less conclusive, argument against the very notion that a logic should be realized in the mind.

3
Logic and Name Learning

There are three principal situations in which a child (or anyone) learns a proper name: (1) The object named is present at the time, (2) the object is absent at the time (perhaps because it has ceased to exist), or (3) there is no object and the name is vacuous, for example, *Santa Claus* and *Goldilocks*. The logic of the first two types of name is the same because logic pays no attention to how a name is learned. Their psychology, however, is rather different. The logic of vacuous names is different from that of nonvacuous ones and so, too, is the psychology. I explore the psychology of all three learning situations, showing the contribution of logic to each. The time has come to pass from generalities about how logic and psychology are related to particulars.

There is a certain number of logical tasks for proper names to do. I specify those tasks and give a theory of how proper names (PNs) perform them. The literature on the logic of PNs is immense, and there are many disputes about how they function. I present what I consider to be the best theory, and although I indicate briefly why I think it is satisfactory, I am not at pains to justify my claims. For that I have to depend mainly on the sources I cite. Fortunately, there is no dispute about the logical tasks themselves. My main object is to show that each logical task places constraints and demands on the psychology of how PNs are learned. I also show that theories of how PNs perform their logical tasks place constraints and demands on psychological theory. It will then be obvious how the psychological theory that I present must be modified by those who do not accept my claims about how PNs perform their logical tasks. There are many aspects of the learning of PNs, such as their phonology, morphology, and syntax, that I do not advert to unless they impinge on the treatment of the semantics.

Logic of Proper Names

Nonvacuous Proper Names
Nonvacuous PNs have five properties: (1) They designate individuals; (2) they pick out individuals across all times and places; (3) the identities

of the individuals are traced by means of sortals; (4) the sortals used denote kinds; and (5) the references of the PNs are not mediated by a Fregean sense. I examine each of these in turn.

1. Designation of Individuals   The main logical function of a PN is to designate an individual. The individuals so designated are often people, pets, streets, or towns. They can, however, be quite complex (for example, Ireland or McGill University) or quite abstract (for example, the number three). Because we are working on the learning of PNs by young children, we confine our attention to names for people and pets (and in the next section names for imaginary people and animals).

2. Time and Place   A PN does not pick out an individual at a particular time or place; it picks it out across all those times and places at which it exists and, furthermore, in all those circumstances in which it might possibly be. To see this, imagine that a PN picked out an individual just at the time it was uttered. In that case it would be alright to say something such as

Joe is in his office now.

If we were to say instead

Joe was in his office yesterday,

our utterance would fail to say anything, because on the imagined theory, the name *Joe* would pick out no individual at a time previous to its utterance. Because in fact we are free to predicate something of Joe at any time or place in which he exists or in any circumstances in which he might possibly be, it follows that his name must pick him out in all circumstances. The rest of the sentence usually makes a selection from among the circumstances by specifying a time, place, or possible set of circumstances. We thus have to make provision in the logic of PNs for the identity of an individual across time, place, and possible circumstances.

3. Sortals and Identity   One of the best supported theories in the philosophy of language, it seems to me, is that the identity of an individual is traced in connection with a sortal (see Dummett 1981; Geach 1962; Gupta 1980; Wiggins 1967, 1980). By *sortal* I mean a count noun in its logical function, that is, a noun used to denote a kind that supplies a principle of individuation and a principle of identity for those individuals that are members of the denoted kind.

The theory to which I allude supports the claim that there is no individuation of entities that is not sortal dependent (see Geach 1962).

This is supported by the fact that individuals cannot be counted without the guidance of a sortal. We cannot count the blues in a room because we do not know what to take as a single blue. (I do not mean shades of blue.) One does not know whether to take a blue shirt as one individual or each of its constituent pieces of cloth (pockets, arms, cuffs) or each thread or each fiber of each thread. I discuss this at greater length in chapter 7.

Sortals, as Gupta (1980) pointed out in his masterly monograph on the logic of common nouns, also supply a principle of identity. No other expressions supply such a principle. We cannot trace the identity of an individual under the guidance of a predicate (adjective), such as *blue*. A blue hankie, used to clean the windscreen of a car, is no longer blue, but it is the same hankie. *Hankie* is a sortal and supplies a principle of identity; *blue*, as a predicate, does not.

Different sortals sometimes supply different principles of identity for a single individual, thus bringing home to us their function in relation to identity. To grasp the idea, imagine that Margaret Thatcher is a passenger on a plane from London to Paris and imagine that, as her exalted status demands, she is passenger number one on the plane. During the trip Margaret Thatcher *is* passenger number one; every property of Margaret Thatcher is a property of passenger number one and vice versa. Margaret Thatcher is prime minister of England and so is passenger number one; Margaret Thatcher is the wife of Dennis Thatcher and so is passenger number one; and so on. When the plane arrives in Paris, Margaret Thatcher ceases to be a passenger. It follows that *passenger* no longer supplies a principle of identity for her, but *person* does. On the flight home again she becomes a passenger once more, and British Airways will count her as two passengers in their annual report. Because the identity of passengers is not that of persons, we count persons and passengers differently.

The PN *Margaret Thatcher* follows the person, so to speak, rather than the passenger. *Person*, tracing the identity of an individual over its whole existence and across all possible circumstances in which it might be, is what Gupta calls a *substance sortal*. Clearly, a PN requires the support of a substance sortal.

To bring home the idea even more forcefully, notice that Margaret Thatcher over her existence can change all her inessential properties, which include all her perceptible ones. Her weight and shape may change; indeed her shape changes every time she moves. Her complexion may change with emotion or illness, as may her temperature. She may even lose a limb without ceasing to be the person Margaret Thatcher. The only properties she cannot lose are those that are essential to a person. And those are precisely the properties that are specified in the kind designated by the substance sortal *person*. We see more of all this in chapter 7.

A note about the expression "to trace the identity of an individual under a sortal." The word "trace" tends to suggest the exercise of a psychological skill, a psychological performance. This is not what the word is meant to convey. The basic notion here is a metaphysical one, that an individual is identical over time, independent of anyone's actual tracking of it (see Gupta 1980, p. 22). Perhaps the notion of a metaphysical principle of identity would make little sense if it were not supported by a general notion of how we can tell identity from one occasion to the next. I do not wish to argue for or against any position as regards the role of such an epistemic criterion. In any event, our presuppositions about the identity of individuals do not require the actual exercise of such a psychological skill or the actual application of an epistemic criterion of identity. We presuppose that there is a truth of the matter whether what we take as Joe today is the same person as Joe of yesterday—independent of whether anyone can actually settle the question beyond possible doubt. It is the metaphysical principle of identity that is supplied by a sortal, not a psychological or even an epistemic criterion. If there is an epistemic criterion of identity, it would have to make essential appeal to a sortal. The sense, then, in which I intend "tracing an individual under a sortal" is an abstract one.

We might wonder whether we need sortals as specific as *person* or even *animal* to supply a principle of identity or whether we might manage with a single general one, such as *thing*, which supplies such a principle for everything. Gupta (1980, pp. 91–94), without coming down definitively on the matter, doubted that we can. His doubts, inspired partly by Gibbard (1975), were prompted by the weakness of our intuitions about how to trace identity under the description *the same thing*.

To see this, imagine this fanciful situation that, though bizarre, is neither logically nor physically impossible. Imagine that all the atoms that formed Ronald Reagan's body at some moment when he was governor of California had been replaced by new ones and that, miraculously, all the old ones had reassembled to form the body of Walter Mondale in 1984. Governor Reagan is identical with President Reagan. But Governor Reagan was identical with a certain set of atoms. If we were entitled to trace identity under the word *thing*, could we not say that Governor Reagan was the same thing as a certain set of atoms and that that set of atoms was now the same thing as Walter Mondale? By transitivity of identity, that would show that Governor Reagan was identical with Walter Mondale. But Governor Reagan is also identical with President Reagan. It could thus come about that Ronald Reagan would stand for election against himself—which is preposterous, and not just on political but logical grounds. Notice that the "argument" does not work if we replace *thing* with *person*. Although it is true that Governor Reagan and a certain group of atoms were once the same person and that Walter Mondale and the group of atoms were later the same person, it does not follow that Governor Reagan and Walter Mondale were ever the same person. The identity of the atoms is traced under the sortal *group of atoms*; the identity of each man is traced under the sortal *man*. The two sortals supply different principles of identity. There is no temptation to make the two men identical merely because each was at different moments identical with an individual group of atoms. It seems, then, that so general a word as *thing* cannot trace the identity of the individual who bears a PN.

Sometimes the role of the sortal appears more elusive. A particular caterpillar becomes a moth, and a particular tadpole becomes a frog. We cannot say that the caterpillar and the moth are the same moth; we cannot say that the tadpole and the frog are the same frog or tadpole. We can and do say, however, that the first pair are the same insect and that the second pair are the same animal (or member of the Ranidae family if we like that sort of thing). So there are sortals to trace their identity. The relation between a live frog and its subsequently dead body is more complicated. A dead frog is not a frog, of course. The identity relation between a live frog and its mortal remains must be traced over some such sortal as *molecule* or *chemical component*, a sortal that applies to something less than a whole frog. The big point that I wish to claim is that there is no identity without some appropriate sortal.

4. Kinds   The main semantic function of a sortal, such as *person*, is to denote a kind. If we say, "Joe is a person," we mean that the individual denoted by *Joe* is in the kind denoted by *person*. It is the kind, really, rather than the sortal, that supplies the principles of individuation and identity. The meaningful use of a PN presupposes the support of a kind that supplies the correct principles of individuation and identity.

5. No Fregean Sense   Proper names do not have a sense of the sort that Frege (1952 [1892a]) posited. Frege, for reasons that need not concern us, held that PNs have a sense as well as a referent. The function of the sense (when the PN was not vacuous) was to designate the individual that bore the name. Frege's doctrine is obscure, but it seems that he envisaged the sense as a definite description or set of such descriptions. All the examples of a sense that he gave were definite descriptions. For example, Frege said that the sense of the PN *Aristotle* is something like "the pupil of Plato and teacher of Alexander the Great." Frege's view caught on and became standard.

Kripke (1982) delivered a phillipic against the theory in its various versions. His main point can readily be grasped in view of the foregoing. It is that a PN has to pick out an individual in circumstances that are not actual as well as in circumstances that are. So, we might want to wonder: What if Aristotle had never studied under Plato and had never taught Alexander the Great? That is, we might want to use *Aristotle* to denote the great philosopher in circumstances that were not actual. If this is to be successful, reference cannot depend on a definite description that does not apply to the name bearer in those nonactual circumstances. This does not rule out essential definite descriptions, such as "the only even prime" as applied to the numeral two; it does rule out those definite descriptions that most people think of as Fregean senses. For further detail the reader should consult Kripke's book.

To sum up this section, a PN (1) denotes an individual (2) across all those times and places in which the individual exists and in all circumstances in which the individual might possibly exist. To supply principles of individuation and identity for the individual, a PN (3) requires the support of a sortal, whose function is (4) to denote a kind to which the bearer of the PN belongs. The reference of a PN is not mediated by a Fregean sense (5).

It is only fair to point out that not all logicians agree with the foregoing account of the logic of PNs. Kripke (1982, 1979) does not accept the account given of identity. Kripke (1979) seems explicitly to reject a role for sortals in tracing the identity of individuals. He is not, however, at all explicit on how identity is to be traced. The point I wish to make in this connection is that the psychology of PNs presupposes a fully explicit account, so that adequate psychological provision can be made for the handling of identity. Because Kripke does not provide an explicit logic, it is not possible to determine what psychological provisions his position entails. If you believe as I do that identity is handled with the support of a sortal, you need to equip the successsful PN learner and user with an appropriate sortal in such a way that it will guide his logical intuitions about PNs.

For those with a taste for formalisms the following schema captures the key elements in my analysis of the logic of PNs:

$$(\exists! P, x) \, \Box \, (\text{Exists } x \rightarrow x = \text{PN}),$$

which is to be read: There is a unique person x, and necessarily if x exists, then $x = \text{PN}$, where PN is to be replaced by some proper name. I follow Gupta in attaching to the bound variable the sortal *person* (*P*), which supplies the principle of identity for x. $\square$ is to be read as "in all possible circumstances," including all actual ones.

Vacuous Proper Names

The vacuous PN that comes most readily to mind, *Santa Claus*, is probably taken by children as a name for an absent bearer, not a vacuous name at all. Others, such as *Goldilocks*, they know relate to fictitious characters.

Unfortunately, I am not sure about the logic of vacuous names. I give them a section to themselves to draw the implications for psychology of not being able to specify their logic. The crux of the problem is that I have no idea how to formulate a psychological theory to handle the learning or use of an element because I have not settled on an account of what that element is.

The Logic of Learning Proper Names

Name Bearer Present

What has been attempted so far is to specify the logic of PNs, but even if that has been accomplished, it is only half the logical job. It remains to specify what is learned when people learn and competently use a PN and what logical resources learning presupposes in the learners. Everywhere in cognition there is a difficult decision to make about which elements to place in knowledge and which to locate in functional devices. I proceed as though each of the identified elements is an element in knowledge rather than in a functional device. That is, I assume for the present that each element must be included in the representation of what is learned rather than in the interpreters that perform operations relevant to the learning and interpretation of PNs. I believe that this is more than convenience; I believe it is what the learner of PNs expresses. At the end of this section I give an argument that the learner does express it. In the meantime I set about identifying the various elements by considering a particular case of a child learning a PN.

Imagine a fifteen-month-old boy named Tom sitting on the living room floor when his father comes in with a new puppy. Naturally, Tom is fascinated by the puppy. He hears his father say several things, many of which he does not fully understand, but among them he discerns the word *Spot* repeated several times. As a result of this experience, Tom learns to call the puppy *Spot* and does so frequently thereafter. He also understands that, when others use the word, they are talking about the puppy.

PNs are among the first words that children learn, and so far as anyone can tell, they understand them in the way adults do, but it is not essential to what follows that they attain adult competence at once. Nothing much more important than timing would vary if at first children used PNs with less than adult logical competence. Moreover, I believe that it is wise psychological strategy to assume that a child's mind resembles an adult's, unless there is evidence to the contrary. That is, I take seriously the obvious null hypothesis—that the two are similar. This places on research the onus of discovering differences between child and adult. Often the differences are obvious, but in the use of PNs they are not. Adults instinctively interpret even one-word uses of PNs by young children as truncated sentences. They tend, for example, to take a young child's utterance of *Spot* as an attempt to say "That is Spot" or "Where is Spot?" or some such thing. I believe the onus of proving that adults are wrong is fairly placed on those who claim they are. For this reason, I am assuming that PNs in the mouths of young children are logical resources with all the logical richness that they have in the mouths of adults.

What exactly happened when Tom learned the PN *Spot* and managed to use it thereafter as adults do? What did the learning presuppose? Here is a list, with explanatory comment. The list and comments raise far-reaching psychological questions, but the reader is invited to suspend skepticism until I have had an opportunity, in the next chapter, to answer them.

The Ability to Refer   Tom understood *Spot* in his father's mouth; he knew what it designated. By his subsequent utterances he showed that *Spot* in his own mouth performed the same task. It follows that Tom was able to perform the act of referring to the puppy by means of the symbol *Spot* and to understand the same act as performed by another. This means that he could use the name to direct attention to the puppy and, on hearing the name used by another, direct his own attention to the puppy.

Notice what is not claimed. In saying that Tom had the ability to perform the act of referring, I do not claim that he had the notion of reference, that is, the notion of the relation that includes the pairing of PNs and the objects they name. Children can perform the act of referring without knowing that notion just as people can walk without knowing the notion of walking. If, however, a person is to *know* that he or any other creature is walking, he needs the notion of walking and also a predicate in some language (for example, *walking*) to express it. I have not claimed that Tom knew that he or his father was referring when he used the word *Spot*. Neither have I claimed that Tom had the notion of a proper name or that he had any such sortal as *proper name*.

The act of referring is the prototype of an intentional act. Brentano (1973 [1874]), to whom we chiefly owe the modern interest in intentionality, described an intentional state as one that involves "reference to something as an object" (p. 271). The important point to grasp about Tom's acts of referring is that their object is not any state, idea, or image in Tom's head but the real live puppy. When Tom uses the word *Spot*, his own attention and that of his listeners goes to the puppy. This is not to deny that all sorts of mental acts and objects are involved. It is, however, to deny that they are the object picked out by the word *Spot*. Hardly a controversial point. It does, however, give entry to perhaps the most impenetrable and also the most discussed notion in cognitive science today, intentional states and actions. In claiming that Tom is able to perform the act of referring, we are attributing to him no insignificant ability.

Demonstrative   In order to learn what *Spot* refers to, Tom has to have some other means of identifying the bearer of that name. The natural candidate for that ancillary role is a demonstrative, such as *that*. Normally, when introducing someone (and teaching his or her name), you say something such as "This is my wife, Joyce." You need some way to let people know which person bears the name, and you do that by using a demonstrative, *this*, supported perhaps by gestures and looks. A demonstrative is not logically essential for name learning. A definite description, such as "the lady by the fireplace," can do the trick just as well. Nevertheless, young children do not normally command enough of the language to grasp the force of such definitive descriptions. It is, then, probably wiser to consider demonstratives. In learning his own PN, Tom must have the use of an indexical synonymous with *I*. In that case, a definite description will not do because no such description will be of any use, unless Tom realizes that it is a definite description of *himself*. But to realize that, he needs an indexical that he knows picks out himself. I will not dwell on the matter here because I return to it in chapter 5.

Many young children have been using a demonstrative, often some form of *that*, for some time before they begin to use PNs (see Gillis and Schutter (unpublished)). My son used a form of *this* at the age of fifteen months, usually with the force of "give me this" (Macnamara 1982, appendix 3). Even if some children do not actually utter a demonstrative, it seems likely that by the age of fifteen months they will have understood at least one. It is another matter to explain how they can learn the meaning of a natural-language demonstrative, such as *that*, but for the present I simply assume that they have learned it.

We might imagine that, because Tom could see the puppy at the moment when he learned his name, he did not need an indexical. There are several problems with this. At the moment, even when looking at the puppy, Tom could see many things, such as the carpet and his own hands and feet. Tom must have had some way of picking out of all these things the one object that was to bear the name. What was that way, if not a demonstrative?

Moreover, as a result of the learning, Tom knew something, and this sort of knowledge depends essentially on symbols. If you know that pigs are dirty, you do not, for all that, have pigs and dirt inside your head but symbols that express the truth. Although this position is disputed, by Davidson (1970) among others, I do not find the arguments against it convincing, and I refer the interested reader to Pylyshyn (1984, chap. 2) for a detailed treatment of the standard position, which is what I am taking.

Tom also needs symbols that express for him that some object is Spot. But cannot the symbol that picks out the object that is Spot be a visual percept or visual image? The idea can be given by this sort of expression that is becoming quite popular for automobile stickers:

I love my 🏠 ,

where the image of the house does duty for the word *house* or *home*. Could the visual image of the puppy not have served Tom in like manner? Perhaps it could, but not without the support of something such as a demonstrative. For as we have noted, Tom had visual images of many things besides the puppy, and he needed some means to pick out the one that belonged to the object that was to bear the name. Or, more precisely, he needed something to pick out that object from other visible ones. That had to be a referring expression. Because he did not have a PN and because among other referring expressions a demonstrative is linguistically the simplest, I opt for it. To use a demonstrative, Tom did not need the notion of a demonstrative.

Identity   Tom learned something that expressed what we express in English by the words "That is Spot" or "This is Spot." For the sake of definiteness, let us choose the first of these two. Note the little word *is*, which here expresses the identity of the objects picked out by *that* and *Spot*. Identity, if I have rightly characterized what Tom learned, is a notion that he must have understood—which is to say that he must have had an appropriate symbol and understood it. This time the crucial element is not an act that was performed but a predicate that was employed, the predicate that expresses identity. In logic and mathematics the predicate is usually expressed by the symbol $=$. It expresses a reflexive, symmetric, and transitive relation, that is, an equivalence relation. In saying that Tom grasped the notion of identity, I do not mean that he *knew* that it was an equivalence relation but that his interpretation of the symbol for identity was in the framework of the logic appropriate to equivalence relations. In other words, the logic of identity does not have to be explicitly represented; it can be left to the interpreter for $=$. For example, if Tom learned that Spot is a certain dog, he would need no further evidence to conclude that that dog is Spot, because the logic of the *is* of identity warrants the inference. Or again, if he decided that Spot on Monday was the same dog as Spot on Tuesday and that the latter was the same dog as Spot on Wednesday, it would not occur to him that Spot on Monday and Spot on Wednesday are different dogs. The claim that Tom grasped the concept of identity is, then, a substantive one and one that can be checked by empirical observation.

Identity is involved with PNs in at least two ways. One, which we have already seen, is the identity of the objects picked out by the indexical and the PN. The other is the identity of the object over time. Tom and his family used the name *Spot* on many different occasions. These usages presupposed the identity of the puppy across all those occasions. Moreover, the name *Spot* does not pick out the bearer at a single point in time or in a single set of circumstances. It is, therefore, necessary to make logical provision for its identity across time and possible circumstances.

Sortal to Supply Principle of Identity   If Tom used the proper name *Spot* correctly over a period of time, he was assuming the animal's identity over that period. He must not have allowed irrelevant properties to decide the identity of Spot on two or more occasions. He must not, for example, have taken Spot's position in space or his posture at the time when he learned his name as essential to identity. Otherwise, he could not have used the name to pick out the same dog when the dog changed his position or when he curled up, stood up, or began walking. Tom could not have allowed size, color, weight, or any other perceptual property to decide identity because Spot was a puppy when Tom first met him and later grew to be an adult dog, changing such properties as his volume, weight, hair, texture, and bark. If he were to lose a leg, have his tail cropped or his ears pointed, he would still have been Spot. Tom at fifteen months knew nothing about molecules, but Spot's identity over time was not the identity of the bunch of molecules or subatomic particles of which he was composed when Tom first met him. These changed continually, but the dog remained the same.

Tom needed to attach to the PN a symbol that supplied a principle of identity for Spot. I have been suggesting *dog,* or some synonym of *dog,* as the sortal that Tom used to supply the principle of identity. Some people are skeptical that so advanced a sortal should be available to a fifteen-month-old. It is possible that the sortal such children actually use is something such as *maximally-connected physical object*—the suggestion comes from Jackendoff (unpublished). I suspect that it is too general. Many individuals that children encounter in the physical environment are maximally-connected physical objects. By the age of fifteen months they are surely making finer classifications. Nevertheless, a general sortal might serve at first and eventually give way to the more accurate *dog* or *animal.* Partly for reasons to be brought out in chapter 7, I would like to opt for the more accurate one right off. Not much in the theory I am advancing for the learning of PNs hangs in the balance.

There is another reason, apart from the logic of identity, to assign an essential role to a sortal in the learning of a PN. A demonstrative on its own is not enough. On its own, *that* might pick out the animal's left forepaw or the gleam in its eye or its visible surface. But what bears the name *Spot* is not any of these things but the entire animal, including the inner organs as well as the visible parts. To guarantee that the PN *Spot* is assigned the correct bearer, we need a symbol that embraces the entire animal, and that is a sortal, such as *dog* or *animal.* The sortal, then, supplies the principle of identity for the bearer, and in addition it plays an essential role in specifying the bearer. Dummett (1981, p. 233) made just this observation.

It is most important to note that there is in this no suggestion that Tom knew what a principle of identity or what a sortal was. Nor is there any suggestion that Tom could have stated the principle of identity for Spot. Consider for a moment the precise principle of identity one would have to know in order to be able to say when someone began and when someone ceased to be a person. When a fetus begins to be a person is, I take it, the bone of contention in the abortion debate. In that debate, everyone agrees that to kill an innocent person is murder. What is disputed is the stage at which one is dealing with a person. Difficulty in deciding reflects difficulty in specifying the relevant principle of identity. Even educated adults need not be able to specify the principles of identity supplied by the sortals they use, so there is no requirement that Tom should have been able to do so for *dog.*

Kind   The sortal *dog* designates a kind of animal, so we have to wonder whether Tom must also have an expression, such as *kind,* that he can use and understand in order to be able to learn the PN *Spot.* The answer seems to be yes. I assume that Tom has had to learn the sortal *dog* or some synonym in the language of thought. In learning that sortal, he must have been directed by something to assign to the sortal the correct referent. Otherwise, he might have assigned to it an individual dog or group of dogs as referent or perhaps some salient impression of dogs, such as their bark. This would be disastrous. So I conclude that Tom's learning of *dog*, or some synonym for it, was guided by the sortal *kind* or a synonym.

Does that mean that Tom also needed another sortal to support the use of his sortal *kind*? This way threatens an infinite and pernicious regress. Fortunately, we can block the regress right here, provided that Tom does not have to *learn* his basic sortal for *kind*. If he does not have to learn it, or how to interpret it, he does not need another sortal. He needs a sortal for "kind" to guide the learning of another sortal, his sortal for "dog." On the assumption that he did not have to learn so basic and so abstract a sortal as a synonym for *kind*, there is no need to endow him with a still more basic sortal.

We should note, however, that in this line of thought we have an argument for allowing the existence of unlearned logical resources. The whole matter is taken up again in detail in chapter 7.

Membership   The kind "dog" supplies a principle of identity only for its members, not for trees or houses or cats. The sortal and kind can do their work only if Tom appreciates that Spot is a member of the kind to which he assigned him. In simpler language, Tom could not have known that Spot was the same dog over time unless he knew that he was a dog. (Remember that we have settled on *dog* for the sake of definiteness.)

Does this mean that Tom had the general notion of membership when he learned Spot's name? The answer would appear to be yes. In assigning Spot to the kind "dog," Tom was expressing, in effect, "Spot is a dog." Here the copula, which earlier expressed identity, expresses membership. Tom could not have understood the sentence "Spot is a dog" (or any sentence expressing the same content) without grasping the significance of the copula, and that presupposes the notion of membership.

To sum up, my analysis of the learning of the proper name *Spot* attributes to Tom the following logical abilities:

To refer to something by a proper name,
To refer to something by a demonstrative,
To characterize the referents of two expressions as identical,
To employ appropriately sortals such as *dog* and *kind*,

> To understand such sortals,
> To assign an object to a particular kind as member.

Another way to sum up this section is to express formally what Tom learned when he successfully learned the PN *Spot*:

$$\text{That} \in \text{dog [kind]} = \text{Spot}.$$

This reads: That [which is a member of the kind dog, which refers to a kind] is Spot. I should note that I am borrowing the symbol $\in$ from set theory and that it does not fit the need exactly. One reason is that the identity of sets is defined over their extensions: same members, same set; different members, different sets. Because the extension of kinds, such as "dog," varies over time, as puppies are born and dogs die, kinds are not sets. Still, the membership symbol for sets is convenient, and for that reason I use it. I should note further that $\in$ and also the English expression "is a member of" are problematic when used to express the relation between "dog" and "kind." It would seem that "dog" is not a member of the kind "kind" in the way that Spot is a member of the kind "dog." Ordinary-language expressions seem inadequate to mark the difference, and mathematical logic does not seem to advert to it. The summary I give has a certain mnemonic value, but it should be read with caution.

Name Bearer Absent

It was not until his twentieth month, when my son Kieran already knew well over twenty PNs, that he learned the first PN for someone who was not present at the time. That name was *Jesus*. Interestingly, as we shall see, at about the time when he learned *Jesus*, Kieran began to use the sortal *name* correctly. He would ask people's names, and when asked his own or a friend's, he would answer correctly.

Every ability that comes into play in the learning of PNs when the name bearer is present also comes into play when the bearer is absent, with the exception of the demonstrative. At least, a demonstrative cannot function in the same way in the two settings because in one it cannot pick out the bearer as perceptually present. And yet the learner must have some means, apart from the name, of picking out the bearer. What might that be?

Well, Kieran was shown pictures of Jesus, and he was told various incidents from his life. He seems to have identified Jesus as the person who is represented in those pictures, the person about whom the stories were told, but especially as the person to whom people refer when they use the name *Jesus*. This is to identify Jesus by means of definite descriptions. Among such descriptions perhaps the most important is

"The person named 'Jesus.' " As far as Kieran knew, only one man was ever called by that name. He would have been able to understand that description or express it for himself in English, though undoubtedly at the age of nineteen months, when he learned *Jesus*, he would have used telegraphese, in which some words, being omitted, had to be understood.

To avoid confusion, we must note the distinction that Kripke (1982) emphasized between the manner in which a name is learned and the meaning of the name. In saying that Kieran probably used some such definite description as "The person named 'Jesus' " in learning the name, I am not suggesting that the meaning or sense of the name is given by that description. That would indeed be fatuous because the definite description itself employs the name *Jesus*; it cannot, therefore, give the meaning or sense of the name.

Notice that the definite description does specify a sortal, *person*, that indicates that it is a whole person who is called by the name *Jesus*, not just a part or property of a person. In addition, *person* denotes a kind that supplies a principle of identity for Jesus, the principle by which an individual's identity is traced. *Person* is an appropriate sortal because the expression "The person named 'Jesus' " entails that Jesus was a member of the kind named *person*. We can represent what Kieran learned as

The person named *Jesus* = Jesus.

This expresses the identity of the objects referred to by the expressions on either side of the equal sign. Notice that on the left-hand side the name *Jesus* is only mentioned (indicated by italics), whereas on the right-hand side it is used. It follows that the expression is informative, in the way that *Jesus* = *Jesus* would not be.

My description of what Kieran learned is, perhaps, less innocuous than it seems because it presupposes that he knew the distinction between the use and mention (italics) of a name and had some device for marking the distinction. It may not, however, be fanciful to suppose that he did know the distinction and had such a device. Children are early treated to reckless switches between the two by their elders, as the following sequence makes plain:

Kieran, this is your cousin, Geraldine.
Shake hands with Geraldine.
Say "Geraldine."

In the first two sentences *Geraldine* is used to refer to a person; in the third one it is used to refer to her name. The difference might be forced on children because they would know that no one would ask them to utter a human person out of their mouths. At any rate, children never seem confused by a switch from use to mention an 1 back again.

On the other hand (as both Anil Gupta and Melissa Bowerman pointed out to me), the relevant distinction may not be between the use and mention of a name but between the use of the name and the utterance of the sounds of which it is composed. In other words, the child may take "Say 'Geraldine' " as a request to utter the sounds Ge-ral-dine rather than to say the name of her name. In either case, the child needs a distinction and, in addition, some means to mark it. If we are inclined to the pronunciation approach, we might represent the content of Kieran's learning of *Jesus* by

The person who is named by saying Je-sus = Jesus.

Not much hangs on whether we take the mention-plus-quotes approach or the pronunciation one.

Vacuous Names
There is little that I can say about the learning of such vacuous PNs as *Goldilocks* simply because I have not satisfied myself as to their logic. The point in mentioning them is to draw attention to the main contention: Cognitive psychology presupposes the logic of the cognitive element to be treated. This is not to deny that cognitive psychology can be done before the last word has been spoken by logicians. Nor is it to deny that empirical observation may lead a logician to a particular logical conclusion. Rather, the claim is that logic is logically prior to cognitive psychology, as I am sure the impasse in my attempt to specify what is learned when a vacuous PN is learned illustrates.

Representation of Logical Elements
There is a certain amount of logical work to be done in connection with the learning of a PN. The individual who is to bear the name must be correctly specified. In fact, the individual must be denoted twice, and the identity across denotations must be catered to. Its identity over time, place, and possible circumstances must also be catered to. The question now is, How is all this done?

This is where the principle stated earlier comes in: A logical resource does not issue from the exercise of logic-free capacities. A PN is a logical resource. So the mere utterance of a sound, no matter how often repeated, does not yield a PN. To grasp this, imagine a Martian without any logical resources who could nevertheless make various sounds. Imagine that it has been programmed to utter *Blik* whenever it is in the presence of a certain dog and *Spik* whenever it is in the presence of any dog. Sometimes it utters *Blik Spik* when in the presence of a particular dog. It does not follow that the Martian is in any intentional state whatsoever. It certainly does not follow that it is in the intentional state of uttering something like what a human would mean by "Spot is a dog." What else needs to be built into the Martian so that it enters intentional states analogous to human ones? I do not think anyone has the slightest idea. It is clear, however, that continuing to utter *Blik Spik* is not enough. It is equally clear that referring is not a computational notion; it cannot simply be programmed into the Martian.

One point that the story of the Martian illustrates is that we do not acquire a PN by learning-how. Learning-how, of which conditioning is a type, is the exercise of previously existing skills. Learning-how is the development of such skills. We can learn-how to refer in some particular way only if we already have the capacity to refer.

We might, however, hope for an account of learning to refer by means of a PN that is causal, in the sense of being framed entirely in the language of natural causality, that is, without the use of any intentional expressions. There are several considerations that undermine that hope. The main one is that referring presents itself to us as a primitive, a structureless simple notion. We have no intimation as to how it might be constructed from elements that can be understood in the language of natural causality. Morever, we can refer to objects that, in the views of many people, do not exist in the physical domain; we can refer to numbers and kinds (universals) as well as to dogs and mountains. It seems that a nonintentional causal account of referring would have to assure us that there are no such causally inert objects, or at least that, if there are, we cannot refer to them. This is a tall order.

But let us suppose that a causal account of referring could be given. It still would not follow that the ability to refer by means of a PN would be acquired by the accretion of causally simpler components at the time that we learn a natural language. In ontogeny, generally, function follows form. On a par with other biological systems, we would expect that so basic an ability as the ability to refer is prearranged by nature. And although lacking insight into the nature of referring, I cannot give a conclusive proof that it cannot be accounted for in nonintentional causal language and that it is not assembled from causally simpler components at the time of learning a natural language; nevertheless I assume as a working strategy that, when children learn a PN, they learn it as a logical element that they can use to refer. This implies that they learn it in a logical context, that is, in an interpreted sentence. It follows that the content specified above as being learned by the child must be catered to by a set of symbols that express that content; it cannot be accounted for by means of functional devices without symbols that have logical structure. Cummins (1983, pp. 94ff) made some remarks that are in harmony with what I am arguing here.

The Effect of Choice of Logic on Proper Names

I conclude by emphasizing that if we adopt some logic of PNs other than that offered, we need to modify the account of what is learned when a PN is learned, the list of logical resources, and the psychology of how it is learned. Suppose that instead of a Gupta-based theory, we adopt a descriptivist theory of PNs similar to that advocated, though in somewhat different forms, by Wittgenstein, Searle, and others. Common to them all is the idea that essential to the logical functioning of a PN is a sense as well as a reference. The sense consists of one or more definite descriptions that fix the manner in which the name bearer is presented to the name user by the name. In some versions of the theory it is enough if a sufficient number of the definite descriptions are true of the name bearer and suffice to specify it uniquely.

We have already considered Frege's (1952 [1892a]) suggestion of a sense for the name *Aristotle*: the pupil of Plato and teacher of Alexander the Great. This contains a number of PNs and is therefore not a good model for the sense of a child's first PN. Perhaps the descriptions of *Spot* required by the theory would be something like "the dog in the living room," "our dog," "the dog we are all playing with." These would not serve well because they are inappropriate for nonfamily users of the name *Spot*. Actually this touches on one of the problems for the descriptivist approach; but my purpose now is not to demonstrate its inadequacy or even to illustrate it by fully acceptable examples of definite descriptions. My purpose is to note that the theory requires on the part of the name learner the logical resources to express and understand a sense or senses in connection with each PN. Clearly this is to presuppose vastly more resources than I have listed. That is one reason for not adopting a descriptivist approach.

On the other hand, each of the logical tasks specified must be performed somehow. For example, the identity of the name bearer through time and nonactual circumstances must be provided for. So nothing can be spared from the list of the logical resources necessary to learn a PN. In fact, the presence of such definite descriptions, as we have seen, are an embarrassment to the task of tracing identity. For example, although Spot certainly was the dog on the living room floor at the time Tom learned his name, he did not cease to be Spot when he left the living room and went out into the kitchen. Note, too, that "The dog on the living room floor" includes the sortal that we thought essential in the theory espoused—a confirmation that none of the logical resources listed can be spared.

The main point is that our logic of PNs has clear consequences for an account of how PNs are learned. The consequences of adopting a descriptivist approach are particularly onerous.

4

Psychology and Name Learning

I have specified certain logical skills that name learners must have if they are to understand the names they learn and to use them meaningfully. There are a number of questions about what I have specified, and I attempt to deal with three in this chapter. The first relates to the language in which children express what they have learned. The chief problem is that, when children first learn to use proper names (PNs), they do not seem to have the resources in their native language to express what they have learned. In particular, children do not seem to have the use of an identity predicate (*is*, *same*, or =) to express the fact that we can express by "That is Spot." In what language, then, do children express that fact? The second question is about the interpreters that I have posited: What are the conditions that trigger their functioning, and what are their outputs? If I can succeed in stating both, I shall have gone a long way toward characterizing the interpreters, at least in the syntactic aspects of their functioning. The third question is about those higher-order notions that might be lacking in young children, such as "refers" (names). If children do not have them when they first learn names, how might they learn them?

Problem of Language

I considered Tom, who at the age of fifteen months learned the name *Spot* for a new puppy. I argued that he needed a demonstrative and a sortal to identify what is to bear the name. The problem is that when children first learn PNs, they usually do not utter anything like the membership symbol ($\in$) or the identity symbol (=). Frequently, they do not give any evidence of knowing or being able to use a sortal such as *dog*. For example, Kieran Macnamara did not use sortals appropriate for supporting the use of people's PNs, like *man, person* (or even *thing* or *object*), until long after he used many names for persons with easy mastery. He also, as a matter of fact, learned our dog's PN six weeks before he learned to use the sortal *dog*. To make matters more complicated, he was already using a large number of PNs meaningfully long before he could string together in speech as many words as we have used to express what he learned. These considerations make the question more critical of how young children manage to express what they learn when they learn a PN.

Clearing the Ground

Twenty years ago a psychologist confronted with this puzzling situation would have made short work of it by saying that children do not express any such thing as I am claiming, that all they learn is an association between the appearance or sound of a dog and its name. This proposal, I fear, just ignores the problems of specifying what receives the name and tracing its identity over time. To begin with, it is not the dog's appearance that receives the name and, besides, the name follows the dog even when its appearance changes dramatically, as when it lies down and curls up or moves about the room. In any case, an association relates two mental objects or events, not an external object, such as a dog, with a mental state or event. The relevant mental objects might be a visual percept of a dog and an auditory percept of its name. That association cannot be the relation of reference, because the referent of *Spot* is the real live dog, not a percept of him in anyone's mind. The theory can be improved by fixing as the referent the physical object (or event) that causes the visual percept. That still does not handle important intuitions about names. The physical object that causes a percept of Spot is the illuminated surface of his body that is visible to the viewer. Yet it is not just that surface, or even the entire exterior, that receives the name. Moreover, intuitions about identity cannot be handled by percepts as proposed. There is nothing to prevent Spot from having a look-alike so similar that he gives rise to percepts that are indistinguishable from those to which Spot gives rise. Yet for all that, we would not judge that Spot and the look-alike are identical. The problem of mistaken identity in relation to people and dogs is familiar to young children. Altogether, it does not seem that much use can be made of associations to solve our problem about how children express what they learn. The problem is to account for intuitions of identity when perceptual tests fail. Our intuitions of identity run deeper than perception.

For many years, after psycholinguists abandoned the learning-theoretic notions of meaning that I have just discussed, they replaced them with semantic markers. The semantic markers that were supposed to constitute a word's meaning consisted of a list of properties that were supposed to determine the word's referent. So on this view the meaning of *Spot* might consist of a list of those properties that were true of Spot at all times and that distinguished him from all other dogs. It was understood that the property of being Spot was not the one that gave the meaning of *Spot*, because, for one thing, in specifying that property, we would be using the word *Spot*, and so *that* property does not advance matters.

Many writers assumed that the distinctive features are abstracted from the perceptual array, but this makes the theory equivalent to the earlier associationist one. Now, however, the associations are among the semantic features and between the set of such features and a percept of the name (or a motor plan for pronouncing the name). It therefore falls prey to all the ills of the earlier theory and some new ones besides. For example, there does not seem to be any set of perceptually given features that must remain true of a dog for it to be the same dog all through its life. It can grow, change color, have its tail docked and its ears and hair clipped, or it can lose a leg. Moreover, the change from a caterpillar to a moth is perceptually baffling, yet we believe that a particular moth is *the same insect* as some particular caterpillar at an earlier stage. This undermines the theory (see Macnamara 1982, chaps. 1, 12).

The theory can be broadened to allow for semantic features that are definite descriptions, such as *John Macnamara's dog, the father of Thady*. Kripke (1982) argued that, because such definite descriptions are not true of a name bearer through the possible circumstances in which we may want to speak of it, they cannot be essentially attached to the bearer's PN. The reason is easy to see. Our dog, Freddie, would still be the same dog if for some reason I gave him to somebody else and he was no longer John Macnamara's dog; he would still be the same dog if he had never fathered a pup. We thus see that such definite descriptions do not help the case, because Freddie would still be Freddie and the same dog even if all such descriptions became untrue of him at once. To avoid confusion, I should note that it is of course possible that Freddie could have been called something else, such as *Towser*. His name, then, is not an absolutely necessary property of his. It is, however, a relatively necessary property, relative to a given language. That is, once Freddie has been assigned to the name *Freddie*, that name can be used to pick him out through all the times and all the circumstances in which he figures.

For these reasons I go back to my claim that PNs require the support of a sortal that supplies a principle of identity to trace the bearer's identity and thus guarantees that such names pick out their referent at all times. How then, to repeat the question, does a young child such as Tom express what we express by

That $\in$ *dog [kind]* $=$ *Spot.*

A Language of Thought

There are two problems, not just one, that have to be solved about the language in which children express what they learn: (1) In what language(s) do they find the necessary resources, and (2) if the resources are in different languages, how do they manage to combine them in a single sentence? The second question arises only if in answering the first we decide that children find the necessary resources in different languages. I therefore tackle question (1) first.

The words *Spot* and *that* are in English and become available to Tom through learning. All the other expressions— ∈ , *dog*, *kind*, and = — are problematic. We begin by looking at ∈ and = . What I propose is that these are available to children in an unlearned language of thought. The idea of such a language is familiar and well presented in the literature, notably by Fodor (1975) and Pylyshyn (1984). For the most part, I rely on the arguments presented there to support the idea, but I can, perhaps, make the argument a little crisper by bringing out some of the details in connection with the learning of PNs.

The standard arguments for a language of thought relate to the economy effected in the number of interfacings among information channels if we posit a central processor with its own language; the claim that cognition must be construed as computational (if only because no one has any other idea of how to conceive of it), which entails (or so it is claimed) that the inputs and outputs to cognition are sentencelike entities; and the current practice among students of image processing of representing information in the visual channel at all levels by means of sentences. None of these lines of argument, however, clinches the claim that there is an unlearned language of thought. It is logically possible, even if we are persuaded by the arguments, that the language in question is a natural language, such as English. To my mind the most convincing argument for an unlearned language of thought takes its departure from the fact of language learning. Fodor (1975, pp. 79–97) made the general point, but I would like to make it in connection with the learning of PNs.

The child we have been considering ended up knowing the content we expressed in statement (1). His learning of it presupposed the logical resources to express that content. We have seen that Tom did not have the resources in English, his only natural language, so he had to have them in another language. It does not follow immediately that the other language was unlearned; it does follow ultimately that Tom must have unlearned logical resources. The first time he engaged in a learning-that event, he needed the logical resources to express what he then learned. Ex hypothesi, Tom cannot have gained them by a learning-that process. Nor, I have argued, can he have gained them by a learning-how process or by any form of conditioning. But that means unlearned symbols with logical structure—sufficient resources to form a sentence or sentences with truth conditions. If I am justified in my conclusion that Tom did not have the use of the English words *is* (=) and *member* (∈) at the time he learned his first PN (*Spot*), he must have been able to express their content in another language. I come back to these expressions later in the chapter.

I do not propose that there is an unlearned expression synonymous with *dog* in the language of thought. In chapters 7 and 8 I discuss the learning of sortals in general; here I give just the briefest statement of what I argue there. The origin of the sortal *dog* is a gestalt supplied by vision. (An appropriate gestalt could be supplied in another modality, but it simplifies things to stick to vision.) The gestalt formed for a particular dog on a particular occasion does not do as it stands for two reasons. First, what is needed is a sortal in the language of thought that can enter into logical construction with other linguistic elements. I do not attempt to decide whether the visual gestalt is subsumed into the language of thought or whether it is replaced there by an appropriate index, say $Sortal_{17}$. If it were subsumed, the effect might be somewhat like

That is a  ,

though I do not advocate the idea that visual gestalten are like pictures. Second, to avoid having different sortals for different views of the same dog and for other dogs, what is needed is a gestalt type. I assume, without attempting to explain, that children have established visual pattern types by the time they begin to grapple with their mother tongue. I assume further that Tom had done this for dogs at the time he learned Spot's name. This means Tom's visual system identified Spot gestalt as being of a familiar type. What Tom needed was an expression in the language of thought corresponding to this gestalt type. Experimental evidence that children are able to classify objects into categories for which they have no natural-language symbols or an inadequately grasped one is beginning to accumulate (Cohen and Younger 1983; Macnamara 1982, chap. 5; and Rosch and Mervis 1978).

What about the sortal that supports the use of the sortal *dog*? I have been assuming for the sake of definiteness that sortal is synonymous with *kind*. It is hardly controversial to say that from their earliest days children seek to assign objects in their experience to kinds. What is controversial is that children have a sortal for the notion kind before they learn a natural-language one. And yet if my analysis of the logic is right, children must have such a sortal—presumably in the language of thought. Children must have it to guide their learning of the sortal synonymous with *dog*. Otherwise they might assign *dog* to the wrong object, to Spot, for example, or to the person who taught them the name *Spot*, or to the members of the kind "dog" as a group. But none of these is the kind "dog"; none is the referent of the sortal *dog*. The claim that Tom had a sortal for kind at his disposal amounts to this: In seeking to assign the individuals in his experience to kinds, his mind kept track of what it was doing and did so by means of a sortal synonymous with *kind*.

Turn back to the expression member ($\in$) and identity ($=$). To say that children seek to assign individuals to kinds and to say that after a little while they experience a particular dog, say Spot, as being of an identified kind is already to have conceded that children have a predicate to express membership in a kind. Remember, there can be no knowledge-that without symbols adequate to express it. The choice of primitives is always a delicate matter, but my preference is to take membership ($\in$) as an unlearned primitive in cognition—that is, a primitive whose employment is guaranteed by a procedurelike device, an interpreter, that is triggered by perceptual experience. To say that an infant has succeeded in identifying a kind of creature and experiences some individuals as belonging in the kind is tantamount to saying (in my language) that the infant has an interpreter that, on suitable perceptual experience of a member a, yields as output an interpreted set of symbols that expresses the content of $a \in K$, where K is a schematic letter to be replaced by a sortal.

Like $\in$, most logicians take $=$ as a primitive predicate, and my preference is to take it as such in cognitive theory. My view is that both $\in$ and $=$ are unlearned expressions in the language of thought whose semantics are taken care of by interpreters.

It is possible that the original resources in the language of thought are extremely restricted and that the language gains expressive power by borrowing—from the outputs of perceptual channels and from natural languages. Among the possible borrowings are PNs from natural languages, such as *Spot* from English. Such borrowing would solve the problem of expressing in a single language the content of what is learned. It is also possible that the language of thought has considerable resources in the form of originally uninterpreted indexes, such as the fanciful $Sortal_{17}$. Another such might be an index for a PN, so that *Spot* might be assigned PN_1, say. Such elements might be assigned content as experience demanded; then there would be no need to borrow elements from other sources. Yet again, the language of thought might possess from the beginning ready-made logical resources to express any thought that a person can possibly entertain. This, I take it, is a position that Fodor (1975) finds alluring. I do not find it so, and in chapters 7 and 8 I attempt to show that it is not forced on us. I do not, however, know how to decide between the first two possibilities. Both are suggestions of how to increase expressive powers, either by borrowing or by utilizing available but uninterpreted resources. But at this juncture it does not seem important to attempt to decide between them.

Interpreters

Interpreters for Proper Names
We have decided that the work of interpreting is done by procedurelike devices that I call *interpreters*. I envisage two major types: (1) those that on the satisfaction of certain conditions yield an interpreted set of symbols as output, and (2) those that take as input a string of uninterpreted symbols and that yield as output the same string as interpreted. Both assign a logical structure to each sentence and an appropriate interpretation to each constituent in that logical structure. The domain into which a sentence is interpreted often consists of entities in the perceptual field that is being surveyed. An indexical is assigned an object. A sortal is assigned a kind. An n-place predicate is assigned an n-tuple of objects: If it is the membership predicate, it is assigned a set of ordered pairs, each consisting of an object and a kind. Readers familiar with model theory will recognize my inspiration for the interpreters. In subsequent chapters I show that I am not content to just borrow from standard model theory, but there is no reason to delay on the reasons here. I begin with some general remarks about interpreters for learning PNs and then go on to empirical data that can guide us in their description.

When children learn a PN for a visible object, an interpreter, call it Interpreter-PN, assigns the PN the same referent as the indexical that is picking out that object. Tom knows what is called *Spot*, can usually pick him out by sight on many different occasions, and on each occasion call him *Spot*. Clearly, when Tom learned the name, he knew that it was the visually presented dog that was Spot, and when he called him *Spot*, on subsequently establishing visual contact with him, he knew that it was the visually presented dog that was the referent of *Spot*. It is necessary, then, that Interpreter-PN register these facts and that its output be, as we have continually asserted, the interpreted sentence

$$That \in dog\ [kind] = Spot.$$

I am not, of course, stating that Tom can use the name *Spot* meaningfully only when the dog is visible. Nor am I claiming that an identity sentence with a definite description (*that dog*) is essential to every meaningful use of the name. All I am claiming is that such a sentence is essential when the name is learned and such a sentence is expressible and interpretable by children whenever they establish perceptual contact with the bearer. I am taking it, then, that the identity sentence is the output of Interpreter-PN, which is the interpreter that assigns bearers to newly learned PNs when the bearer is visible.

If the bearer is not present when a PN is learned, a definite description is required to fix the bearer. Without being categorical on the matter, I think that the main definite description is "The S named X," where S stands for sortal and X for proper name. For Kieran learning *Jesus*, I thought it might be "The person named Jesus." In that case the output of the interpreter would have been

The person whose name is "Jesus" = *Jesus*.

Another view we discussed, instead of depending on the distinction between the use and mention of a name, depended on the distinction between the use of the name and its pronunciation. On that view, what Kieran learned was the content expressed by

The person whose name is pronounced Je-sus = Jesus.

Kieran was much older when he learned *Jesus* than when he learned his first PNs for visible objects, and by then he already had the words *man* and *name* and the copula *is* to express identity. Further, he had had something like the use/mention distinction thrust on him by being asked to pronounce names that had been used to refer to their bearers. He must have realized that a single sound could be used to refer to its bearer and to the bearer's name or to the sounds in the bearer's name. This means that the ambiguity of the word was thrust on him, and the ability to note it means that he must have had some device for marking the distinction. Kieran, therefore, had the resources to express that output in English, though it would have been a long sentence for him at the age of nineteen months, his age when he learned *Jesus*. I do not know if he expressed what he learned in English or in the language of thought. However he expressed it, we have to distinguish the interpreter that assigns a visual object to a PN from the one that assigns an invisible object to a PN. Just as we call the former *Interpreter-PN* we can call the latter *Interpreter-PN$_a$* (*a* for absent).

Alternatively, the definite description that fixed the referent of *Jesus* might have been prompted by a picture. Kieran was shown pictures of Jesus and was quite familiar with the representing function of pictures. He could by then name the people in photographs, though he clearly did not think that people in photographs really were photographs. He expressed the representing function of pictures by the copula *is*, saying things such as "That is Lisa" and "That is Dad." If he used pictures to ground definite descriptions (rather than mentioned PNs), we could express the content of what he learned as

Jesus = the man that is represented by that picture.

This would call for a slightly different interpreter, which we might call Interpreter-PN$_{a'}$.

Since Kripke (1982), there has been much talk about a "causal theory" of reference. To be fair, Kripke did not propose a theory but a "picture." The picture is that our grasp of the referents of PNs does not require a definite description, that it can be achieved through "a certain passage of communication" (p. 91), placing a PN user in intentional contact with the individual who assigned a PN its bearer. Nevertheless, even here a definite description does seem to play a part:

> When the name is "passed from link to link" [in the communication chain] the receiver must, I think, intend when he learns it to use it with the same reference as the man from whom he heard it. (Kripke 1982, p. 96)

This suggests that some such definite description as this lurks in the background: the individual that X (my informant) intends when X uses a PN. More probably it is closer to the individual that my speech community intends when they use a PN. Quite rightly, Kripke pointed out that all this has to do with fixing the referent of a PN, not with giving the sense of a PN. I go into this to show that the position I have outlined is in the spirit of Kripke's causal picture of reference.

Empirical Evidence from Child Studies
Even if we are disposed to accept that fully competent speakers have the logical resources of which I have been writing, we may be astonished to learn that very young children, about fifteen or sixteen months old, have them also. Is there any empirical evidence, then, that such young children have a fully competent grasp of PNs? There are several lines of evidence to suggest an affirmative answer. The reader should realize, however, that psychological investigations inspired by the theory of this book are in their infancy, so the empirical evidence is not nearly as rich as I would like.

Part of the evidence was obtained by Nancy Wargny (Katz) and myself and presented in detail in Katz et al. (1974) and in Macnamara (1982, chap. 2). We conducted a series of experiments with children ranging from about twenty-eight months to younger than seventeen months of age. The children, all Montrealers, belonged to English-speaking families and were tested individually in their own homes.

Table 4.1
Percentage Correct Responses over Three Experiments on Proper Names

Object	Sortal	Number of subjects	Proper names	Number of subjects
Dolls	49.8	25	75.6	25
Blocks	44.0	5	51.1	15

Each took part in only one cell of an experiment; in other words, we are not dealing with repeated measures of the same children.

The idea of the test was to see if the children would accept a PN for a block as easily as for a doll. We felt that they would see dolls as surrogate people, and we suspected that they would readily accept a PN for one of a pair of dolls. This gave us two conditions: dolls or blocks. We also wanted to see if children were sensitive to syntactic clues that mark PNs. This gave us two other conditions: presence or absence of articles (*a* and *the*) with the name. Our original idea was that young children would be influenced by the cognitive factor (dolls or blocks) but not by the linguistic one (presence or absence of articles).

The procedure was to introduce each child to either a pair of dolls or a pair of blocks. The dolls differed in color of dress and hair color; the blocks differed in shape and color. The experimenter, in introducing a pair of objects, applied a name or a sortal to one and only one of the pair. Nonsense syllables were employed to preclude the effects of familiarity with the symbols. For example, the experimenter under the proper-name-plus-doll condition called one doll *Zav* and referred to the other doll as *the other one*. Under the non–Pn condition the experimenter introduced one and only one doll as *a Zav* and subsequently spoke of it as *the Zav*. She spoke of the other doll as *the other one*. The pair of objects were spoken about five times during the introductory period. Each child, remember, took part in only one condition.

Then testing proper began. The tester engaged in some such operation as drawing a house, and as she worked she asked the child to hand her Zav or the Zav (depending on the condition) so that she could place it in the house. Each child was tested at least seven times in this way. We were thus able to compute for each child the proportion of times he or she handed the "correct" object, that is, the object to which the nonsense syllable had been applied. As there were only two objects in any test, the probability of a child's handing the correct one by chance was 0.5. Table 4.1 gives the results over three experiments for 70 children.

The central finding is that only under one condition did the children tend to hand the correct object more frequently than random performance would warrant. That was in the proper-name-plus-doll condition. This surprised us, because we expected only the cognitive factor to influence responses. In fact, the linguistic and cognitive factors influenced the children equally. The results fit the interpretation that the children did not take a word to be a PN unless (1) it was applied to a doll *and* (2) it was syntactically marked as a PN. Nevertheless, the results give grounds for thinking that children as young as seventeen months can, under favorable circumstances, distinguish PNs. In doing so, notice how they coordinated the notion of individual and kind. It is the individuals of some kinds, not of others, that are the likely bearers of PNs. This suggests, of course, that the children had appropriate sortals to support PNs in some language.

These results have been replicated by Gelman and Taylor (1984) and Mitchell (1984). These authors extended the study usefully to check on whether children are also able to distinguish sortals, and they found strong indications that they are. That is, under certain circumstances children are led to take some words as PNs and in others to take words as sortals. I do not dwell here on the learning of sortals.

These observations are suggestive, but I do not find them as convincing as a linguistic record that I kept of my son, Kieran, in his early language-learning days. Never in his speech, to my knowledge, did he confuse a PN with any other kind of word, even a sortal. It was uncanny how, when he was introduced to a person, he took the word he then learned as a PN for that person. When given a sortal for an object, he never hesitated to apply it to other members of the kind. For example, when I told him that one of the fasteners on my pajamas jacket was a button, he ran his finger over each button, saying *button* of each. Or when I told him that an object standing on the footpath was a tree, he said *tree* of every object of the same kind as we walked along. He never did this with PNs. He never seemed to fumble even at the earliest stages of learning. His ability to discriminate PNs showed no signs of growing more sure.

And Kieran's PNs behaved like rigid designators across time from the start. Having learned that our dog's name was *Freddie*, he applied the name to Freddie, and only to him, no matter where Freddie was, no matter whether he was standing, walking, running, sitting, or curled up. Even when the veterinary surgeon had to shave Freddie's head to help clear up an abscess, making his head look like a badly abused tennis ball, Kieran showed no hesitation in calling him *Freddie*.

Jill and Peter de Villiers, who also kept linguistic records of their son, told me that he, too, never once, to their knowledge, confused PNs and sortals. This does not, of course, even suggest that the *linguistic category* of proper noun is either unlearned or functional at the early stages of language learning. Rather, I take the diary data combined with the results of our experiments as indicating that, when children begin to learn language, they are already able to understand and use PNs as adults do and that they use this semantic skill to discover a linguistic subcategory of nouns. And they seem to do so quickly, because seventeen-month-olds in our experiments showed sensitivity to the presence or absence of syntactic markers, the articles.

When I present these observations, people sometimes ask whether *Dada* is not a frequent exception. As a matter of fact, Kieran did not in our hearing call other men *Dada*. Many children do, however; but I should note that *Dada* is not a PN but a function word. Children early know that the child next door also has a Dada, and they hear stories in which there is a Dada bear or a Dada lion. So even if children do misapply *Dada*, it does not follow that they are confusing a PN with another category of word. For a fuller discussion of early comprehension of *Dada*, see Greenfield (1973). I am not claiming that young children cannot confuse a PN with a sortal or that they never misapply a PN. Leopold (1948) records that his daughter used the name *Rita* for a girl who visited the Leopolds occasionally and also for Rita's friend, who always came with her. Leopold explains this by the marginal significance of both girls in his daughter's life. What I am claiming is that such misapplications and confusions are extraordinarily rare.

Moreover, parents interpret certain of a child's expressions as PNs, and from all that we have seen they are fully entitled to do so. Now, Quine (1960) has convinced us that there can be no apodeictic demonstration that a word in the mouth of an informant should be translated just one way and not another. True, but neither can there be an apodeictic proof that Quine is a real person, not a fictitious one. Parents simply take it as obvious that children are intentionally employing certain expressions as PNs. I believe that the parents are right and would place the burden of proof on anyone who would claim that the matter is in doubt.

I would like to return for a moment to the availability of a sortal to support PNs before children have a natural-language sortal. Owing to the work of Cohen and Younger (1983), there is now some experimental evidence that suitable sortals are available. They cite an unpublished study of seven-month-old infants carried out by Cohen and Caputo. The design of the study is what is called a *habituation design*. If infants are shown the same object over and over, they cease to be interested and their eyes wander; they habituate. Then, if shown a new object, they reveal whether they can tell that it is new by showing or failing to show a revival of interest. Cohen and Caputo set up careful controls, but we will look only at the essential data. One group of infants was shown a single stuffed animal for ten trials; a second group was shown a series of ten different stuffed animals in ten trials. Both groups habituated equally. Then came the test trial, in which the infants were shown a new stuffed animal, the same one for both groups. There was a large and significant difference in the way they reacted. The group that had seen a single stuffed animal for ten trials showed a marked revival of interest. The other group showed none; they took the test animal as just another in the series. Here is evidence that seven-month-old infants can form a category. Habituation to the series of ten different stuffed animals and failure to show increased interest when shown the test animal strongly suggests this conclusion. They grew tired of looking at different instances of a single kind, thus showing that they had spotted the kind.

Cohen and Younger speak of the children as forming a concept, which we might refer to as *stuffed animals* or *toy animals.* Can we be sure that they did form such a concept? And did they have a sortal to refer to the kind? There must be some doubt. For example, the infants may have spotted something, say a texture, common to all eleven toy animals. If that were the case, they could have represented the kind by means of a predicate. On the other hand, I think it much more likely that their attention was directed to each stimulus as a whole and that each was seen as an example of a familiar type of toy. Unfortunately, Cohen and Younger do not say whether their subjects had stuffed animals of their own. In any case, the likelihood is that they saw these stuffed animals as something like toys; in which case they must have had a sortal to express that.

I am inclined, therefore, to take these data as tentative evidence that even seven-month-olds have sortals that could support the learning and use of PNs. I might add that anyone observing seven-month-olds has the distinct impression that they already know many categories of objects: animals, bowls, cups, hands, bottles, and so forth. By that age, for example, they behave differently toward cups and toward their contents. I see Cohen and Caputo's work as supporting this impression. Those who share this impression of infants in the second half of their first year are implicitly attributing to them a range of sortals. Some of these sortals could support the learning and use of PNs.

Inputs and Outputs

The empirical studies with dolls and blocks suggest some of the input conditions for Interpreter-PN to perform its operation. They tell us, for example, that with young children the interpreter has a tendency to work only when they are attending to members of certain classes, such as people, family pets, dolls, and perhaps stuffed animals.

Besides, a word probably needs to be isolated and brought to the children's attention at the same time as they are attending to the appropriate objects. Then, if they have not already assigned a PN to those individuals or assigned that word to another individual as PN, the interpreter functions and assigns those words as PNs to those individuals.

The name normally needs to be isolated for children. The segmentation of an utterance into words is itself an immensely complex task. There is some empirical evidence that it is greatly facilitated by the parental practice of isolating and repeating key words (see Macnamara 1982, chap. 6). There is also some suggestion in the literature that children in the early stages of language learning are reluctant to assign to a new acquaintance a PN that they have already assigned to another person (Macnamara 1982, chap. 2). Against the suggestion is the evidence that children accommodate readily to several PNs and nicknames applied to themselves. On the other hand, it seems plausible that Interpreter-PN is less likely to work if the children already know a PN for the individual, because once they have learned a PN, they can use it to learn other words, such as attribute words. Children are frequently told, in the simplified language that adults use with them, "Spot happy," "Spot sick," "Spot gone." It seems plausible that the probability of Interpreter-PN's operating should diminish once children have learned a PN. Perhaps the probability diminishes further with the appearance of the already learned PN in an utterance.

There is a great deal more to be said about these triggering conditions than can be said here, mainly because it is unknown. Perhaps there are special supersegmentals, tones of voice that indicate a proper name and help to invoke Interpreter-PN. There surely are several attention-fixing devices, such as pointing and holding an object out to a child. I have made some preliminary studies of such factors (Macnamara 1977a, chap. 2). There may also be a prolonged preparatory period in which children and adults learn each other's ways of signaling which individual they are attending to (see Gillis and Schutter (unpublished)). Clearly, a great deal of research is possible in this area, and it is not difficult to design it. All one has to do is experiment with the conditions under which words are applied to individuals of the privileged kinds.

One thing that seems clear about the conditions that lead interpreters, such as Interpreter-PN, to function is that, once they have been set in place, they must last through life. A person may learn a second language well after childhood and employ the same interpretative biases in doing so as he did when a child. To see that this is so, perform the following mind experiment. Imagine that you are in a country in which the language is utterly foreign to you. Imagine you have somehow secured a teacher who, while looking at a third party to whom you are attending, isolates the phonetic sequence *Sigla*. Would you not automatically take *Sigla* as that person's name? Or if, to take an example made famous by Quine, as a rabbit passed before you, the teacher said *gavagai*, would you not be inclined to take that word as naming the kind "rabbit"?

Just imagine for a moment that such interpreters disappeared or became altered by age fifteen and that we retained none of the interpretative biases of childhood. Then, we would be quite likely to make the language learning of our children impossible by working at cross-purposes with their interpretative biases. Adults need to have a pretty good idea of how children will interpret their linguistic instruction; otherwise, children could scarcely learn a language from them.

One reason for mentioning this is to suggest that research on the triggering conditions for Interpreter-PN and its cousins might actually be conducted on adults who are learning a new language. The advantage of studying adults is that it is much easier to conduct experiments on them.

Learning Metalinguistic Predicates and Sortals

Kieran Macnamara did not use any English word, such as *name, call,* or *refer*, to designate the relation between PNs and their bearers at the time when he learned his first PNs and could employ them with obvious meaning. We have been exploring the possibility that at that time he did not have the notion of reference or any symbol to denote it. When he was nineteen months old, he began to use the word *name* much as an adult does, answering correctly when asked for people's names, including his own, and asking us for names. It seems, then, that at the age of nineteen months or perhaps a little earlier he learned the word *name* and what it means. We must now ask ourselves how he could have managed to do that. The answer is of necessity speculative because the matter has not, to my knowledge, been closely studied. Nevertheless, it is interesting to explore what the ideas being developed here suggest.

Because *name* is a sortal, we should begin by asking how young children learn sortals in general. It would seem that the main way is ostension of members. For example, a child is shown a number of dogs and told that each is a dog. He concludes that dogs are creatures in the same basic-level category (see chapter 7) as those individuals that his parents have called *dogs*. He establishes a pattern or gestalt type for dogs and assigns the English word *dog* the same extension as the visual type. I have attempted to work out some of the details of a theory based on this idea (Macnamara 1982, chap. 12), and in chapter 7 of this book I develop the same ideas further. Undoubtedly, something along these lines is a basic form of conceptual learning. Before exploring this notion, however, it will help if we take a brief look at a definition of PNs to see what light it might cast on the learning of the sortal *name*.

To begin, it does not seem at all likely that a child of nineteen months or less could pick up the sortal *name* by definition. Most attempts at definition would probably use a synonym for *name* and thus presuppose the notion that *name* expresses. For example, it would not help to say, "A name is what a thing is called."

Tarski (1956) showed how to get around this difficulty and gave a proper definition of *name*, at least for formal languages in which each name is assigned a single bearer distinct from the bearers of all other PNs. Although Tarski's idea is unlikely to be intelligible to nineteen-month-old children, it is instructive to examine the idea in a little detail because it throws light on how children can learn the notion of a PN by ostension. The restriction to a one-to-one function from PNs onto objects may not be much of a distortion when we are dealing with young children. Kieran, as a matter of interest, was using PNs for about four months before he learned that a single PN could have several bearers.

To understand Tarski's idea, let us choose a restricted domain of three boys, Tom, Dick, and Harry, and let us suppose that each has only one PN, *Tom, Dick,* and *Harry* respectively. Although we could construct the definition of *name* in a less roundabout way, we can best serve our purpose by following Tarski closely. So we determine an ordering for our three boys: Tom first, Dick second, and Harry third. We call the ordering a *sequence*. Next we specify that x will be a variable over the objects in the domain and x_i will the ith member of the sequence.

The definition of *name* will be a success if it captures all cases that can be exemplified by

> *Tom* is the name of x_1 if and only if $x_1 =$ Tom

and if it rules out all other cases. Notice that to the left of the "if and only if," "Tom" is in italics and on the right it is not. The definition can be given, somewhat simplified, by

> *Name*(α,x) if and only if $\ulcorner x_i = a \urcorner$ satisfies the sequence.

Here, α is a schematic letter for which a name in italics can be substituted and a is to be the same name not in italics. The use of Quine's corner quotes ($\ulcorner \ \urcorner$) enables us to mention, rather than use, a sentence. The expression $\ulcorner x_i = a \urcorner$ satisfies the sequence just in case the substitutions made for x_i and a refer to the same individual.

The definition succeeds because it captures all and only the desired cases. Notice that *name* is defined in terms of identity ($=$) and the satisfaction of a sequence. We will not be further concerned with the notions of satisfaction and sequence; we needed them just to highlight the role of identity. The idea that guided Tarski's use of identity can best be given by an ordinary-language sentence, such as *"Tom* is the name of somebody if that somebody is Tom." There is essential use of the use/mention distinction for a name and also of identity—two notions we have on other grounds attributed to young children. We now have to see if children can use them to learn the notion of a PN by ostension.

If children can learn the kind *dog* by ostension, it is because they have a perceptual system that can discover gestalt types in the perceptual array. The function of ostension in the early stages of language learning is not so much to help them discover a gestalt type as to show them which gestalt type is associated with a particular sortal. If children are to learn the notion of a PN by ostension, they must have the ability to discover the relevant type to which members of the type (such as ordered pairs consisting of *Spot* and a certain individual) belong. We have just seen that they have resources that could enable them to do so: identity and the use/mention or the use/pronunciation distinction. (We confine ourselves to the hypothesis that children have the use/ mention distinction. The modifications required for the use/pronun- ciation distinction as the effective one are obvious and straightforward.) What the children have to be able to do is employ their resources together with some means other than a PN for picking out the name bearer. Because we have already dwelt on the use of a demonstrative, let us confine our attention to it.

At those times when children are learning PNs, a demonstrative presents name bearers to them one at a time. Demonstratives can, therefore, serve the same function as Tarski's sequence and indexed variable. Interpreter-PN presents children with interpreted expressions, such as

$$That \in dog \ [kind] = Spot.$$

The children note that people use the same word, *Spot*, to speak about the dog and also about the dog's name: "This is Spot" and "Say 'Spot.' " This prompts Interpreter-PN to go into action again and yield the content we express by

$$That \in name \ [kind] = Spot.$$

Spot is in fact the PN of the name. This time the demonstrative picks out a pattern in auditory perception and establishes its identity with the name *Spot*. To do this children need a sortal to supply a principle of identity for the name; I have used *name* with supporting sortal *kind*. *Name* in fact denotes a relational kind consisting of ordered pairs of PNs and their bearers. The process is repeated with many PNs, whenever an attempt is made to teach pronunciation. Meanwhile, the children are hearing much talk about what the parents call *names*, and the children have an opportunity to notice that *name* serves as a sortal that will supply a principle of identity for names. The parents say things such as "Your name is *Tom*," "This girl's name is *Nuala*," "The dog's name is *Spot*." This is a case of ostension combined with a sortal, just like the teaching of the sortal *dog*. The ability to mention a word as distinct from using it constitutes a metalinguistic awareness. It is this awareness coupled with the learning of several PNs that enables children to identify the type we call *name*; and because we use the sortal *name* in connection with that type, they learn the meaning of *name*. Thus the learning of *name* can easily be accommodated within the set of ideas that have been developed to handle the learning of PNs and basic-level sortals, such as *dog*. We have to put off further discussion of the learning of sortals to chapters 7 and 8.

To show that young children do grasp the notion of a PN distinct from sortals, the following quotation, given to me by Maureen Shields, bears dramatic witness. The source, a working-class two-year-old boy in England, is older than the children we have been considering and his mother's language is offensively racist, but the sequence is so dramatic that it merits citation here. The conversation begins when a black man appears on the television.

Boy:	What's *he* (emphasis) called?
Mother:	A golliwog. A coon.
Boy:	Coon
Mother:	Coon
Boy:	Coon
Mother:	Coon
Boy:	Not coon
Mother:	Wog
Boy:	Wog
Mother:	Yeh. Black man
Boy:	Black man. And what's he *called* (emphasis)?
Mother:	Coon
Boy:	And what's he *called*?
Mother:	Coon
Boy	And what's he *called*?
Mother:	I just told you—a wog.
Boy:	And what's he *called*?
Mother:	(no response)
Boy:	Me want barley water.

5

Self-Reference

The personal pronoun *I* is in many ways similar to a PN and in some ways not. It is similar to a PN chiefly in that it is an expression that denotes an individual; it is unlike one mainly in that whom it denotes depends on who uses it. Its logic, then, is interestingly different from that of a PN, in that the interpretation of *I* makes essential appeal to a context of use. The interpretation of PNs generally appeals to context, too (see Barwise and Perry 1983, p. 34), but that is owing to the fact that there are not enough PNs to go around and that many of us are called *John, Peter,* or *Mary.* If there was a one-to-one correlation between PNs and their bearers, the interpretation of a PN could proceed without taking account of context. Not so the personal pronouns.

The learning of the personal pronouns, too, is interestingly different from the learning of PNs, mainly because we wonder if we can account for the learning of indexicals themselves, in the same way we can account for the learning of PNs. I posited a role for a demonstrative, *that,* in the learning of PNs; do we also need a demonstrative in order to learn an indexical such as *I?* Our attention will be focused mostly on the learning of *I* because the learner must understand that in his own mouth *I* designates himself. The interesting question is, How, apart from the word *I,* do learners pick themselves out as the referents of *I?* We might have done as well by choosing *you,* as addressed to the learners, because then, too, they have to learn that *you* designates themselves. It makes matters a little simpler to concentrate on one indexical, and somewhat arbitrarily I have chosen *I.*

We also look in this chapter at the logic of learning our own PNs, because they, too, presuppose a means for designating ourselves. It would seem right off that we cannot, in learning our own names, use the same perceptual indexical as we used in learning other people's names. So the learning of our own names raises some of the same questions as the learning of *I,* and it is convenient to deal with the two together. Some of the psychological insights are deeply interesting.

We begin by looking systematically at the similarities and differences in logic between PNs and the indexical *I.* Even when I do not say so, the work will be guided by Kaplan (1977) and to a lesser extent by Perry (1979). They have much in common and, so far as I know, come the closest to supplying the logic that is needed. I then work out the psychology of the ability to use and understand the pronoun *I* and also the psychology of our learning it. It transpires that it greatly facilitates the work if we assume that children know their own names at the time they learn *I*, but it is convenient to begin with children's learning of *I* and end with their learning of their own names.

The inquiries provide us with another opportunity to illustrate how logic and psychology are related. That great topic, rather than the particulars of the logic and the psychology I work out, is the main reason for the inquiries here. I believe that the logic I present is quite solid, and I believe that, together with the empirical observation of children, it argues for the psychology I offer; but I realize that, even if the logic is correct, the psychology is speculative. What I am sure about is the depth and complexity of the psychology that is needed to account for children's learning of their own names and of *I*. If anything, the account presented here is likely to err on the simplistic side.

Logic of Proper Names and of I

Referring Expressions

Contrary to Anscombe (1975) and Malcolm (1984, p. 44), *I* is a referring expression, as is also a PN. That is, each usually has the semantic function of picking out an individual. On the other hand, just as there are vacuous PNs, such as *Goldilocks*, there are vacuous uses of *I*, as, for example, in the story when Goldilocks says to herself, "What shall I do?" Being unsure of the logic of vacuous PNs, we will not trouble ourselves with vacuous uses of *I*.

The key move that Kaplan makes, the move on which his whole logic of indexicals depends, is to distinguish what he calls the *content* from the *character* of indexicals. Perhaps the best way to introduce the distinction is to consider the sentence

> I am here now.   (1)

That is a logically valid sentence because no matter who says it or where the utterer is, it is true. So take sentence (1) as used by John Macnamara in his office on 10 June 1985. So used, the sentence is true, yet its truth is not a necessary truth. If I were a more sensible person, I would be with my family enjoying the warm summer weather. So sentence (1) as used by me on that occasion does not express a necessary truth. How can we handle the fact that sentence (1) is valid but not necessary?

The first point to note is that, no matter who uses sentence (1), its meaning remains the same. That must be so, because we can all understand what the person who uses it means. It follows that we all have the same rules for interpreting it, and in that sense sentence (1) has the same meaning for us all. Yet the information it conveys varies with the context of use. When you and I use it, we express different content: You are talking about yourself; I am talking about myself.

The *content* of sentence (1), then, is a function of particular uses, whereas its meaning—or *character*, to use Kaplan's word—is a general rule for interpreting it that remains unchanged from context to context. Just as we can talk of the content of an assertion, we can talk of the content of a meaningful expression in an assertion, such as the expression *I*. Being a referring expression, *I* picks out an individual as its content. The character of *I* is given by the following general rule: "In each of its utterances, *I* refers to the person that uses it" (Kaplan 1977, p. 44).

How does the content/character distinction help us to account for the difference between valid sentences and necessary truths? The answer is that necessity attaches to content, whereas validity attaches to character. The sentence "I am here now" is valid; it is true no matter where, when, or by whom it is uttered because the character that assigns content to the indexicals is such that it makes it true. But if we wish to study necessity, first fix content, and then see whether *that* content is true in all possible circumstances. Thus sentence (1) as used by me on 10 June 1985, is true in the set of circumstances that are actual; it is false in the circumstances that I stay with my family all day. Note that this shows *I*, as used on a particular occasion, to be a rigid designator, in the sense that, as so used, it picks out the same individual in all circumstances in which the individual exists. (Here I part company with Kaplan, who takes rigid designators to pick out the same individual in all possible circumstances, whether or not the individual exists in them. I stay with Kripke (1982) and with Gupta (1980), but the point is not of great significance for the picture I am presenting.)

A similar point can be made about some other types of linguistic expression, as Steven Davis has pointed out to me. If I use the expression *the table* in circumstances in which just one table is picked out, I can distinguish the content thus picked out from the character or meaning rule that enables me to interpret the expression. Although this is both true and important, the distinction does not apply to a sortal on its own. *Table* does not refer to any table or group of tables but to a certain kind. With Putnam (1975) I take it as rigidly designating the kind. We do not, then, get the distinction, to which Kaplan draws attention, between variable content and fixed character.

Because *I*, as used on a particular occasion, is a rigid designator, the identity of the content must be provided for in the logic of *I*. This, in the light of my remarks in the two preceding chapters, tells us clearly that we need to consider a sortal to back up the use of *I* and to supply a principle of identity for its referents. It also tells us the main things that children learn when they come to understand *I* fully. Children learn a general rule that tells them to assign to *I*, as referent, the person who uses it on any particular occasion. They also learn to apply that rule and, having applied it, to treat the interpretation of *I* as rigid for the purposes of evaluating assertions.

Kaplan also says that *I* and PNs refer directly, by which he means that the relation between them and their referents is not mediated by a Fregean sense. Earlier we considered Kripke's (1982) arguments against such senses in connection with the semantics of PNs. His basic argument is that PNs are rigid designators and must continue to pick out their bearers even in circumstances in which any proposed sense (definite description) that does not assign an essential property is false, indeed in which all such senses are false. Kaplan is at pains to make the same point about indexicals, such as *I*. In particular, he is anxious to quell Frege's (1968 [1918]) mysterious theory that *I* has a radically incommunicable sense, namely that "particular and primitive way" in which "each person is presented to himself." Remember that a sense is "a mode of presentation." In fairness, Frege saw the danger of such a sense, which, being incommunicable, would have demolished his theory of sense, so he tried to sidestep it. His attempts at sidestepping, however, have met with less than general approval. Although the problem is wider in scope than these remarks indicate, Kaplan finesses it by abolishing the need for a Fregean sense for such indexicals as *I*. The arguments are similar to those advanced by Kripke against Fregean senses for PNs. Just to avoid confusion, Kaplan's character is quite distinct from a Fregean sense. A Fregean sense expresses the manner in which an individual is presented by a PN, and in opaque contexts, such as those that follow the verb *believe*, the sense, not the individual, is the referent of the PN. Kaplan's character is a rule that enables us to pick out the referent of *I* as used on a particular occasion. The character is not a description of the referent, and in opaque contexts the character is not the referent of *I*.

PN's, too, share with *I* the fact that their interpretation depends on a character that marks their context dependence (see Barwise and Perry 1983). If my mother is asked about her children and says, "John is in Montreal," the context determines me as the referent of *John*. If, however, we are talking about situation semantics and its authors, the sentence "John is in Montreal" would be about John Perry, not me. Although this is true, PNs are not nearly as context sensitive as *I*, and in the experience of young children PNs will probably not be context sensitive at all. The interpretation of the personal pronouns will be.

One or two other points about the referent of *I*. The learning of *I* is closest to the learning of a PN when the bearer is present. If the learner uses *I* himself, he must be present when he uses it; if the learner hears someone else use it, that other person will also be perceptually present to him at the time. Moreover, linguistically competent users of *I* cannot fail to recognize its referent, namely themselves. I do not mean that users never fail to recognize themselves in a photograph or in a mirror or even that they never fail to recognize parts of their own bodies. What I mean is that if people are conscious enough to use the word *I* and understand it, they must recognize themselves as the distinct individuals that it designates. To avoid confusion, it will help to add that, though the referent of *I* is the entire person, users need not be (perhaps cannot be) aware of their entire persons at the time they refer to them.

Now consider PNs, including one's own. Others besides me who happen to know the name *John Macnamara* need not recognize me if we meet. If I were to suffer a certain type of memory loss, I myself might fail to realize that *John Macnamara* refers to me. I might, for example, know that it refers to the only Irishman in McGill's Department of Psychology and use it competently to refer to that person—without realizing that that person is me. I do not see how I could fail to recognize myself as the referent of *I*, even in such a memory loss, as long as I still knew English and remembered *I*'s character.

Identity

The learning of a PN depends on a sortal to specify what will be the bearer, and the use of a PN depends on a sortal to supply a principle of identity. The matter of identity arises in connection with *I* much as it does with PNs. Take the sentence

I promised that I would, and I will.

The referents of the three *I*s are identical, so there must be a sortal supplying a principle of identity over time. The *I* who promised is the same *person* who now repeats the promise and the same person, he claims, who will at a later time keep that promise. Notice that a sortal such as *speaker* will not do, because the promiser may not be a speaker at the time he fulfills the promise.

Identity also figures in the learning of the personal pronoun *I*. If the learner is to represent to himself what he is learning, he needs some means other than *I* of indicating the referent of *I*, and part of what he learns is that the person thus indicated and the referent of *I* are identical. At this time, too, there is need of an appropriate sortal to support the logic of identity.

Finally, the learner needs a sortal to pick out the referent of *I*. In other words, even if he succeeds in locating the referent in his own person, he still needs to know that the referent is his entire person—not just his feet, hands, mouth, or even his mind. It is the sortal, with its principle of application, that settles on the entire person as the referent for *I*.

Kaplan (1977) speaks of some indexicals as having a "built-in sortal," notably *he* and *she*, which have *male* and *female* as built-in sortals. Many languages signal the speaker's status relative to the listener by choice of pronoun—witness *tu* and *vous* in French. I am not sure whether Kaplan would say that *I* has a built-in sortal, but then it is not clear what he means by "built-in." Whatever his position on the matter and whatever he means by "built-in," we know from our study of PNs that *I* needs the support of a sortal both at the time when it is being learned and subsequently during use.

It is clear, too, for reasons parallel to those given in connection with the learning of PNs, that the person who is learning *I* must understand the sortal employed in connection with *I*. For the sake of definiteness, let us say a sortal synonymous with *person*. That is, the learner must appreciate that the referent of *I* is a person. As with PNs, this further presupposes the learner's having the notion of membership.

The Indexical

The learner needs some means other than *I* itself of picking out the referent of *I*. What can that be? In the learning of PNs a definite description will do. No definite description on its own can guarantee that function in the learning of *I*, as Perry (1979) shows so vividly. He tells a story in which he is wheeling a shopper's cart about a supermarket when he notices a thin trickle of sugar on the floor. He guesses that someone has a leaky sugar bag and is trailing sugar. He sets out to find the sugar trailer by following the trail. After a time he notices the trail becoming heavier and it dawns on him that he is that person. He had an entirely appropriate and true definite description of that person that picked him out uniquely. Yet he did not, in another sense, know who that person was; he did not realize that it was himself. Not even the definite description *The person who is speaking now* suffices for the learning of *I*, unless the learner appreciates that he is that person. The learner needs some means of representing that fact, some means other than the definite description.

Perry goes on to consider two modifications of the story. Suppose he somehow knew, when he first noticed the sugar, that John Perry was the sugar trailer; he still would not have known that it was himself unless he also knew that he was John Perry. So if he had been in a somewhat unusual fugue state, suffering from memory loss, he could have known that it was John Perry he was looking for without realizing that that was himself. To have been told that the man he sought was John Perry would have been illuminating only if he had some other means, not a definite description, of identifying himself as himself and knew also that John Perry and the person so designated as himself were one and the same.

The second modification of the story is that Perry is able to indicate the sugar trailer by a demonstrative, such as *he* (pointing to a man in a mirror or pointing to a part of his own body). Even that would not force the illumination on him unless he knew that he was the man in the mirror or that the body part belonged to him. So he needed something other than a definite description, a PN or a demonstrative, to designate him precisely as himself. Perry's candidate for that role is the English word *I* (or *me*), which he has thus shown cannot be replaced without loss by any other expression. I believe that the point is both correct and important, so long as we are confining our attention to English (or a natural language). But how do children identify themselves as themselves before they learn the English word *I*, and how do they do so at the point when they learn it? This neither Perry nor Kaplan answers, but it is a focal point in my inquiry. The crux of the matter is to find a symbol by which children can identify themselves before they have any natural-language symbol to do so. This will become pressing when I consider the learning of one's own name.

Time

The main difference between a PN and *I* is that a PN picks out its referent no matter who uses it (at least for young children), whereas *I* picks out a particular person only when that person uses it. There is what looks like one exception to this rule that must be mentioned just for the purpose of allaying suspicions. It is the direct-quotational use of *I*, as in "Mary said, 'I am tired.' " In that case the *I* refers to Mary and not to me if I report what she said. But the rule has not been violated, because when I report an expression, I do not *use* the words in quotation marks, I *mention* them. My report specifies Mary as the person who uses the *I*, and the rule assigns her as its content. Notice, however, that in indirect quotation there are no quotation marks, as in "Mary said that I am tired." If I am the reporter, I *use* the words with which I report her observation, and I am rightly assigned to the content of *I*.

To express the character of *I*, we cannot escape some device to indicate time, because the character of *I* makes essential reference to time. The point can be confusing. *I* does not assign the user to any particular moment; that is not the way time enters in. Rather, the character of *I* is a rule for searching events in time to determine a referent. Informally, the rule says: At each moment when *I* is used, see who is using it, for that person is the referent. It follows that children who understand the character of *I* must have at least a primitive grasp of time together with some symbol to indicate position in time. To the extent to which PNs have fixed character, and we are so treating them for the purposes of studying early child language, they can be understood without regard to the time of utterance. Perhaps that is one reason why children usually learn at least to understand their own names before they learn the personal pronouns.

Let me summarize the findings of the comparison of PNs and *I*. Both PNs and *I* are directly referring expressions that rigidly designate their referents. Both need sortals in support to specify the referents and to supply principles of identity for them. Both are context sensitive and require characters to guide interpretation, but *I* is far more dependent on context for its interpretation. There is an essential temporal component in the rule that specifies the character of *I*. To the extent that PNs have fixed character, we can dispense with considerations of character and so with any essential temporal component in assigning them a content. Finally, there is something special about *I*, in that the competent user cannot fail to be conscious of its referent in the manner in which we are conscious of ourselves, whereas the competent use of a PN does not presuppose or imply any intimate acquaintance with its bearer. For this reason we need not consider conditions for the learning of *I* analogous to those in which the referent of the PN is absent or nonexistent.

Psychology and I

Empirical Observations
Here is the entry in my diary that records the first use of a personal pronoun by my son, Kieran, when he was fifteen months and nineteen days of age:

> When I came home this evening, Joyce told me that she showed Kieran several photos in which he appears. When he saw himself, he pointed to himself and said *me*, once. I tested him and once

he looked at a picture of himself and then pointed to himself—but I was not sure that he really was indicating himself because he often puts his finger on his chest. When I was putting him to bed, he pointed to himself many, many times and said *me*. Nothing to do with pictures! I was not sure that this was a pronoun and self referring. Though Joyce assures me that he looked at the photo for a long time and spontaneously said *me*, pointing meanwhile to himself.

Subsequent entries confirm that Kieran could use *me* correctly to refer to himself. This was a great step forward, prefigured by nothing that Joyce and I had noticed in his speech. It was not, however, the end of the road. On a few occasions about that time, he also used *me* to refer to another person. Later, he systematically reversed the pronouns in certain contexts, calling himself *you*. It was easy to see why he did this. He had developed a strategy for answering yes/no questions: He said *no* if he wanted to give a negative answer and repeated the last word of the question if he wanted to give an affirmative one. At this stage, if we showed him a photograph of himself and asked, "Who is that?" he would answer *me*. If, however, we asked, "Is that you?" he would answer *you*. This occurred when he was eighteen months old and lasted about a month. Again, when he was twenty months old, he began to say things such as "I help you," where he meant us to help him, usually with his food. These reversals lasted for about two months. They seemed to occur only when he was attempting to say what we often said to him, as for example when with the words, "I'll help you," we undertook to feed him. It was as if to utter so long a string and also make the necessary reversals was too much, so he just repeated the words without the reversal and trusted us to understand.

Although we cannot be sure of the matter, my wife and I never doubted that all his uses of personal pronouns, even the erroneous uses, picked out an individual as a whole and that the individual was seen as being identical over time and space and also through those manifold transformations that most individuals undergo continually. One reason for thinking so was the close connection between personal pronouns and PNs. Personal pronouns seemed to substitute for PNs in his speech. And PNs, as we have seen, are supported in child language by an identity-supplying sortal. The success of most children in identifying the referents of personal pronouns as complete individuals is highlighted by occasional failures. Oshima-Takane (1985) tells of one small boy whose parents sought to teach him the meaning of *I* (*me*) by means of a pointing gesture. For a short time the boy seemed to interpret *I* (*me*) as meaning just the neck, not the whole person.

Many children seem to begin their use of the personal pronouns in a certain confusion. Oshima-Takane (1985) found evidence that many children initially use I (*me*) to refer to either the speaker or the addressee. But their confusion is not obvious, because they usually use the addressee's PN (or an expression like *Daddy*) when they intend to refer to the addressee. Oshima-Takane could not be certain whether such children thought that I (*me*) could refer to either of the participants in a conversation or whether they were simply unsure of the semantic rule. To illustrate, think of the confusion children often experience with the meaning of the words *left* and *right*. When asked, "Show your right hand," they will sometimes show the right and sometimes the left. Yet they do not seem to think that the matter is undecided. Their response merely reveals uncertain grasp of the rule. Similarly, Oshima-Takane was not sure whether these children were uncertain about the rule or whether they imagined that I (*me*) could refer to either participant. I must confess that I favor the uncertain-grasp interpretation, if only for the reason that, if children are naturally inclined to interpret I (*me*) disjunctively, we would expect to find such singular pronouns in some languages. So far as I know, we do not.

Oshima-Takane (1985) also found a small number of children who systematically reversed the pronouns, using I (*me*) to refer only to the addressee and *you* to refer to themselves. Petitto (1983) documented an even more dramatic reversal in the signing of I (*me*) by a deaf child. This was the child of two deaf parents whose own first language was American Sign Language. The finding is the more dramatic for the fact that in sign language the correct sign for I (*me*) is made by the speaker's pointing to himself with the index finger; that for *you* is made by pointing to the interlocutor with the index finger. What is more, before this child had begun to use sign language, she had been using her index finger, as we all do, to designate objects, including people, that interested her. For a time after beginning to learn to sign, she refrained from using such gestures to designate participants in her conversations. In fact, she gave no indication of using the sign language indexicals for *I* and *you*. When she began to sign I (*me*), she reversed the sign, despite the transparency of its content. That is, she pointed to the wrong person systematically—a dramatic demonstration of Perry's point that an indexical such as *I* is not just a demonstrative. Incidentally, Petitto has found two other deaf children, one of whom showed a similar confusion but less consistently, and another who showed no confusion at all.

The most interesting thing, however, is not how some children sometimes reverse the pronouns but how all children (with the possible exception of certain autistic ones) soon come to get them right. It is something each child must learn without the benefit of a rule formulated by his instructors. There is no use saying to a child, "You must say *I* when I say *you*." For reasons parallel to those we considered in chapter 3, operant conditioning is no help either. The most we could hope for from such conditioning is to get the child to utter the right indexical, not to understand it. The learning-theoretic approach has nothing interesting to offer to the student of child semantics. That is not to say that a parent's response to an expression containing an indexical has nothing to do with the learning of the indexical, just that learning theory is a hopelessly wrong approach. So how do children learn the personal pronouns?

Obviously they have to listen to the speech of others and guess its intent. Over a month before his first use of *me*, Kieran gave some evidence of beginning to understand the personal pronouns when we spoke to him. If either Joyce or I said "Kiss X," where X was a variable ranging over the PNs that he knew, he would do it; if either of us said to him "Kiss me," he would do it. He also gave indications at the same time that he understood *you* when it was addressed to him. The particular question I am focusing on is, How did he come to understand that *I* (*me*) in his mouth referred to himself?

The full answer must include an account of an inductive leap on the basis of a few examples, but induction is not my concern here. My concern is how Kieran came to conclude that *I* (*me*) could refer to him at all, because in all his earlier experience it never did. Even more important, what precisely did he learn when he reached that conclusion, and how did he express it? We must keep in mind that he may at first have misunderstood *I* (*me*), taking it to mean either participant in a conversation. The logical resources needed to reach and express that conclusion are even more extensive than those needed to express its true meaning or character. The misunderstanding requires the availability of a disjunctive, *or*; the correct rule does not. But let us not worry about those children who first reverse the pronouns completely. They need exactly the same logical resources to express their mistake as to express the correct rule. Instead, we concentrate on children who, if Oshima-Takane is right, may initially think that *I* (*me*) can mean speaker or addressee. How might they come to that conclusion, and how might they correct it?

Well, first they may well observe that many different people who speak to them use *I* and, when they do, it refers to that person. This might be apparent from their actions—"I'll do it, pet," followed by an action performed by the speaker. That would mark off *I* from PNs, of which children know many but each of which picks out a different person. How do children know that *I* is not a sortal, seeing that it can be applied to many individuals of a kind, just as *dog* and *person* can? Perhaps they can rule that out by noting that *I* is a referring expression, that its syntax in a noun phrase is quite similar to that of a PN. So they hear such sentences as "Freddie wants to go to sleep" and "I want to go to sleep." If they can make such comparisons, they might rule out a sortal interpretation.

In any case, children probably listen to their parents talking to each other, especially when the children themselves are involved. They might then notice that the referents of *you* and *I* depend on who is speaking. That would also help to exclude the sortal hypothesis if they ever entertain it. Oshima-Takane (1985) gives some evidence that children do benefit from the exchanges between people other than themselves in their efforts to understand the personal pronouns. If this is right, as it seems to be, it provides us with an important clue. It tells us that children notice that the referent of *I* is a function of which person is speaking. *Person that is speaking* supplies children with a key to the character of *I* and also with the sortal (*person*) that helps to specify the referent and supply the principle of identity. It will do those things, however, only if the child realizes that he, too, is a person and that, when he uses *I*, he is the person that *I* refers to.

This is not the place to inquire how children know that they are persons; that they are in the same kind as their mothers and fathers, brothers and sisters, cousins and neighbors; that they are not in the same kind as walls, floors, rocks, plants, dogs, and cats. I assume that this is a basic discovery helped along by all the social and nurturing contacts between children and their caretakers. I allowed earlier that children have identified gestalt types for dogs by the time they come to learn PNs for them. It would be odd if by the same time they have not done the same for people and managed also to fit themselves in the kind that such a gestalt type designates. To do that, however, they have to have some way of designating themselves as the entity that is the relevant person.

Self-Designation
At the point when children are learning the force of *I*, as used by themselves, they cannot use *I* to designate themselves because that is what they are learning. There are four other types of natural-language expression that might serve the purpose: the child's proper name, a definite description, a function expression, such as *oldest child of*, and a demonstrative or indexical other than *I*. We know Perry's (1979) arguments that *I* is not eliminable in favor of any or all of these; nevertheless the four alternative expressions might serve the function of fixing the referent of *I*. We should note that fixing the referent of a

term may be quite a different matter from giving its character (or meaning). Fixing the referent of *I* on a particular occasion is merely indicating its content. Its character is different from its content, and, although its character also helps to indicate its content, there are many other ways of indicating it. So I can tell you the content signaled by a particular use of *I* by telling you that *Ronald Reagan* picks out the same content. Yet *Ronald Reagan* does not invariably pick out the content of *I*, whereas its character consists of a general rule that specifies how to do just that—how to pick out the content of *I* in all its uses as a function of context. The distinction between fixing the content of an expression and stating its meaning has been urged by Kripke (1982).

Neither does the fixing of its content supply *I* with a Fregean sense. So, even if we employ a definite description to identify the content of *I* on a particular occasion, the definite description does not mediate between *I* and its referent in the way that Frege seemed to imagine. For example, suppose that a teacher hears the words *I'm bored* and asks, "Who said that?" And suppose a tattletale says that it was the girl in the red sweater near the window (and that picks out just one girl). It still does not follow that *The girl in the red sweater near the window* expresses a Fregean sense of the word *I*. The definite description is just a means of indicating to the teacher who said "I'm bored."

At the time when Kieran first used *me* to designate himself, he had not used any other English indexical or demonstrative and he had never uttered a string of such length or complexity as "the person who is now speaking" or "the eldest son of *x*." If he did employ a natural-language expression to indicate himself when he learned the meaning of *I* (*me*) as used by himself, almost certainly it was his own name. Though he himself did not utter his name, he understood it well at the time. Quite often young children get around the complexities of the pronominal system by using PNs in their place. So Kieran could have used his own name to express what he learned. If he did, he could have expressed part of what he learned at that time by a sentence that has the same content as

$$Kieran \in person \ [kind] = I.$$

In what follows I drop explicit mention of *kind*, as it makes the formalization of what is learned too complicated.

The content just noted, however, must have been only part of what Kieran soon learned, because he had to realize that *I* also designates other people. On the assumption that, when he first learned *I*, he was confused, thinking that it could be used to refer to both speaker and addressee, we can express his earliest rule as

$$I_{t_ip_i} = \imath(P, x)(x \text{ utters } I \text{ at } t_ip_i \lor I_{t_ip_i}) = \imath(P, y)(y \text{ is addressed at } t_ip_i).$$
$$(2)$$

This is to be read as I at a time t_i and place p_j refers either to the unique person x who utters it at t_ip_j or to the unique person y who is addressed at t_ip_j. The sortal that specifies the referent and supplies the required principle of identity for the referent is *person* (P). Of course, if the addressee were a cat or a teddy bear, the sortal for y would have to be altered accordingly. The indexes for time and place are essential. The one for time is needed to signal that the child does not take the referent of I as fixed in the way that the referent of a PN is. The index for place is necessary to signal that, if at the same moment when the child itself utters I in one conversation, someone else also utters it within earshot (or out of earshot for that matter, though that possibility may not occur to the child), the referents are nonetheless distinct. Remember that of itself I does not pick out the speaker at either a time or a place; time and place, however, are essential elements in the rule that assigns to I a particular content. The rest of the sentence may specify the referent at a particular time and place. For example, the clause "When I was last in London," as used by me, picks out that part of my existence that was passed in London when I was last there. The sortal that specifies and supplies the necessary principle of identity for the referent is *person* (P).

The rule that soon replaces expression (2) is simpler, although the final rule must be complicated in ways that I do not specify fully—to take account of the use/mention distinction and also of possible worlds. We shall be satisfied with

$$I_{t_ip_i} = \imath(P,x)(x \text{ utters } I \text{ at } t_ip_i).$$
$$(3)$$

This reads just like expression (2) except that all mention of the addressee is dropped.

Let us now look at the logical resources necessary to express sentences (2) and (3). I will not dwell on the disjunctive $\lor$; I deal with all such sentential connectives in chapter 6. The new logical resources, beyond those demanded for the learning of PNs, include an indexical for time and a tensed verb, *utters* or *addresses*. Quite early, Kieran had a large number of expressions that showed he had a concept of temporal ordering. For example, he used *all gone* to say that something or somebody that had been present was present no more. And he had a large category of words that anticipated the future, a category that I labeled *action demands* (Macnamara 1982, appendix 3). It's just that he lacked any convenient natural-language device to mark the temporal aspect of a verb such as *speak*. He was well into his eighteenth month when he first used the present progressive morpheme, *-ing*, to indicate contemporaneous action. That was three months after he learned *me*. How then could he have expressed the temporal element in the character of *me*? Although the question demands an answer if the psychology of learning personal pronouns is to advance, I am not confident that I have the answer. Nevertheless, in the spirit of these inquiries I prefer to be clear rather than cautious, so I venture the following.

In some basic sense children do not *learn* the capacity to see events as temporally ordered. This may not be saying much more than that memory and the power to anticipate are natural. If children are naturally to recall some events as past and anticipate others as future, as Kieran clearly did, they have by that very fact the capacity to order events temporally. I take this much as relatively uncontroversial. In particular, I take it that the learning of a natural language does not force the concept of time on children but that the prior concept of time enables them to learn the meaning of the temporal elements in a natural language. But how do children represent temporal ordering before they have natural-language devices to do it? Well, if young children know some events as past, they must have a symbol that represents them as past; if they are knowingly able to anticipate some events as future, they must have a symbol that so represents them. Because children do not yet have natural-language symbols to serve these purposes, they must have them in some other language. The one that comes to mind is the language of thought, for it is in that language that children must express the character of *I* (*me*) at the point when they are learning it. Allow children symbols to express past and future, and it is not much of a concession to allow them a symbol to represent an event as present. Children surely know present events of which they are aware as present. We have, then, allowed children a symbol with which they can express the temporal element in the character of *I* (*me*). This is all, even in the spirit of daring I have adopted, that I feel capable of contributing at the moment.

Another logical resource essential to the expression of *I*'s character is an index for place. This, however, we have already allowed children in our discussion of PNs. In endowing them with demonstratives in the interpretation of vision, we have already implicitly endowed them with the means of representing place. One problem with expressions (2) and (3) is that Kieran said no word, such as *speak* (*speaker*), *talk* (*talker*), *say*, or *tell*, for a long time after he had what seemed like adult competence in his use of *I* (*me*). I do not know what importance to attach to this. He certainly understood *say* as a command quite well at the time, but he never uttered it himself. So perhaps he employed the word *say* in his mind to express the meaning of *I* (*me*) as used by himself. It hardly seems too fanciful to claim that, by the time he came to use the first-person pronoun, he already understood what it was to say something to someone. To concede that much is to allow that he had symbols that expressed that content, exactly what he needed to express the character of *I* (*me*). What is not at all clear is that he had those resources available to him in English.

Correcting Error

Apart from the persuasiveness of Oshima-Takane's (1985) evidence, the acceptance of initial error in children's understanding of the personal pronouns enables me to make a number of observations about error and its correction and the relation of both to logical competence.

We are assuming that some children's initial understanding of *I* (*me*) is such that it can be used to designate either the speaker or the addressee. This, it should be noted, is an error in English, not in basic logical competence. There is, for example, no evidence that children are confusing themselves with their addressee or that they are failing to trace the identity of each appropriately. This means that in some language they are able to represent the relevant state of affairs correctly. They are making a mistake in the logic of English—quite a different matter. Further, Oshima-Takane, in giving us her interpretation of the children's confusion, is assuming a basic consistency in their thought. She found that in experimental sessions many children use *me* while pointing either to themselves or to an addressee, whereas in ordinary conversation the same children use *me* only of themselves, replacing it with a PN or an expression such as *Mommy* when they refer to an addressee. The assumption of logical consistency suggests that they interpret *me* as having the same meaning in the experimental sessions as in ordinary conversation.

In due course the children got the meaning of *I* (*me*) right, presumably because they spotted how others were using the expression or because others failed to understand their (the children's) utterances that inappropriately included *I* (*me*). The change required no revision of basic logical competence.

This type of revision finds no place in the development of logical systems by logicians. Logicians set up a language, specify some axioms in it, and use rules of inference to add new propositions, the theorems of the system. The picture is of monotonically increasing systems, in the sense that there is never any need to backtrack, to revise the language, or to expunge error. Although this makes perfect sense for finished systems of logic, it is not satisfactory as a picture of how those systems are actually developed, let alone of how we build our knowledge of our language and of the world. For this reason a number of cognitive scientists have been attempting to formulate more realistic systems— systems that are not monotonic in one way or another (see, for example, McDermott and Doyle 1978, McCarthy 1980, and Reiter 1980). For reasons that need not detain us, I have misgivings as to whether any one of these writers has yet captured the intuition here satisfactorily. One feature of McCarthy's work, however, interests me greatly. His strategy is to define something, which he calls *circumscription*, that is designed to constrain the application of predicates to just those individuals who are relevant to a particular discourse. Circumscription, however, is not a modification of logic. He says: "In our opinion, it is better to avoid modifying the logic if at all possible." In the language we are using, circumscription is defined for a performance model, leaving the logical competence or idealization untouched. This, I think, is altogether wise, and I have attempted to abide by it in my account of children's error and its correction.

Basic Self-Reference

When specifying Kieran's first step in the learning of the character of *I*, we assumed that he knew his own name. It was not absolutely necessary, though it was absolutely necessary that he have some expression he could use to pick himself out, knowing that it was himself. Several researchers have noted that some children begin by using their PNs, whereas in adult life they would use *I* (*me*), but many, like Kieran, use the pronoun first (Oshima-Takane 1985). This does not mean that the pronoun users do not understand their names, but nothing in the theory presented here demands that they should have. In any case, Kieran could have used his name with profit to learn the meaning of *I* only if he knew that he himself was Kieran. How, then, did he learn to understand his own name? No use thinking that he said to himself, "Kieran is me." We are supposing that he did not yet know the meaning of *me*. Yet to express the meaning of his name, he needed a symbol like *me*. When he learned the first natural-language word that picked himself out in the appropriate way, whatever that word was, he must have had some other symbol that did the same thing. What can that symbol have been?

For an answer I am thrown back to Frege's (1968 [1918]) remark: "Now everyone is presented to himself in a particular and primitive way, in which he is presented to no-one else." The notion of presentation (*Vorstellung*) in German philosophy is a portentous one, but we need not become entangled in it. What Frege meant is that, just as in vision my wife is presented to me as a visual object, so in consciousness we are presented to ourselves precisely as selves. We are aware of ourselves in a special way in which we are not aware of anyone else, as the beings that are aware. All other persons and objects are presented to us as other. We are presented to ourselves as selves. Once again, if we are to know ourselves in that way, we need a symbol that so represents us. We need that symbol, and we need to be able to understand it in order to learn any natural-language symbol as referring to ourselves.

So I conclude that Kieran had command of a symbol for himself in the language of thought when he learned his own name. Let us call that symbol *ego*. Though he was twenty months of age before he first uttered *Kieran*, he understood the name, perfectly as far as we could see, from the time of his earliest utterances. Presumably Interpreter-PN came into play at that early time and yielded as output in the language of thought an expression synonymous with

$$\text{Ego} \in \text{person [kind]} = \text{Kieran}. \tag{4}$$

There is little point in considering whether *ego* is learned, because if it were, it would have to be learned on the back of some other symbol that performed the same semantic function. Because there is no point in beginning on a regress, let us assume that *ego* is unlearned and that it is available to children by the time they begin to tackle language seriously, sometime after the age of about twelve months.

In keeping with Kaplan's (1977) logic of the indexicals, we should note that equation (4) does not give the meaning of *Kieran*; it merely specifies its content. Having learned the name as referring to himself, Kieran could use it to designate himself in the appropriate manner. That is why *ego* does not appear in Kieran's first specification of the character for *I* (*me*). A final remark is that, by the logic of identity ($=$), Kieran would have understood that because *ego* is a person, so also *Kieran* is a person. That logic embodies the principle that if $a = b$, then any property of a is also a property of b. So if *ego* and *Kieran* are identical and if ego is a person, so is Kieran.

One result of these meditations is that children do not in the most basic sense learn the notion of self and the identity of the self. Psychiatrists often speak about learning our true identity. By this they seem to mean that we have to learn what it means to be male or female, white or black, Catholic or Jewish. But in the most basic sense, the self that is male, white, and Catholic is not identified through learning, nor is its basic identity, under a sortal synonymous with *person* or *animal*, learned. This would seem to be the psychological lesson of Perry's theory of the essential indexical. Strangely, though, the basic symbol, *ego*, by which people identify themselves is not an indexical. It is a proper name.

6

Truth and Truth-Functional Connectives

Tucked away in the analysis of how children learn proper names and personal pronouns is the assumption that, from their earliest attempts to speak, children have the notion of truth. To begin with, it is tucked away in the use of intuitions about truth conditions to yield an analysis of the semantic functions of those expressions and in allowing the results of the analyses to guide the construction of psychological theory. That approach consists of studying the contribution of expressions to the truth conditions of sentences in which they occur. Suppose that a child had no understanding of any sentence or no grasp of the concept of truth; then a word that we regard as a proper name could not be a proper name for that child. It might have the function of designating an individual, but it could not have the function of combining with other expressions to form a sentence that the child would regard as truth valuable, that is, capable of being evaluated as true or false. This would follow directly from the assumption that the child does not have the notion of truth.

The assumption that young children have the notion of truth is, perhaps, more obvious in the statements of what they learn when they learn a proper name or a personal pronoun. These statements consist of sentences that children are thought to understand. Part of the understanding is appreciating that the sentences relate to states of affairs in the manner that I call describing them truly. For example, Tom was taken as representing to himself such a sentence as

$$That \in _{dog\ [kind]} = Spot.$$

He was also taken as understanding the sentence as being about a particular animal, and he was also taken as asserting the sentence for himself. Assertion presupposes a grasp of the notion of truth; it presupposes a judgment of truth. Thus, if children can make assertions, they must have the notion of truth. To do so, of course, they do not need any natural-language predicate, such as the English word *true*.

Many psychologists and philosophers to whom I have talked about cognitive development have expressed surprise at my attributing so abstract and so deep a notion as truth to one-year-old children. For this reason we should consider the grounds for the attribution. It is all the more necessary to do so, as we are about to discuss the learning of truth-functional connectives. They cannot be understood without the notion of truth. It was, I hope, possible to discuss the learning of proper names and personal pronouns without tackling the notion of truth head-on. It was desirable to begin in a more tangential way so that the reader might obtain the general idea of how logic illuminates projects of narrow scope before going on to questions that involve a predicate that is claimed true of an entire proposition and to relations among entire propositions.

Truth

Learning

Learning-that, as we have seen, presupposes the ability to form and understand a sentence in some language. Learning-that results in a belief, and all belief must be expressed in language. Further, belief involves judgment; the believer judges that some proposition is true. Even if an individual judges that some proposition p is not certain but only possible, he is still judging that the proposition *possibly* —— is true. In any case, *possibly* here means possibly true. It follows that learning-that presupposes the concept of truth. The learner does not need the concept of judgment because he can perform the act of judging without knowing that he is judging. But the learner must have the concept of truth; there is no action that can stand in its place.

Psychologists and computer scientists sometimes talk as if this is not so; they talk about putting certain sentences in a belief box and leaving others out. It might seem as though the placing of a sentence in a belief box is an action of the sort I have just ruled out. When, however, we look at what it means to have a sentence in a belief box, how it interacts with other sentences and how it relates to behavior, it is clear that the phrase "placing a sentence in a belief box" is merely a metaphor for judging it true. Although a judgment is in the strictest sense an action— explained by reference to beliefs and desires—the predicate *true* that it involves is no such thing. It is a predicate that must be *used* in judging the sentence true. It must therefore be understood.

Do people need the concept of a proposition in order to engage in learning-that? It would seem that they do not, because it is an individual proposition that is judged to be true. At any point learners will be confronted with a particular proposition, which they judge true. Just as we can judge an object to be hot and not know what sort of object it is, we can judge a proposition to be true and not know what sort of object it is and in particular that it is a proposition.

I lay aside for the moment the question of the language in which the truth predicate is available to children who are successful learners-that.

Another way to look at the impossibility of learning the concept of truth is to consider the form that the learning would have to take. It is worth doing so for the purpose of considering how children might learn the English predicate *true*. The proposition that would express the learning would have to have a form similar to

A proposition is true if and only if ———,

where the line would be replaced by some suitable definition. The definition need not be of the sort that the logician seeks. It might, like the learning of the concept of dog that we considered, involve a demonstrative—"is of the same kind as that and that," where the demonstratives pick out true propositions. Even so, the definition uses a truth-functional connective *if and only if*, whose understanding presupposes the notion of truth. The same holds even if we were to endow children with the notions of reference and true of (as pertaining to predicates) and imagine that, Tarski-like, they defined *truth* for themselves. To do so, they would employ a truth-functional connective, which they must understand, so they would have to have the notion of truth. This brings out in a new way how the purported learning of the concept of truth would presuppose the concept of truth itself.

Negation

Truth is of its nature opposed to falsity, so we cannot have the one without the other. To bring this out, think of truth as one pole on a dimension whose other pole is falsity. Just as we cannot grasp the notion of top without grasping that it has an opposite, bottom, we cannot grasp the notion of truth without grasping that it has an opposite, falsity. Medieval people used to express the point in a philosophical adage: *eadem est scientia oppositorum* (opposites are understood in a single insight). This leads us to the conclusion that young children also have a predicate for falsity. Because the most likely candidate for the falsity predicate is *not true*, it seems likely that they have a one-place sentential connective that is synonymous with *not*. In any case, because they have truth and falsity predicates for propositions, children understand the relations among sentences that we express by means of the one-place connective *not*.

Principle of Contradiction

The position I have reached prompts the question of whether someone ignorant of the principle of contradiction could learn it. The principle is intimately related to the fact that truth and falsity are opposites, and I have concluded that children are endowed by nature with an understanding of both. To grasp the question, imagine a child who has no knowledge and no use of the principle of contradiction. Not only would this child be unable to state the principle, he would have no means of applying it. The child's mother, noticing this, tells him that for any proposition p, it cannot be that both p and $\sim p$ are true at the same time. She might even back up her general principle with a number of examples, such as, it cannot simultaneously be true that *Dobbin is a horse* and *Dobbin is not a horse*. Is it *logically* possible for such a child to learn the lesson that the mother wishes to teach? The word "logically" is important. I do not wish to consider miracles or cases in which the utterance of that sentence by the mother triggers a prepared mental device to form the conclusion that the mother desires the child to form.

Several considerations argue that the child could not learn the lesson. One that comes to mind first can perhaps be surmounted: To teach the lesson, the mother must use a proposition. If the child did not apply the principle to the proposition in which the principle is enunciated, he could not learn the principle, for there would be at least one proposition that the child took to be possibly both true and false. Heaven knows how he would apply a proposition so taken to other propositions. In other words it must be made clear to the child that the proposition is self-referring. Making that clear is not easy, but it does not seem impossible. It could be done in an additional clause to the effect: "and that applies to the proposition stating the principle itself, whereas this whole addendum is itself true and not false." It is worth spelling out, because the cumbersomeness of the statement suggests the unlikelihood of children learning the principle.

Although this first difficulty is not, logically, insurmountable, there is no lack of others that are. In stating the principle, the mother has to use the words *proposition, true*, and *false*. Is it possible to understand the word *proposition* and not know that it cannot have both truth values simultaneously? Is it possible to understand the word *true* without realizing that it is opposed to *false* in such a way as to exclude their both applying simultaneously to the same proposition? It would seem that those words form a system that must be grasped all at once if they are to be grasped at all. It follows further that, although a child might indeed learn from an informant that the English words *true* and *false* are opposed in the manner expressed by the principle of contradiction, the child could not learn the truth that the principle expresses.

Even if we could get a child with no knowledge of the principle of contradiction and no mental machinery for applying it to appreciate the principle's universal applicability, even if we could manage to have the child understand the words needed to express it, there is something odd about the idea that he might learn so basic a logical principle. My analysis of learning would then imply that the basic principles of logic might have, in their basic mental realization, the status of beliefs. If they were beliefs, they would have to be expressed in symbols that need to be interpreted. Interpretation, if it is to be consistent (not to say sensible), must conform to certain logical principles. Therefore such interpretation demands the availability of basic logical principles, which, in turn, presupposes the availability to the mind of the very principles we are imagining to be learned. Thus the basic form in which logical principles are available to the mind cannot be as beliefs.

The conclusion that forces itself on us is that neither the concepts of truth and falsity nor the fundamental principles of logic are learned.

Truth-Functional Connectives

Suppose, then, that by nature children have the notions of truth and falsity together with a few fundamental principles of logic, such as the principle of contradiction. The question I now wish to ask is, Can such children learn the logic of the entire set of two-place truth-functional connectives that are employed in logic? Examples of such connectives are *and* and *or*, which can be used to form a single large sentence from two smaller ones. Thus, from the two sentences "John sells bagels" and "Joyce eats cream cheese," we can form the single large sentence

John sells bagels and Joyce eats cream cheese.   (1)

To say that a connective is truth functional is to say that the truth value of the large sentence depends only on the truth values of the smaller sentences. Thus sentence (1) will be true just in case it is true that (a) John sells bagels and (b) Joyce eats cream cheese.

I begin the inquiry by determining certain uses of sentential connectives that are common to logic and ordinary language and by distinguishing these from other uses. Then I discuss the interpretation of the sentential connectives in the uses I have isolated. Only then do I pose the question of the learnability of the entire set of sentential connectives. To make the work manageable, I confine attention largely to the connective *and*. I might point out that psychological work in the area is quite unsatisfactory, so my "psychological" remarks are going to be largely critical.

Clarifications

These introductory remarks about sentential connectives are in need of several modifications and clarifications. First some clarifications, which for brevity's sake can be confined to *and*. They are inspired by a celebrated work by Grice (1975). The purpose of these remarks is to isolate the truth-functional uses of *and* and to limit attention to these alone.

Formal logic defines the two-place connective & without any reference to the content of the sentences it conjoins. It would be odd if someone in ordinary conversation were to say

> The day is fine *and* seven is a prime number.   (2)

What is odd is to conjoin two sentences that have so little to do with one another. We seem to be constrained by a maxim, which falls short of being a law, to conjoin only sentences that have to do with one another, a non–truth-functional constraint. Nevertheless, we have no difficulty in understanding sentence (2) and in interpreting the *and* truth functionally.

Formal logic is insensitive to the order of the conjoined sentences, whereas ordinary English is not. Sentences (3) and (4) express rather different states of affairs:

> Mary got married *and* she had a baby.   (3)

> Mary had a baby *and* she got married.   (4)

Nevertheless, there are many occasions in which ordinary English pays no attention to the order of sentences, as, for example, sentence (1). Formal logic has simply isolated those uses of *and* that are truth functional and laid the rest aside.

English often abbreviates by dropping part of one of the conjoined sentences. Sentence (5) can be taken as short for sentence (6):

> John *and* Joyce came.   (5)

> John came *and* Joyce came.   (6)

Sentences similar to (5) cannot always be taken as abbreviations, however, as sentences (7) and (8) illustrate:

> John *and* Joyce are a married couple.   (7)

> John is a married couple *and* Joyce is a married couple.   (8)

Once again, logic has based its & on those cases in which what is conjoined are entire sentences, not constituents of simple sentences.

There are also idioms in which *and* ceases to function as a logical connective. We can quite sensibly say that Smith is a member of Jones and O'Keeffe, where *Jones and O'Keeffe* is the name of a legal firm. As a general rule, names, when functioning as names, do not have logical structure. A somewhat different example is *good and ready*. The child who is told to wait until Mother is good and ready does not have to wait for moral improvement as well as leisure on Mother's part. *Good* in the idiom seems to function logically as an adverb. The force is similar to that of *properly* in the expression *properly ready*.

It is important to clear the decks by mentioning these uses, because if the logic of & and of the English *and* were completely different, some might assume that the natural-language connective expresses the function that is operative in everyday reasoning, whereas logic's & expresses a special-purpose function. This would set a great distance between the two and support the view that we have to learn the connectives of propositional logic from books or teachers. The distinctions noted enable us to see that the two share a purely truth-functional set of uses, as many linguists have said (McCawley 1980, Gazdar 1979).

Focusing the Question

I am now in a position to bring the question of learning into sharper focus. The question is, Can children who have a notion of truth and falsity but no truth-functional connective learn the entire set of such connectives that are found in propositional logic? The question is not about the learning of the English connectives that come closest to matching the truth-functional connectives of logic. Natural-language connectives vary from language to language and must be learned. I am interested, rather, in whether the entire set of functions that such connectives express can be learned.

The word "entire" is important, because it is well known that it is possible, given some of the connectives, to define the remaining ones. For example, it is possible with *not* and *and* or with *not* and *or* to define all the remaining two-place connectives. A fortiori, with *not*, *and*, and *or* it is possible to define the remainder of the set. This suggests (without demonstrating it) that, given certain connectives, children can learn the others by defining them. My interest is in whether they can do the more basic thing—learn the lot.

The question before us is complicated in several ways. There is not complete agreement on how to interpret intuition in logic. In particular, intuitionist logicians (for example, Heyting 1956) argue that classical logic misrepresents intuition by taking truth to be bivalent. Intuitionists replace the *true* of classical logic with the predicate *provable*, where proof is to be carried out by (constructivist) means that intuitionists accept. This gives rise to at least the following categories of propositions: provable, refutable, and unproven. The point to note is that *provable* and *refutable* do not exhaust the set of propositions in the way that classical *true* and *false* do. This difference entrains differences among all the connectives of intuitionist and classical logic. It is not part of my job to decide between the two theories. The main position toward which I am working stands for intuitionists as well as classical logicians. Because classical logic is more familiar, I work with it.

Relevance logicians (for example, Anderson and Belnap 1968, 1975) also claim that classical logic misrepresents intuition, particularly the intuition on which implication is based. Relevance logicians, however, generally accept the truth tables of classical logic and seek to place constraints on the use of premises in proofs. Because I am concerned mainly with the truth tables, I can afford to leave aside the issues that exercise relevance logicians.

Some logicians, influenced by current theories in quantum physics, think that, whether or not classical logic represents prescientific intuition correctly, the connectives of propositional logic need some modification in view of empirical findings. The issues here are difficult, and I deal with them in chapter 9. If the reader so wishes, he can regard this chapter as dealing with prescientific logical intuition, which certainly demands attention because scientific investigation presupposes it. In the final chapter, however, we will see that there really are no empirical grounds for revising logic.

Some psychologists argue that children do not manifest ability to handle propositional logic until the age of twelve or older. This position I must confront because, if it were justified, it would seem extremely plausible that children have to learn the logical force of the truth-functional connectives. It seems plausible that the absence of such a basic logic is due at least in part to the inability to understand its connectives. Dealing with this psychological position has the advantage of putting us in touch with a considerable body of psychological literature and sharpening the psychological side of our work.

By limiting the scope of the inquiry to the truth-functional uses of *and*, I manage to sidestep one of the most ticklish issues in the logic of natural languages—the proper interpretation of the conditional (*if . . . then*). It seems clear that the natural-language conditional does not match classical logic's material implication ($\supset$) at all well. Material implication can, however, be easily defined in terms of truth-functional *and* and *not*:

$$(p \supset q) \text{ if and only if } \sim(p \text{ and } \sim q).$$

Clearly, children who know both *and* and *not* and in addition can express definitions can learn the function that I call *material implication*. But the question posed is not whether children can learn that function but whether they can learn the entire set of truth-functional connectives.

We shall see that there are grounds for taking *and* as psychologically more basic than material implication.

Learning: Preliminaries
The main guide to the meaning of *and* is the following truth table, in which T stands for *true* and F for *false*:

p	q	p *and* q
T	T	T
T	F	F
F	T	F
F	F	F

The table reveals the truth-functional force of *and* because it assigns a truth value to *p and q* as a function of the truth values of *p* and *q* taken individually. This is what must be grasped by anyone who can use and understand *and* correctly in the manner that interests us. It is not necessary that we should have the table in our heads or be able to state it in anything like the given form.

There is a point to note about this truth table and others like it: its conciseness. The size of the table depends on the number of places assigned to a connective and the number of truth values allowed. Classical logic allows only two of each. Ordinary language, however, seems to set no limits on the number of sentences that can be conjoined by a single *and*. It is quite acceptable to say

> He went into the shop, looked around, caught an attendant's
> eye, and bought a pair of shoes.   (9)

If we keep the number of truth values at two, the number of rows in the truth table for a three-place connective is eight; for a four-place connective, sixteen. This does not cause much difficulty to the user of either *and* or *or*. Sentences with *and* in them are true only when all the conjoined sentences are true; those with *or* in them are true only when one of the disjuncts is true. Those rules are easily mastered and managed. The constraint imposed by propositional logic—that & be allowed only two places—does not distort things for psychology.

Things would become more complicated if we were to allow more than two truth values. For example, a two-place connective in a three-valued logic would have nine rows. The general formula is: If k is the number of places allowed a connective and n is the number of truth values, the number of rows in a connective's truth table is n^k. Being a three-valued logic, a three-place connective has twenty-seven rows, and they cannot be summarized in the same way we summarized the effect of increasing the number of places for *and* and *or* in a two-valued logic. We do not know the practical limits on human storage and processing powers for truth-functional connectives. Nevertheless, on the assumption that reasoning is normally conducted on material in short-term memory, the limits would seem to be tight indeed. This poses a problem. Some logicians think that truth, as applied to vague predicates, such as *tall* and *handsome*, has many values; some would even say that it has nondenumerably many values (that is, more values than there are natural numbers). We simply have no idea how the mind would process truth-functional connectives for so many truth values. Yet logical claims about the nature of the truth predicate place strains on psychological theory, and eventually logic and psychology must be shown to be compatible. I raise the matter for its interest and importance, but I fear I am unable to say any more about it.

Misconceptions of Piaget's Position

Piaget claims repeatedly that children do not command propositional logic until the age of adolescence, and he claims to have proved it empirically. If we were to inquire no further into what he means by this, we might conclude that the logical force of the connectives *and*, *or*, *not*, etc. is unknown to children before their teens. Those are precisely the connectives that Piaget (1953) and Inhelder and Piaget (1958) speak about. Now, if Piaget's claim means this and if it is correct, the door would be open to a strong case that youngsters must learn the entire set of sentential connectives. It is difficult to know whether Piaget himself would have called the claimed transition to propositional logic *learning*. It is difficult to make sense of the mechanisms to which he attributes cognitive growth, that is, accommodation and assimilation. It is in fact doubtful that Piaget had any shareable insights into the fundamental processes of cognitive growth (Macnamara 1976). Nevertheless, if children, though they use such connectives as *not*, *and*, and *or* from the age of two, did not grasp the logical functions that they express, it would be at least likely that they learned those functions in the interval.

For several reasons it is improbable that Piaget is saying that children younger than twelve lack all elements of propositional logic. It is far too obvious that at a much earlier age they employ such words as *and*, *or*, and *not* much as adults do. Besides, what Piaget claims adolescents can and younger children cannot do is something much more than just use each connective correctly on its own. What he is talking about is mainly combinations of connectives. In particular, he is talking about the system of possible combinations of two propositions (p, q), with *not*, *and*, and *or*. The set forms an elaborate and complicated algebra. A lucid analysis and trenchant criticism of Piaget's account of how this algebra develops and of his methods of testing whether youngsters control it can be found in Ennis (1977). Fortunately, we need not go into the important issues raised there, for the algebra of combinations presupposes the connectives that are combined. We are not discussing later developments of propositional logic, such as the ability to handle entire logical algebras of connectives; we are examining only the most basic logical connectives themselves. It follows that Piaget's claims about the algebra do not touch my claims about basic competence. It is important to note this well, for there is widespread misinterpretation of Piaget on the point.

There is, however, one element in Piaget's thinking that we should examine, not just for its relevance to the truth-functional connectives but for its relevance to the whole question of whether basic logical skills develop. Piaget says that before adolescence youngsters cannot form a hypothesis and reason from it. The typical form of a deductive proof is from hypotheses to conclusions, and it is expressed by means of the connective for implication. Schematically it has the form $p \supset q$. Inability to reason from hypotheses would have far-reaching consequences. Here are Piaget's own words, in which the *fourth stage* in his schema is supposed to be reached by most children only in adolescence:

> The new feature marking the appearance of this fourth stage is the ability to reason by hypothesis. In verbal thinking such hypothetico-deductive reasoning is characterized, *inter alia*, by the possibility of accepting any sort of data as purely hypothetical, and reasoning from them. (1953, p. 18)

I do not know what importance to attach to "any sort of data." In arguing with adults, we frequently find that it is difficult to get them to assume, for the sake of argument, a proposition that runs counter to their interests. Little wonder if children should also balk at hypotheticals under similar circumstances.

What would be interesting would be a finding that at some stage children are incapable of entertaining any proposition unless they judge it true; for that would mean that their minds differ profoundly in their logical aspects from those of adults, and it would pose the problem of explaining how children acquire so basic a capacity. What appears to be at stake in Piaget's words is whether children can understand a sentence independently of believing it.

Is there any evidence that before adolescence children cannot understand without believing? Emphatically no! Piaget (1964) wrote a book called *La formation du symbole chez l'enfant* in which he documents among other things young children's ability to conceive of imaginary situations and use them in their play. Many other researchers have gone further and shown that three- and four-year-olds are well able to make elaborate deductions from hypothetical propositions (see Ennis 1977 and references therein). Macnamara (1977b) showed that four-year-olds can accept descriptions of imaginary scenes and deduce from them a variety of inferences, including such logically complicated ones as presuppositions. The only sensible construction to place on Piaget's claim is that in it, too, he is thinking about the elaborate algebra of propositions and connectives, not about the ability to entertain simple propositions as hypotheticals. More telling still, Bowerman (to be published) has documented a number of utterances and nonverbal events that showed her daughters to have a lively appreciation of the possible apart from the actual by the middle of their second year.

There are, however, in the body of Piaget's work, suggestions that could be construed as claiming that children below the age of about seven do not have any grasp of the fundamentals of propositional logic. I am not sure that Piaget himself would make that claim. Inhelder and Piaget (1958), to choose just one of many possible sources, claimed that Duc, a seven-year-old, could not "give an objective account of the experiment" (p. 69). He was experimenting with weights, cord lengths, and force of impetus to determine the factor(s) that influence the period of a pendulum. There are several references to the lack of objectivity of the young children, although Duc's difficulties were attributed to problems with "serial ordering" and "exact correspondence." More telling, we are informed that Duc was unable to "even give consistent explanations which were not mutually contradictory" (p. 69). It would, of course, be incoherent to claim that children can be satisfied with explanations that they appreciate as contradictory. It must be remembered, however, that Duc was faced with a complicated induction problem and simply became muddled. There is nothing in the evidence to even suggest that he was so totally lacking in logical intuition as to knowingly assent to both a proposition and its negation.

Although nothing in the foregoing would countenance the extreme interpretation that I am countering, there are several passages in Piaget's work that do lend themselves to the extreme interpretation. Piaget (1963) and Inhelder and Piaget (1964), for example, claim that before the age of about six or seven, children generally do not have a "true concept" of an individual in a class. If that were the case, it would follow that they would not have the ability to predicate either, because predicating assigns an individual or individuals to a class. Lacking that, they would not be able to form or understand a sentence; so it would follow that they could not have an adequate grasp of a sentential connective, such as *and*. Piaget's test for a true concept of class is a tough one that he construes as turning crucially on the quantifiers *all* and *some*. Actually, we will see in chapter 7 that the findings turn crucially on a rather bizarre use of the connective *or*. We must simply anticipate here the conclusion of the next chapter and say that, even by the standards of Piaget's tough test, young children do have sufficient command of the logic of simple sentences to sustain the grasp of a sentential connective.

The only explanation for Piaget's underrating of children's grasp of the basic logic of sentence constituents is his neglect of child language. Although he early studied the communicative functions of child language, he gave the relation between language and logic scant attention. He simply warded off objections to his theories based on observations of what children say and obviously mean. The following passage from Inhelder and Piaget (1964) expresses this attitude:

> The main finding of these investigations may be stated thus: the fact that the language of adults crystallizes an operational schema does not mean that the operation is assimilated along with the linguisitic forms. Before children can understand the implicit operation and apply it, they must carry out a structurization, or even a number of successive restructurizations. These depend on logical mechanisms. (p. 4)

Now it is reasonable to be suspicious of children's (or anyone's) language. They can certainly use expressions without any proper grasp of what they mean. Nevertheless, it is folly to disregard spontaneous speech to the extent that Inhelder and Piaget did. They never examined the conditions under which a person who lacks the ability to predicate might acquire it. We might be tempted to explore the fact that with the notions of reference and truth we can define predicates as those constituents that, when combined with referring expressions (in certain ways), yield objects that have a truth value. Truth, however, is itself a predicate. How, then, could someone who lacks the ability to predicate succeed in predicating *true* or *false*? We must not, however, get ahead of ourselves, for these issues are more properly held over to the next chapter, in which I deal with the first-order predicate calculus.

To sum up, there is no empirical evidence that children at one stage are incapable of grasping the logical force of the most basic sentential connectives, such as *and*. Lack of such evidence, however, is no proof that they do not have to learn it. So I turn to the conditions under which it might be learned.

Conditions on the Learnability of the Logical Connective And

At the beginning of this chapter I laid down some quite general conditions on the learnability of *and*. Because *and* is a function from truth values to truth values, learning its meaning presupposes the notion of truth and an ability to identify at least some of those objects that can fill its argument places, namely, interpreted sentences. I am asking now whether with that much children can learn the logical function of *and*.

It is easy to define *and* in terms of other sentential connectives, say *not* and *or*. It would follow that someone who has the notions *not* and *or* together with the ability to define can learn the logic of *and*. I have, however, decided not to take that route because it merely pushes the interesting questions onto the learnability of *not* and *or*. We can also define *or* in terms of *not* and *and*. Because my interest in *and* is mainly as an exemplar of what bids fair to be a fundamental connective (for reasons we shall see), I might as well stick with it and ignore the fact that it can be defined in terms of other connectives.

There is another definitional approach, one that digs deeper into logical structure. It is possible to define *and* with the aid of a number of notions borrowed from logical algebras. For example, *and* can be defined as the greatest lower bound relative to two propositions in an implication lattice. The mind stalls, however, at the thought that children should follow that route in acquiring so simple a connective as *and*. Moreover, our definition presupposes the truth-functional connectives *if and only if* (for definition) and *implies* (for the implication lattice). If we insisted on that approach, we would solve our problem for *and* by presupposing other connectives. Because the main objective is to decide whether the entire set of propositional logic's connectives can be learned, we would not, by appealing to lattices, advance the program. In a more general way, the path would lead nowhere. We would be moving away from a connective, *and*, which has a lexical equivalent in almost every natural language (see Gazdar 1979) and moving toward symbols that are technical and not lexicalized in any but a few languages.

I am taking it for granted that all English speakers come by the logical force of *and* without benefit of instruction in formal logic. Such instruction might well distinguish what I call the purely logical or truth-functional force from the associated Gricean implicatures. But I am taking it for granted that people do not need logical instruction to grasp the force of *and* in such uncomplicated occurrences as

> Peter came and Paul came.
> There's one biscuit for you and one for your sister.
> I want you to pick up your doll and your Teddy.

The conclusion I have reached, then, is that the entire set of truth-functional connectives cannot be learned. Because I am regarding *and* as a basic connective, for reasons that will be given shortly, I conclude that children do not *learn* the function that is expressed by *and* in its truth-functional role.

Learning the English Word And

Children still have to learn the English word *and* and its meaning. Let us now ask: Under what conditions can children learn the English word *and* in its truth-functional uses?

The first condition is that there must be some means available to children to distinguish the truth-functional uses of *and* from its associated Gricean implicatures and from its occurrences in names and idioms. It seems as least possible that parents and other informants could guide children here. I am not aware of any empirical evidence that parents do this for children. It would be an interesting topic to examine empirically.

The second condition also permits of empirical examination. Something would have to tell children that the interpretation of *and* is radically different from that of proper names, predicates, and quantifiers, in fact that it makes no contribution to the truth conditions of the simple sentences to which it is added. They must also spot that it is quite different from other words, such as *well* and *however*, which do not alter the truth conditions of the sentences in which they occur either. Children must notice that *and*'s contribution to interpretation depends on the truth values of the sentences that it conjoins. But even that is not enough, because they must spot that its semantic function is to map (pairs of) truth values onto truth values.

The point can be made dramatically in an instructive manner by imagining a child who has guessed that the interpretation of *and* depends on the truth values of the sentences it conjoins. The child might still form such hypotheses as are expressed in the following table:

p	q	p and q
T	T	*It's odd that p*; it's odd that q.
T	F	Imagine p; don't imagine q.
F	T	It's naughty to say p; it is good to say q.
F	F	It is silly to say p; it is silly to say q.

Because there is a large number of such hypotheses, the child who actually goes about testing them would be lost. Why does the table look so utterly implausible? It must be that the human mind is constrained not to advert to the full range of interpretative possibilities.

Gazdar (1979, pp. 69ff) makes an observation that, if it turns out to be empirically correct, may well throw light on the issue. He claims that, of the sixteen possible sentential connectives (for bivalent truth and two-place connectives), only two are lexically encoded in any language and that they are encoded in nearly all such language: *and* and (inclusive) *or*. The reader must turn to Gazdar (1979) for the evidence on which the claim is based. If it is right, it suggests a broad solution to the problem children have in learning the word *and*. Gazdar's claim suggests that there is something about the human mind that demands a convenient expression for the logical functions we express by *and* and *or*—that there are symbols for them in the language of thought. It suggests further that the number of two-place connectives in the language of thought is very small, say three or four. Children will be on the lookout for truth-functional connectives in their mother tongue. It will not occur to them that there are any connectives of the sort illustrated in the table just given. Once they spot that a word is truth functional, all they have to do is determine, from the evidence of ordinary conversation, which of the three or four connectives *and* is. This they can do relatively easily by watching how their parents react to their behavior when the parents say such things as "Pick up your truck and your Teddy." If the child picks up just the truck, the parent is likely to say, "I said the truck *and* the Teddy." That should be enough to show which of the connectives *and* is.

If you agree with the foregoing, there still remains the enormous task of giving an account of how children learn the meaning of the English word *and*. If *and* expresses an unlearned connective in the language of thought, it still remains to explain how the unlearned connective's meaning is expressed. We know that it is futile to think of *and* as being expressed in terms of other expressions in the language of thought—for that way lies a vicious regress. Earlier we decided that ultimately the semantics of the language of thought must be expressed by means of interpreters—devices that perform the task of interpreting. If I were to give a full account of the learning of *and* (in its truth-functional aspects), I would have to specify the conditions that trigger the relevant interpreter—call it *Interpreter-&*. I would also have to show how these conditions mesh with occurrences of the English word *and* so that children are able to attach the word to the connective that the procedure invokes.

A further task is to specify the output of Interpreter-&. The output must be to predicate *true* of the complex sentence if the simple sentences are taken as true; otherwise to predicate *false*. For this to be possible, children must have the concepts of truth and falsity, but they do not need the concept of a sentence. When Interpreter-& functions, there will always be simple sentences as well as complex ones, before the children and the truth predicates can be applied to those sentences without the intervention of the concept of a sentence. Neither do children need anything that looks like the truth table for *and*. All that is required is that Interpreter-& compute the function expressed in that table.

It is interesting to speculate on whether children who can understand *and* have anything like the *and*-introduction rule of some natural deduction systems (see, for example, Thomason 1970, chap. 4). Such a rule might be applied by what I have called an *implicator*. It would permit the inference to *p and q* whenever *p* is assumed true and *q* is assumed true. Something of the sort is extremely likely when children have begun to use *and* correctly. We can also speculate about a possible implicator to apply an *and*-elimination rule. There are problems, however, as the following scenario illustrates:

Child: What can I have before going to bed?
Mother: You may have a cookie and a glass of milk.
Child: I think I'll just have the cookie.
Mother: No you won't. No milk, no cookie!

Still, children do have to learn the meaning of English *and* by noting the truth values of sentences. The whole logic of generalizing on the basis of observation is poorly understood, so it is difficult to make a distinction between logical generalizations and empirical ones. Nonetheless, there is an important distinction to be made—one that is at the center of Frege and Husserl's polemic against psychologism. If the laws that express the logic of *and* are empirical generalizations of the sort that psychologists find attractive, they have at best the modal status of empirical laws. But logic, the most basic discipline of all, is assumed in all empirical investigation. Accept this, as we have agreed to, and we must accept that the laws that express the logic of *and* cannot be explained in whatever way empirical laws can be explained.

The line I have been following might suggest that children first learn *and* in the role of a conjunction between sentences, as in

Mary sang and Jane played.

Hakuta et al. (1982), however, present evidence that children first produce *and* in the role of a phrasal connective, as in

Mary and Jane sang.

Hakuta et al. give few examples of child speech. Lust and Mervis (1982) cite many examples of conjunction in the speech of two-year-olds. All but one ("five and five make six") of the clausal conjunctions were reductions in the sense that their truth conditions could be expressed as the conjunction of two simple sentences, such as

Mary sang. Jane sang.

Even the phrasal uses, then, might result from the reduction of a pair of simple sentences that are conjoined in the language of thought.

Even if, however, it transpired that many children first learn to understand and use *and* in phrasal settings that are not reductions—such as

Tom and Mary are married

—it still would not follow that the account I have given is wrong. What would prove it wrong is a finding that an understanding of unreduced phrasal *and* was essential to the learning of *and* as a conjunction. Because of the logical independence of those two uses of *and*, it is quite unlikely that such a sequence in learning could be established or indeed that it could be true. It follows that the account I have given of how the conjunction *and* is learned is unlikely to be disturbed by observations of how phrasal *and* is learned. This is not to say that my account could not be falsified on other grounds.

I have concentrated on young children and the logical resources they need to express the meaning of *and*. There has been a certain number of empirical studies of the ability of older children to understand *and* and draw inferences in propositional logic from it. These studies throw light on development beyond the point I am focusing on. They are summarized in Braine and Rumain (1983, pp. 276ff).

7

Basic-Level Sortals

Sortals are the counterpart in logic of common nouns in syntax. The expression "basic level" is borrowed from prototype theory, where it has the status of an empirically based theoretical construct. The easiest way to convey the idea is to begin with some examples. Take the hierarchical series of sortals: (1) *furniture, chair, Shaker rocker, Shaker rocker owned by Harry Stanton*; (2) *plant, flower, rose, Mrs. Miniver Rose*. In these series, *chair* and *flower* are the basic-level sortals, because as we descend the hierarchy, they are the first that readily evoke an image of a typical member at that level; they are also the first level at which we expect to find conventional drawings of typical members. For example, we are much less likely to be greeted with a puzzled frown if we ask children to imagine or draw a chair than if we ask them to imagine or draw an article of furniture. The construct of basic level has proved its usefulness in a variety of psychological tests (see, for example, Rosch et al. 1976), and the distinction between basic-level and higher-level sortals (such as *furniture* and *plant*) is a useful one in psychology.

In this chapter, after an interval on sentential connectives, I continue the study of the logic and psychology of simple sentences, by taking up sortals. In this chapter I deal with the logic of sortals in general and the logic of learning of basic-level ones; in the next I deal with higher-level sortals, the logical relations among hierarchically related sortals, and the logic of the quantifiers *all* and *some*. I begin this chapter by laying out the logic of basic-level sortals. In doing so, I distinguish three principles that are of fundamental importance in cognitive psychology. In the psychological part of the chapter I discuss the interrelated tasks of concept formation and sortal learning.

To the logical expression *sortal* corresponds the linguistic expression *common noun*, so fundamental in syntax. We will not, however, be concerned with syntax except insofar as it is relevant to sortal learning. Instead, we concentrate on the logical role of sortals as they combine in various ways with proper names, personal pronouns, demonstratives, and (in the next chapter) quantifiers to form clauses and sentences.

One common use of sortals is in the formation of definite and indefinite descriptions:

> The dog that bit me,
> A dog that bit me.

Most of all, however, we concentrate on even simpler uses in which a sortal is used to assign individuals to a category:

> Freddie is a dog.
> I am a person.

Logic of Sortals

Principle of Application
Among the individuals we encounter, some are dogs and some are not. What decides the matter in each case is the principle of application for dogs. The principle is familiar to psychologists under various guises. It is sometimes called the set of *necessary and sufficient conditions* for category membership, sometimes the set of *criterial attributes*, and sometimes the *concept* that determines category membership. Whatever the name, the idea is the same. The judgment that everything either is or is not a dog depends on there existing a principle of application sufficiently sharp to determine the truth of the matter in each case. A principle of application, therefore, is implicit in our most ordinary acts of judgment.

Things are not always clear-cut. Frege (1952 [1893–1903], p. 159) wondered whether the concept *Christian* has boundaries so sharp that it makes sense to hold that each person either is or is not a Christian. There surely is no sharp boundary between childhood and adulthood. So, some sortals are inescapably vague, as are some predicates, such as *tall* and *old*. But vagueness does not deprive a sortal of a principle of application, only of a sharply defined one. Many of our everyday sortals, such as *dog* and *water*, may be vaguer than we imagine. Jackendoff (1983) made great capital out of the vagueness of many everyday sortals and built a central part of his theory on the vagueness of intuition. Although there is more to be said for his position than I say here, I prefer to work on another set of intuitions that strikes me as more basic. We have intuitions that there is a truth of the matter of whether or not an animal is a dog, though we may not be able to decide which in all cases. It is this intuition, which may turn out to be erroneous, that I wish to be guided by.

A proper name denotes an individual in a domain of discourse; a sortal denotes a kind to which individuals belong if they satisfy the principle of application for the kind. Just as a proper name is a rigid designator of an individual, in the sense of picking that individual out in all possible circumstances, so a sortal is a rigid designator of a kind. This is one of the theses proposed by Putnam (1975). It means that if we have some means other than the sortal of specifying a particular kind and if we fix up a sortal to refer to it, then the sortal will continue to pick out that kind so long as the language remains unchanged. So long as the language does not change, no matter what revolutions happen in science and no matter what creatures come and go in nature, the sortal will continue to pick out the same kind. And so long as children who are learning the language intend to conform to standard usage, the sortal in their mouths will pick out the same kind. They may, of course, apply the sortal to some wrong individuals, but so long as they intend it to mean whatever adults mean by it, it picks out the same kind as it does for adults.

It is a great question in metaphysics to decide what sort of entities kinds are (see Armstrong 1978 for a detailed discussion). It is not my purpose, however, to discuss the issue. All that I need to note is that there is a fairly obvious sense in which a sortal refers to something, as Frege (1952 [1892a, 1892b]) said. Dummett (1981, chap. 7) gave a formula that makes this particularly clear. For example, we can say

There is something that Julius Caesar and Cicero were,

namely a Roman citizen. And we can say

There is something that Julius Caesar was and Cicero was not,

namely a Roman general. We need not be any more explicit about what sort of things are being referred to, but our way of talking brings home to us that *Roman citizen* and *Roman general* do refer to something.

The principle of application is associated in the first instance with the kind, not with the sortal. The principle consists in a set of descriptions that must be satisfied for membership in the kind. Logicians usually call the membership the *extension* of the kind. There is a modal element in the principle of application as I am construing it. Any creature that is a dog must satisfy all the conditions in the principle of application for *dog*, for so long as it remains a dog and in all the possible circumstances in which it is a dog, it must satisfy them all. This stands even if some of the conditions are vague. Vagueness means that it may not be fully determined whether or not something is a dog. If, however, it is a dog, it must satisfy the principle of application for dogs.

The theory of sortals just given conflicts, unless I am greatly mistaken, with one of the key ideas of prototype theory. That theory, too, recognizes the vagueness of many everyday sortals, but it adds something new. Like the standard theory, just described, it allows that the principle of application for a kind consists of a set of conditions, but it does not require that members of the kind satisfy all the conditions (see Rosch 1975, 1977). The theory may even rank order conditions, so that the satisfaction of some counts more toward membership in the kind than the satisfaction of others. For example, a robin seems to be the proto-typical bird in North America. A penguin, the theory goes, is a bird because it shares a sufficient number of important features with a robin. This makes a robin's features the principle of application for the kind, bird. The theory is backed, its sponsors claim, by the fact that people can reliably rank subspecies for typicality.

The intuition I have been plying is that (to continue with the example) anything that is a bird has all the properties that are necessary to be a bird. Judgments of typicality by this intuition have nothing immediate to do with the principle of application; they have to do instead with the frequency with which different subspecies are encountered or with the exemplars used to teach children a sortal or some such thing. That this is correct is supported by the fact that we can obtain, among other things, reliable typicality judgments about exemplars in a kind, even when there exists a well-understood set of necessary and sufficient conditions for membership in the kind.

Armstrong et al. (1983) found that subjects rank individual odd numbers for typicality as odd numbers in much the same way as they rank varieties of vegetables for typicality as vegetables. Their subjects also gave a whole range of responses for odd numbers that paralleled those that had been given by Rosch's (1973) subjects for such kinds as birds. Prototype theory has leaned heavily on the patterning of such responses. The results of Armstrong et al. show that such patterns extend to cases in which subjects are well aware of the set of necessary and sufficient conditions that must all be satisfied for membership in the kind. This suggests that, even when such a set of conditions is unknown, the patterning of responses is independent of whether or not subjects think a set of necessary and sufficient conditions for membership in the kind exists. At any rate, it shows that the data collected by proponents of prototype theory do nothing to support the main claims of the theory.

Even more important, we have a strong intuition that if a penguin really is a bird, then it must have everything that marks an individual as a bird. Otherwise we would only be entitled to say, "A penguin is like a bird." Yet our intuition is that saying "A penguin is like a bird" is simply wrong, because a penguin is a bird. Osherson and Smith (1981) made this intuition the basis for a formal analysis of the prototype theory of kinds, which led to their rejection of it.

It is necessary to emphasize that my theory (that sortals supply a principle of application) does not imply that average competent users of a sortal know how to apply the associated principle of application. They do not need to be able to tell in hard cases whether, for example, foxes and wolves are members of the kind *dog*. In other words I distinguish the principle of application from any *test* that might be based on it for membership in a kind. Such a test I call a *criterion* of application.

One of the major reasons for the demise of logical positivism is the finding that it is not, in general, possible to find perceptual features that are distinctive of a kind. To take one example, water is perceptually different as it goes from being ice to being liquid and from that to being vapor and from that to being snow. What is definitive of the natural kind *water* is H_2O. And though the elements in the definition are known through empirical experience, the road from such experience to the specification of the elements is long, tortuous, and poorly understood. Moreover, we cannot discern perceptually the hydrogen or oxygen in water, the proportion of one to the other, or the bonding between them.

Now, I am not saying that the kinds of science map nicely onto the kinds of everyday speech, but there is overlap. In at least some of its uses, the ordinary-language word *water* picks out the same kind as does the scientific use of the word or H_2O), allowing for some impurities. In any event, most of the kinds of ordinary language cannot be defined in terms of perceptually given features alone. Nor is there implicit in the use of ordinary-language sortals a condition that they be definable in such terms. I have dealt with the matter elsewhere (Macnamara 1982, chap. 12) and do not pursue it further here.

We should not confuse knowledge of the specifics of the principle of application for dogs, say, with knowledge of the meaning of the word *dog*. We would all wish to say that we know what the word *dog* means, though we would insist that we do not know the specifics of the principle of application for dogs. On the assumption that we are right to do so, the two are distinct. The meaning of *dog* is its reference to a particular kind. The convenience of reference is that it does not demand detailed knowledge of what is referred to. I can refer to an individual number as the least prime greater than 1,000,000 without being able to pick it out in any other way from the successors of 1,000,000. So detailed knowledge of the kind dog and the principles it supplies are not required for the meaningful use of the word *dog*. What is required is that the user have some way of picking out the unique kind dog. I come back to this in the psychological section of this chapter.

Both predicates and sortals supply a principle of application. There is a set of necessary and sufficient conditions for being prime (a predicate) as there are for being a number (a sortal). The property of supplying a principle of application, then, does not distinguish the two.

Time to sum up. A sortal supplies a principle of application that must be satisfied by all those individuals that are members of the kind that the sortal designates. Such principles are implicit in our most everyday judgments assigning individuals to a kind. It is not required that the competent users of a sortal be able to state its principle of application or to decide in all cases whether an individual is a member of the kind it designates. The principle of application for a sortal is not an image of a prototypical member of the kind designated by the sortal.

Principle of Individuation
The basic-level categories typically embrace a number of readily discriminated, distinct individuals. There are many individual flowers, chairs, dogs, and persons. The individuals of some categories are not so readily distinguished as, for example, individual ideas. The individuals of yet other categories may be unspecified in the language, or "unbounded" in the expression of Jackendoff (1983, chap. 3, fn. 9). Of a body of water, such as a lake, we can say that it is all water, but the sortal *water* does not specify any such body as lake or tumblerful. The logic of mass sortals is obscure, and I simplify our inquiry by confining attention to individuals we can readily recognize as such—individuals we can bump into, such as dogs, bicycles, and persons, individuals that fall under a count noun.

Frege (1959 [1884]) argued at length that there is no counting objects without the support of a sortal to specify what is to be counted. He noted that the same physical objects yield different counts, depending on the guiding sortal. A pack of cards, for example, contains four suits but fifty-two cards. A single shopping basket typically contains different numbers of vegetables and varieties of vegetable. Remove the sortal altogether and, as Geach (for example, 1962, p. 153) has frequently told us, there is no counting at all. For example, if asked to count the red things in my room, I do not know whether I should count my shirt as one red object or two, because it has a sewn-on pocket, or as many, in that it consists of many threads. The trouble, as Geach observed, is not that we cannot make an end of counting in such a case but that we cannot even make a beginning.

It follows that count sortals and predicates (such as *red*) are logically distinct categories, though logicians do not usually distinguish the two. The difference I am drawing attention to is that, although sortals supply a principle of individuation, predicates do not. The difference is underlined in ordinary language by the fact that quantifiers combine freely with count sortals with or without predicates (*two dogs, many tall men*), whereas whenever they combine with predicates, they require the support of a sortal, explicit or implicit, for example, *two black dogs, many of the poor* (people). The fact that quantifiers combine with count sortals is due to the fact that such sortals supply a principle of individuation. This aspect of sortals must, then, be accounted for in the psychology of how count sortals are learned and understood. For interest's sake, note that mass nouns reveal their sortal status by the fact that certain quantifiers combine with them. For example, we say *lots of water, plenty of porridge, large quantities of beer*. These quantifiers do not presuppose any perceptually salient reflex of a principle of individuation. Matters are complicated by the fact that certain mass nouns embrace individuals that are easily distinguished in perception—*furniture, money*. But I do not pursue the matter. I merely wish to indicate that mass nouns might yield to a modification of the theory being offered here for the learning of sortals.

Counting presupposes distinct individuals, but how are the individuals made distinct from one another in the first place? The answer depends on the type of individuals in question. Ideas are individuated by their contents. For example, we know that the ideas of water and salt are distinct because they contain different descriptions: H_2O and $NaCl$. This will not do for two distinct dogs, which insofar as they are dogs are indistinguishable. In other words, being dogs marks them as similar; something else marks them as different individuals. We need not pursue this great metaphysical question—the question of the one and the many. All we need to do is note that the manner of individuating individuals depends on the kind of individuals they are. Because the business of a sortal is to designate a kind that requires individuals to be individuated in a particular manner, we can speak of a count sortal as supplying a principle of individuation.

We must distinguish sharply the principle of individuation from what might be called the *criterion of individuation*. The principle is a metaphysical one that is independent of whether or not we can specify it. It is a puzzle to say what makes two poodles distinct—whether it is prime matter, geographical location, or something else. It is altogether another matter to have grounds for judging that we are dealing with two poodles, not one. Often, appearances help, and indeed two poodles normally look distinct. Sometimes appearances are a poor guide, as when a caterpillar turns into a butterfly while remaining one and the same insect. What the logic of sortals presupposes essentially is the metaphysical principle, not the criterion, though it is unimaginable that we would ever have developed the logic of sortals with its principle of individuation if we did not have serviceable criteria of individuation to invoke the logic. The principles and criteria are nonetheless distinct.

The point just made brings out the distinction between the principle of application and the principle of individuation. The principle of application for *dog* consists of a set of conditions that anything must satisfy to be a dog. Such conditions do not specify what it is for there to be two dogs rather than one, nor do they give any indication of how this is to be possible. That work is done by the principle of individuation.

Though it is outside the scope of this study, I note for completeness that sortals often supply a principle of individuation for events. Thus the event of the performance of a Vivaldi flute concerto on one occasion is individuated from its performance on another occasion by the principle of individuation for concerto performances. We also individuate actions by reference to the individuals who perform them. For example, if John Wayne is presented diving from a cliff into a torrent beneath, appearances notwithstanding, what the film presents is not one dive if the individual leaving the cliff is John Wayne and the individual entering the water is his stunt man.

To sum up, count sortals supply a metaphysical principle of individuation for the individuals that are members of the kinds they designate. In this they differ from predicates, the two being logically distinct categories. A principle of individuation is distinct from a criterion of individuation. The logic of sortals presupposes the principle; the effective use of sortals may well presuppose a serviceable criterion that users of sortals are normally able to apply.

Principle of Identity
Besides principles of application and individuation, a sortal supplies a principle of identity for members of the kind it names. Identity is recognized in developmental psychology as a fundamental element in our construal of the environment. It is not widely understood in psychology that all identity statements presuppose a sortal. As we saw in chapter 2, just as there is no counting individuals without the support of a sortal, there is no identity of individuals without the support of a sortal. I begin with some informal observations that are aimed at illuminating what is meant by a principle of identity and at showing it to be different from the other two principles we have studied. Then I attempt briefly to lay out certain key aspects of the logical role of sortals in relation to identity. For further details about this role of sortals and for more comprehensive motivation for the conclusions reached, the reader is referred to Gupta's (1980) *Logic of Common Nouns*. Because the number of points to be made is rather large, I number them as I go along.

1. Time and Possible Worlds   First, there are really two distinct principles of identity, one related to time and one to possible circumstances or possible worlds. The two are seen to be distinct by observing that individuals are judged to be the same over time in a single world, say the actual one; they are also judged to be the same across possible circumstances at a particular time. The two are closely related, and because our intuitions about time are somewhat stronger than those about possible worlds, I confine attention mainly to identity over time and speak as though there were only a single principle of identity.

2. Metaphysics   Judgments about the identity of individuals over time, such individuals as oneself and one's dog, make an important metaphysical claim about them: the claim that, despite changes in such perceptually given properties as size, color, shape, weight, and location, the individual is truly the same. I am not concerned with the truth of such claims but with their logic, that is, their general truth conditions. Such claims play so crucial a role in our mental life, with their ramifications into social, legal, and ethical structures, that it is difficult to see how mental life could survive their rejection. Nevertheless, I do not endeavor to establish the truth of such claims but to explore the logic that is implicit in them. The main aim is to show how that logic is essential to the psychological tasks of accounting for the understanding of sortals and their use in everyday language.

3. Distinction between Principle of Individuation and Principle of Identity   It is easy to see that the principles of individuation and identity are distinct. Consider two dogs at a moment t_1 and again at a later moment t_2. At each moment the principle of individuation has applied, because at each the dogs are distinct. But that does not establish which dog at t_2 is identical with which at t_1. Establishing that is not the function of the principle of individuation at all; it is the function of the principle of identity. The principle of identity presupposes that of individuation; it makes sense to talk of the identity of individuals only when they are already individuated.

4. Distinction between Principle of Application and Principle of Identity   Appreciation of the distinction between the principles of application and identity is due more to Geach (1957; 1962; 1972, sec. 7), perhaps, than to any other logician. I can bring the distinction home by considering the example of the two dogs of the last section. The principle of application merely determines that each dog at each moment is a dog. It does not determine which dog at t_1 is identical with which at t_2, so the two principles are distinct.

Gupta (1980) sealed the argument by showing how the principles of identity and application for certain sortals vary. He pointed out that *adult* and *child* share a principle of identity, for the same person is a child at one time and an adult at another. Yet *adult* and *child* do not share a principle of application, for if *adult* is true of some individual, *child* cannot be. On the other hand *passenger* and *person traveling in a vehicle* share a principle of application. They do not share a principle of identity. *Person traveling in a vehicle* supplies the same principle of identity as *person*. A person who travels in a vehicle was a person before he entered the vehicle and continues to be the same person when he leaves it. The person ceases to be a passenger at the moment he leaves the vehicle. *Passenger* supplies a principle of identity for the person only for as long as he is a passenger. The principle of identity logically presupposes the principle of application and is distinct from it.

The arguments for distinguishing the two principles are overwhelming. The distinction is of prime importance for psychology, because the learning and use of sortals presuppose a certain appreciation (to be specified) of each. So far as I know, the distinction is almost unnoticed in the psychological literature.

5. Principle and Criterion of Identity   A criterion of identity would be an ideal test to decide whether x at t_1 and y at t_2 are the same object. Many people feel that Liebniz's law can be made to yield a criterion of identity. The law can be formulated as the claim that a and b are identical just in case everything that is true of the one is true of the other (subject to certain conditions that are discussed later in the chapter).

A common source of confusion in the literature on identity is due to the failure to distinguish this criterion from the principle of identity. The confusion is so fundamental that strenuous efforts must be made to eradicate it. What seems to happen is this. We have a at t_1 and b at t_2, and we wish to see if they are identical. To that end we apply a criterion of identity. If (subject to conditions to be discussed) every F that is true of a is also true of b, then and only then is a identical with b. This looks like an operational definition of identity and might appear to be all we need.

But it is not. A criterion of identity is logically posterior to and distinct from actual identity. A criterion is something that, if valid, decides whether a and b are identical. The criterion does not make them identical. Something else does that. We have been calling that something else the metaphysical principle of identity.

The logical dependence of the criterion on actual identity can be brought home by a close look at Leibniz's law. Formally, the law is

$$(\forall x)(\forall y)[x = y \equiv (\forall F)(Fx \equiv Fy)],$$

where F is a second-order variable ranging over predicates and sortals (standard logic does not distinguish them). Consider how we might apply a criterion of identity based on this law in a particular case. Imagine that on one occasion you have been introduced to a man as Samuel Clemens (c) and on a later occasion you have been introduced to a man, suspiciously like c, as Mark Twain (t). Acting on the similarity you seek to discover if c and t are the same man. For simplicity, suppose that only two predicates are relevant in the case: being an author (A) and being famous (F). Questioning reveals $A(c)$ and $A(t)$ and also $F(c)$ and $F(t)$, so you decide that $c = t$. Notice, though, that while the result proves that $c = t$, the application of the criterion presupposed that the c that was seen to be A is identical with the c that was seen to be F and that the t that was seen to be A is identical with the t that is seen to be F. The application of the criterion of identity presupposes identity. It follows that the grasp and application of the criterion of identity cannot be the source of children's notion of identity.

6. Principle and Psychological Skills   The criterion of identity that we have been discussing, based on Leibniz's law, is an idealization. It and any psychological skill that people have for tracing identity presuppose identity. Such skills do not constitute the identity that they trace. I am, of course, assuming that the identity of individuals over time is objective. Strange as it may seem, that position is contested by Carnap (1967 [1928]), Quine (1961, essay 4), and Noonan (1980), among others. I feel, however, that the position I am taking has sufficient footing in the intuition that we sometimes call common sense that I do not here defend it against its adversaries. Instead, I rest content with referring readers to Geach (1972, chap. 10.2), who does the job of defense well. Besides, my strategy is not to extend myself establishing the truth of the logical positions I adopt but to illustrate the dependence of psychology on logic.

For us, the main point is that the integrity of our everyday mental structures presupposes the identity of a myriad of individuals under the sortals to which we assign them. Psychological skill at tracing identity depends on such factors as the perceptual resemblance of a single individual from one occasion to the next and the continuity of movement through space. We all know, however, that appearances are sometimes deceiving and that memory can let us down; we sometimes fail to recognize an acquaintance and sometimes mistake a stranger for an acquaintance. The continuity of an object's movement through space presupposes both the identity of the object as it moves and the identity over time of the places through which it moves. There is really no need to say more at this point about psychological skills.

7. Role of Sortal   Geach (1957, 1962) has long insisted that talk of identity makes sense only in association with a sortal. He has argued that it makes no sense to ask if *a* and *b* are the same absolutely. We have to ask if *a* is the same dog or cat or bicycle as *b*. Geach seems to have an important truth here. We can speak of a person as being the same weight or the same color over time, but the force of *same* is different from when it is used with person. We describe a person's cheeks as the same color on two occasions, though in the interval they varied. One says that one's weight is the same if on two occasions it reads 170 pounds, though in the interval it shot up to 190 pounds. *Same weight* on two occasions is short for *the number that specifies the weight is the same number* on the two occasions. *Same dog* is short for nothing. Moreover, outside fairy tales, a dog cannot be a cat or a canary in the interval between two occasions when it is a dog. The basis of the difference between sortals and predicates (such as *red*) is that sortals supply a principle of identity and predicates do not.

We have already seen that different sortals supply different principles of identity for the same individual: *Person traveling in a vehicle* and *passenger* do; so do *dog* and *set of molecules*. The same set of molecules over time will not be the same dog, though at any one time a dog consists of a set of molecules. To handle certain problems that arise in this connection, we will shortly address ourselves to the topic of time and identity. In the meanwhile, note that the supplying of different principles of identity by different sortals draws attention to the fact that a sortal does supply a principle of identity.

Peter Denny has pointed out to me (in a letter) that some principles of identity permit of interruption. For example, my last reading of *Brideshead Revisited* may have been interrupted by sleep and all sorts of daily activities, yet I am entitled to speak of it as a single reading, distinct from previous readings. It is important to note, however, that the principles just given still apply. It is not that my reading of *Brideshead Revisited* changed into something else when I fell asleep and became itself once again when I awoke. Perhaps the point to make is that principles of identity can be quite different from one another and enormously subtle and complex.

Gupta (1980) proposed that sortals as well as quantifiers engage in the technical business of variable binding. To begin, notice that we count only under sortals (*three dogs*). In expressions like *three reds*, *reds* is a sortal. *Three reds* is short for something like *three shades of red* or *three red balls* or *three persons of Marxist views*. *Three dogs* is short for nothing. The manner in which Gupta has sortals engage in variable binding is this. The logical form of expression (1) is expression (2):

John is a man.   (1)

$(\exists M, x)j = x.$ (2)

The way to read expression (2), in which $M = man$ and $j = John$, is: Some man is identical with John. This achieves an end that logicians have long felt necessary, the restriction of quantification. Each quantified variable in Gupta's logic is restricted by a sortal. His proposal has another advantage in that it makes explicit what is only implicit in standard predicate logics. Take expression (3) whose standard logical form is expression (4):

A man is tall and straight.   (3)

$(\exists x)(Mx \ \& \ Tx \ \& \ Sx),$ (4)

where $M = man$, $T = tall$, and $S = straight$. One purpose of variable binding is to ensure that an x that is M is identical with an x that is T and S. The standard systems achieve this by stipulation. Gupta is more explicit, for he would replace (4) with (4'):

$(\exists M, x)(Tx \ \& \ Sx).$ (4')

The sortal M binding the variable x specifies a principle of identity.

There are certain well-known "paradoxes" of identity, such as the famous ship of Theseus in which each plank is replaced until none of the original remains. The problem is whether the identity of the original ship survives all the replacements. Gupta is led by a consideration of such examples to abandon the thesis that identity is absolutely transitive. Instead, he allows cases in which changes are cumulative and the identity of the original individual is lost. I do not have time to discuss the "paradoxes" or Gupta's ingenious solution of them. I mention his solution merely to allay any fears that the notion of identity is incoherent. Gupta has shown a simple way to avoid the incoherence that threatens.

8. Time and Identity   Insensitivity in handling the definition of identity creates spurious problems. The definition states tht a and b are identical just in case whatever is true of a is true of b. Consider this example, originally proposed by Perry (1970). An artist sells a patron a clay statue of George Washington, but what the artist delivers is a statue of Warren Harding. In the interval between selling and delivering, the artist has reworked the clay and made a new statue. To the patron's protests, the artist replies, "That's the same thing you bought last week." In a loose sense the artist is right; it is the same clay. Yet the patron has a right to feel aggrieved; it is not the same statue.

The problem for the definition is this. The clay is identical with the statue of Washington at one time and with that of Harding at a later time. Yet the statue of Harding is not identical with that of Washington. What was identical with the clay at one time is not identical with it at another. We need to be able to say that it is the same clay on the two occasions. Superficially, the definition seems to prevent our claiming identity of the clay over time, for what was identical with it on one occasion (statue of Washington) is no longer identical with it at another (when it is a statue of Harding). How do we hold onto the claim about identity of the clay and also to the criterion of identity?

Wiggins (1967, 1980) showed how to do both. We must employ the tense system of our language. Of the clay at t_1 we can say that it *is* identical with the Washington statue and that it *will be* identical with the Harding one. Of the clay at t_2 we can say that it is identical with the Harding statue and *was* identical with the Washington one. By this means we avoid having to relativize identity. We satisfy our intuitions about the identity through change, and we hold onto the definition of identity.

One implication for psychology is that the learning and use of sortals involves not only distinctions among related identity principles but also the development of a temporal framework in the use of such words. Although the temporal aspect of verbs is well appreciated, it is not generally realized, at least in psychology, that common nouns, too, require a temporal framework for their interpretation. The clay loses its identity with the Washington statue and acquires identity with the Harding one. The clay cannot be identical with both at once. Part of learning to understand sortals is learning their temporal aspects.

Now to sum up this logic section as a whole. Count sortals supply three major principles that are of consequence for logic and hence for psychology:

1. Principle of application, which explains why a sortal is true of some individuals and not of others.
2. Principle of individuation, which explains why quantifiers combine with sortals as they do.
3. Principle of identity, which implicates sortals in all statements of identity over time (and across possible worlds).

Different sortals sometimes supply different principles of identity for a single individual, and the difference shows a hidden temporal dimension in the semantics of identity statements and hence in the semantics of sortals.

Psychology of Basic-Level Sortals

What the Learner Learns

Consider again the little boy Tom at the time when he is about to learn the sortal *dog*. His family has a dog with which he is familiar, and he has frequently encountered other dogs. He even knows his own dog's proper name, *Spot*. He has noticed certain resemblances among dogs that enable him to distinguish them from other such entities as walls, carpets, doors, chairs, tables, cups, grass, water, trees, rocks, motorcars, and clouds. He is also able to distinguish dogs from cows, but he has not yet succeeded in distinguishing them from cats. Perhaps he has even heard the word *dog* on a number of earlier occasions, but he has not paid close attention. Then the moment arrives when Spot comes before him and his mother says *dog* in such a manner that Tom connects the word with Spot. This is the moment when Tom grasps the word *dog* and learns that Spot is a dog and that other creatures that are like Spot in certain ways are dogs. He learns the sortal *dog* as referring to the kind.

There are certain constraints on the functioning of the word *dog* that I must attempt to specify. These are constraints on how the word is to be understood—constraints constituted by the logic I have just outlined. My task is to translate that logic into a statement of logical work that must be accomplished in the competent learning of the basic-level sortal *dog*.

We are assuming that Tom knows a name for the animal, Spot, and that the name enjoys the support of a sortal in all his use of it. I have opted for a sortal synonymous with *dog* rather than with, say, *mammal* or *animal*, because *dog* is a basic-level sortal. As we proceed, I need to argue for a psychologically salient and privileged position for such sortals. For the moment, just assume that they are both salient and privileged.

The main item that Tom learns is that *dog* in English refers to the same kind as the sortal that has been supporting his use of *Spot*. We can express this informally as

> There is a unique basic-level kind of which Spot is a member and *dog* refers to that kind. (5)

More formally statement (5) can be expressed as

$$(\exists!B, K)(\text{Spot} \in K \ \& \ (\forall A, x)(x \in \text{dog} \equiv x \in K)), \tag{5'}$$

where B means basic-level kind, K is a variable ranging over basic-level kinds, A means animal, and $\exists!$ is read "there is a unique." Statement (5') reads: There is a unique basic-level kind, of which Spot is a member, and any animal is a dog if and only if it is a member of that basic-level kind. I have arbitrarily employed *animal* in sentence (5'). Some sortal that includes dogs is necessary for my theory; but a more general sortal, such as Jackendoff's *maximally connected physical object* would also serve. Note that the theory involves quantifying over second-order objects, that is, kinds. The logical role of B is considered in more detail later in this chapter.

We have assumed that Tom knows other dogs besides Spot and has noted the similarities among them, even though he has as yet failed to distinguish cats from dogs. We must be on our guard lest this confusion become irremediable. The best way I know to handle the problem is to have Tom identify the kind referred to by *dog* as the basic-level kind to which Spot belongs and allow its extension to be whatever it is. This avoids any regimentation that would press some cats into its extension. It also avoids having to express in the formalisms anything so complicated as an intention on Tom's part to assign to the sortal the referent that the speech community assigns to it. I have accomplished this by including in statement (5') the expression $(\forall A, x)(x \in \text{dog} \equiv x \in K)$. This move has the further advantage of avoiding the temptation to say any such thing as $K = \text{dog}$. The problem with this is that it treats K and *dog* as proper names that pick out an object. For notoriously ensnarled reasons, Frege (1952 [1892b]) denied that sortals in predicate position (for example, *is a dog*) denote an object. By using $\equiv$ instead of $=$, I have sidestepped the problem; I have assigned K and *dog* the same extension instead of the same object as referent. The solution was suggested by Dummett (1981, chap. 7) and is discussed in greater detail later in this chapter.

There is some uncertainty that the semantics of sortals can be thus handled extensionally. There are examples where, it is claimed, the extension of two sortals happens to be the same and yet the two do not refer to the same kind. For example, *creature with a heart* and *creature with a kidney* are supposed to have the same extension; every individual that is in one kind is in the other. Yet there seems to be no law that nature cannot produce a creature with only one of the two organs. This objection, if it were raised, could be overruled by introducing a modal operator, as in

$$(\exists! B, K)(\text{Spot} \in K \ \& \ \square \ (\forall A, x)(x \in \text{dog} \equiv x \in K)). \tag{5''}$$

In this way the extensions of K and *dog* are necessarily the same. Probably, however, the modal operator is not required in the representation because it seems unlikely that it would ever occur to a child that the basic-level category to which Spot belongs would have different extensions when denoted by (K) and *dog*. In effect, it seems reasonable to locate the modal operator in the "functional architecture" of the mind (Pylyshyn's phrase) or in the interpreter for sortals.

Sentence (5′) specifies the principle of application for *dog* as grasped by the learner: being in the same basic-level kind as Spot. It does not specify what it is about Freddie that makes him a dog. It does not need to.

A further logical element that needs to be provided for relates to the principle of identity for *dog*. The principle of identity roughly guarantees that, for as long as a creature is a dog, it is the same dog. The qualification "roughly" is needed because the paradoxes of identity (see Gupta 1980, chap. 4) suggest that the principle of identity needs to be slightly modified if it is to achieve full generality. My inquiry, however, can safely ignore the modification. I capture the principle of identity for dogs informally in

> Throughout the time that any creature *d* is a dog, it remains the same dog. (6)

More formally this can be expressed by

$$(\forall D, d)(\exists ! K, y) \,\square\, (\text{Exists } y \supset d = y). \tag{6′}$$

This reads: For any dog *d* there is a unique member *y* of the basic kind *K*, and as long as *y* exists, it is identical with *d*. Here, in keeping with the decision to ignore possible worlds, $\square$ is read as "at each moment" or "as long as."

We now bring together statements (5′) and (6′):

$$(\exists ! B, K) \, [(\text{Spot} \in K) \,\&\, (\forall A, x)(x \in \text{dog} \equiv x \in K)$$
$$\&\, (\forall D, d)(\exists ! K, y) \,\square\, (y \text{ exists} \supset d = y)]. \tag{7}$$

Children's Logical Resources

People who accept the account given in the first part of this chapter of the logic of basic-level sortals can hardly fail to agree with statement (7), which gives the logical work that needs to be accomplished in the competent learning of the sortal *dog*. We are assuming that Tom, who is serving as our example, will use and understand *dog* in accordance with the principles just stated. It does not follow that he knows, in the sense of knowing-that, all that is specified in those principles. On the other hand, Tom must know some of it because statement (7) includes what one knows when one understands *dog*. Although we cannot with certainty distinguish what children know explicitly from what is implicit in their interpretation of, say, *dog*, it is interesting to attempt some division and study its implication for developmental cognition.

The main thing that the child Tom learns is expressed in statement (5): Spot is a dog. Tom learns the English word *dog* from his mother, and I am positing that as a result of his mother's saying it on this occasion, Tom understands the word. Because *dog* denotes a particular kind, Tom must know which one. To manage that, he needs some means other than the sortal *dog* of picking the kind out as that which is to be denoted by *dog*.

A second thing that Tom has to learn is that *dog* is synonymous with the sortal that has been supporting his learning and use of proper names for dogs. Here, *synonymous* means having the same extension (because of having the same principle of application) and having the same principles of individuation and identity. In describing the learning of the first proper names, we decided that children can learn names only for individuals whose perceptual gestalt types they have succeeded in identifying. We decided further that to each such gestalt type they must assign a sortal in the language of thought and that they represent certain individuals in their experience as falling under those sortals. What I now suggest is that in learning a basic-level sortal, such as *dog*, children merely have to represent the synonymity of the English word and the sortal in the language of thought. This is to treat the learning of such natural-language sortals as a form of translation. Later in this chapter I return to reasons for believing that the gestalt type for dogs elicits a basic-level sortal rather than any of a host of logically possible alternatives.

Sentence (7), then, should be seen as attempting to capture the logical competence of the sortal learner, not necessarily as stating the content of what is learned and actually represented. Much of that content is already implicit in the working of the interpreter that performs the task of interpreting the language-of-thought sortal associated with the gestalt type for dogs: It assigns to the kind, dog, any individual that satisfies that gestalt type and it handles the individual's identity under that kind. This is little more than saying that certain individuals appear to Tom as dogs and that among them he recognizes that some are the same dogs over time. In psychological jargon, certain individuals elicit the dog response and some of those elicit the same-dog response.

It seems unlikely that children have to represent the rule for tracing identity under the sortal *dog*, that is, statement (6'). It may perhaps be applied by the interpreters and implicators that handle sortals and apply them to individuals. What children do have to represent in some form is the synonymity of *dog* with the basic-level sortal for dog in the language of thought. This is the core content of statement (5'). It contains four elements that deserve special comment: K (kind), B (basic-level kind), the quantifiers, and the symbol ≡ (logical equivalence).

Kind   In discussing the psychology of learning a proper name (chapter 4), we decided that children need in their representation an expression synonymous with *kind*. The work that *kind* does cannot be tucked away in the "functional architecture"; it cannot be tucked away in the interpreters. The reason is that children need it to learn the sortal synonymous with *dog*, which is needed to support the learning and use of the proper name. But now we are squarely confronting the learning of *dog*, so there is a certain amount of tidying up to do.

Children who learn the sortal *dog* end up understanding it, which means that they must have some understanding of what it refers to, namely, a kind. Suppose that they think that *dog* refers to an ordinal number or to one of the moon's craters or to an individual dog; we would say that they do not really know its meaning at all. Suppose, however, that they can say that *dog* refers to a kind, in fact to the "main" kind that Freddie and Rover belong to; we would be satisfied that they know the meaning. It follows inevitably that the learners must have some symbolic means of representing this information. They must, therefore, have an interpreted symbol synonymous with *kind*.

It would seem that the sortal synonymous with *kind* is supplied by nature, that it is unlearned. The reason is that otherwise an infinite regress would threaten. If we say that the learning of *dog* must be guided by a sortal, *kind*, then the learning of *kind* would also have to be guided by another sortal, say, *kind'*; and if *kind'* were learned, the learning would have to be guided by yet another sortal, say, *kind''*; and so on ad infinitum. The regress would be pernicious because the learning of each sortal would depend on the next sortal down. Hence the learning could never begin. Obviously an unlearned sortal is required, and I suggest that we take the first *kind* as that unlearned sortal.

A second observation brings to light a hitherto unnoticed piece of evidence in favor of Frege's (1952 [1891], 1952 [1892b]) doctrine that the referent of a sortal is an "unsaturated" or incomplete entity. Just imagine that, contrary to Frege's view, the referent were a complete object; then the sortal would be the name of that entity, in fact its proper name. Now we have seen that a proper name needs the support of a sortal to supply a principle of identity for its referent. But that sortal, itself ex hypothesi a proper name, would need yet another sortal to supply a principle of identity for its referent, and so on ad infinitum. Once again the regress is pernicious because the identity of each referent is catered to by the next sortal down. It follows that the identity of no referent would be catered to. This time the way out of the regress is suggested by Frege. The referent of a sortal is not the sort of thing that requires a principle of identity. In fact, sortals are not the sort of words that can properly flank the identity sign (=) on their own. It is not correct, for example, to write anything such as

dog = chien.

That is part of what it means to be an unsaturated object. That is the main reason why I account for the synonymity of two sortals by saying that their extensions are the same (see sentences (5') and (5")). Yet this notion of synonymity is sufficient to permit quantifying over sortals, as Frege did and as I do in sentence (7). *Dog* supplies a true principle of identity for those creatures that are dogs and, strictly, that is the only sort of identity that we have to deal with.

Basic-Level Kind   In sentences (5') and (7) the symbol B represents basic-level kind. It is improbable that young children need to represent B as part of what they learn. The whole idea of basic-level sortals is that they are the ones that occur to children at certain moments, especially when learning a word for a kind of object (see Rosch and Mervis 1978 and Markman and Hutchinson 1984). In other words, there is no need for children to distinguish the many kinds to which Spot belongs; only the basic-level kind, dog, occurs to them. This is borne out by evidence from studies of how parents teach sortals.

Anglin (1977) and Shipley et al. (1983) have shown that parents tend to use basic-level sortals when telling young children the kind to which an individual belongs. Shipley et al. added that parents use higher-level sortals (1) when explaining an unfamiliar lower-level sortal to a child ("a tiger is an animal like a large cat") or (2) when speaking about a plurality of individuals. Macnamara (1982, chap. 5) presented evidence that two-year-olds also tend to take *animal* as a word that is applicable only to a plurality of individuals. Wales et al. (1983), in reporting a study that supports this general position, made the interesting observation that, although parents use ostension to teach basic-level sortals ("that is a cow"), they do not generally use ostension to teach higher-level ones. The idea seems to be that one way to teach higher-level sortals is by employing several basic-level sortals, for example, *animals*: Well, cows are animals, horses are animals, and so are pigs. We ought, however, with Shipley et al., to observe that parents sometimes describe a group of different kinds of animals (horses, cows, sheep) simply as animals, which may be a form of ostension.

Perhaps we should not have attached the symbol for basic-level sortal to the existential quantifier binding K in statements (5') and (7), because K is not the sort of object that requires a principle of identity. Add to this the fact that in both sentences the principle of "identity" (identity of extension) is spelled out, and the temptation to require B diminishes further. Finally, kinds, unlike dogs, are not the sorts of things that are ever thought of as changing, especially by theorists who see kinds as outside the realm of space and time. All in all, it seems reasonable to dispense with B from the content of what children learn.

This is not to deny, however, that what is a basic level for a child may change with age (see Mervis and Mervis 1982).

Quantifiers   Sentences (5') and (7) carry both sorts of quantifier. We will see in chapter 8 that children do not have to learn these or how to apply them meaningfully. What we see now is that they must be available to children at a young age because sortals are among the first words they learn. All this is on the assumption that quantifiers are necessary to learn the synonymity of two sortals. The universal quantifier in these sentences serves a function analogous to that of the sortal *dog* in the learning of the proper name *Spot*. The universal quantifier helps to express the counterpart of identity. The referents of proper names have true identity, which is supplied by a sortal; the referents of sortals can have identical extensions, and the universal quantifier is required to express that notion. The existential quantifier is needed to achieve reference to the general notion of a kind and to bind the variable K that expresses that reference.

Logical Equivalence   In sentences (5') and (7) logical equivalence is represented, uncomfortably, by $\equiv$. It is well known that logic's $\equiv$ is not a good match for such natural-language expressions as *just in case* or *whenever* (see Strawson 1952). Thus it seems probable that $\equiv$ is not a good match for the language-of-thought equivalent of *just in case*. In the last chapter we saw that children cannot learn the entire set of natural-language truth-functional connectives. Without being dogmatic, the language-of-thought equivalent for *just in case* seems a likely candidate for unlearned status. That status is made all the more likely by the fact that children need the expression so young—on the assumption that my whole approach is on the right lines. For evidence of an early understanding of the notion we express by *just in case*, see Bowerman (to be published).

There is no need to go into the language in which children express what they learn when they learn *dog*. The problems are parallel to those we encountered in connection with the learning of proper names. If the account of language given there was adequate, it can serve here as well with a few modifications.

Mobilizing Competence

I do not need to dwell in detail on how the logical resources that children need to learn a sortal are mobilized. I appeal to procedurelike devices, which I call *interpreters*, to do the work. The main part of characterizing the interpreters that enable the learning of a basic-level sortal is to identify their input conditions and their output.

A few remarks on input conditions are interesting, in that they lead to empirical predictions. How do children know that they are being confronted with a sortal and not with a proper name or a predicate? We have imagined that children are possessed of a proper name for the individual used to teach the sortal. That might lead them to suspect that the word now applied is of a different kind. But they need not have had a proper name; most sortals are learned without benefit of a proper name. In chapter 4 we saw evidence that children have a marked tendency to take a word applied to individuals of certain kinds as a proper name. I do not go back over it here. In the past few years evidence has been accumulating that young children tend to take a word applied to individuals of unfamiliar kinds as sortals for the kind. Gelman and Taylor (1984), in an interesting extension of Katz et al. (1974), found strong suggestions that two-year-olds take a common noun (*a Zav*) applied to a doll-like object and a common noun or a word without a determiner (*Zav*) applied to blocklike article as category words. Their findings are corroborated by Mitchell (1984), who carried out similar experiments with somewhat older children. These are interesting results, but they do not tell us whether the children were taking the category words as sortals or predicates.

Identifying the Kind

Predicates

When dealing with a sortal, how do children know that it is not a predicate? If they knew the English quantifiers (*all, some, many, one,* etc.) and knew that quantifiers combine with sortals, not with predicates, they could tell the sortals. But then, how would they learn about the quantifiers? The answer that is debarred on this approach is the one that gives the sortals a key role in the learning of the quantifiers, because I am imagining that the quantifiers guide the learning of sortals. How children learn sortals is an empirical matter, and the evidence is that they grasp many basic-level sortals long before they seem to pay attention to natural-language quantifiers. It can hardly be that such quantifiers give the children the clue to the presence of a sortal. It is probably the other way about.

How, then, do they distinguish sortals from predicates? In my 1972 paper I noted that children in fact learn sortals before they learn predicates such as verbs or adjectives. I based my observation on diary data, and later my records of my son, Kieran, bore out the common pattern. His early words included a negative (*no*) and a general directive for something to be done for him (*nana*), but apart from that it was sortals rather than predicates all the way. Goldin-Meadow et al. (1976) bear out the evidence of the diary studies with the findings of a longitudinal experiment. They tested at intervals, starting at the beginnings of speech and continuing to beyond the age of two years, the ability of children to understand and produce sortals and action words. Sortals were well in advance in comprehension and scarcely present in production. Gentner (1982) presented evidence that the finding holds cross culturally— for children learning German, Kaluli, Japanese, Mandarin Chinese, and Turkish as well as English. She also took the trouble to rule out such possible explanations as sortals being in the preponderance over predicates in the speech addressed to children. There seems to be no escaping it: In the early stages of language learning children are far more likely to pick up sortals than words of other kinds. It is not that they fail to perceive attributes and events but that they construe them, individuate them, conceptualize them on a foundation of substance sorts, and direct a large part of their first linguistic efforts to the task of learning words for such sorts.

It should be possible to put this to more rigorous test by introducing children to members of some kind unfamiliar to them, say, grasshoppers. If I am right, children even under twenty months ought to take a nonsense syllable applied to them as a substance sortal for the object as a whole rather than as a sortal for any of its parts or a predicate for any of its attributes or activities, whether or not the nonsense syllable is accompanied by a quantifier (*a Zav* or *Zav*). Some experiments along these lines are being planned at present. They are all tests of the hypothesis that, in the early stages of language learning, sortals are psychologically more privileged than predicates and that children assume that words for kinds are sortals rather than predicates.

There are other even more difficult problems to which we must now turn, leaving behind the problem of predicates as one whose solution can be glimpsed even if somewhat vaguely.

Fixing the Interpretation
One problem for Tom and his instructors is that Spot belongs in many kinds besides dog. He is a pal and sometimes a pest. How does Tom know that *dog* is not such a sortal? I would predict, in fact, that he would treat the first English sortal he picked up for Spot as a substance sortal. And, if that sortal was the English word *pal* or *pest*, he would not be long in changing his view, because if he said *pal* of each dog he met, he would be corrected by his parents. He would also notice that, although Spot is sometimes called a pest, he is not always one. If Tom had taken *pest* as a sortal synonymous with the one that supported his use of *Spot*, he would have been surprised to find that his parents sometimes disallowed his being called a pest. That would have

been a clue that put Tom right. But here again there is ample scope for interesting empirical observation.

Neither *pal* nor *pest* is a substance sort because neither supplies a principle of identity for an individual throughout its existence. Spot can be a pest on Monday and again on Friday and be an angel in between. It even sounds odd to say that Spot is the same pest on Monday and Friday. I could speak of Jane as being the same pal I had years ago even if we had a falling out in the interim. What I would mean, though, is that Jane is the same person who was my pal years ago and is now again. A substance sortal is more basic than other sortals in the sense that it supplies a principle of identity for an individual over its entire existence.

This is apparent with phase sortals, such as *child* and *adult, pup* and *dog, caterpillar* and *butterfly*. Such sortals embrace only part of an individual's existence. *Person* is a substance sort because it covers childhood, adolescence, and adulthood. It makes sense to speak of *a* as being the same child as *b*; the little girl in the corner as being the same child as the one you just saw in the street. But you would also want to say that the striking young woman on the podium is the same as the little child who once lurked shyly in the corner. Obviously *child* cannot be the sortal that is supplying the requisite principle of identity. It must be supplied by a substance sort that embraces both phases of the individual's existence—a sortal such as *person*.

Now, children who learn a new sortal for an individual cannot always know there and then whether it is a phase or a substance sortal. In fact young children may not know that puppies grow up to be big dogs and that every big dog was once a pup. It is conceivable, then, that some children would take the English word *dog*, if learned in connection with a pup, as a substance sortal covering an individual's entire existence but not realize that the creature grew up to be an adult animal. If that were the case, they might be surprised to hear the word *dog* applied to large dogs, and that should provide them with a clue to their mistake. They do not even have to wait until the pup grows up to discover it. The error to which I allude is far more likely to occur in connection with tadpoles and frogs or with caterpillars and moths—as Jackendoff has pointed out to me.

But there are many substance kinds to which an individual dog belongs: poodle, dog, quadruped, mammal, beast, animal. Most of these are at different levels of a hierarchical tree. How do children know which one the English word *dog* is, which level it belongs at? More realistically, how do they manage to place *dog* at the right level? The answer depends on there being basic-level sortals that are psychologically salient and privileged. The idea here is that children attend to the similarities among dogs before they subclassify them and before they attend to the attributes dogs share with other species of animals. If this is right, and there is some evidence from child language that it is (see Anglin 1977 and Mervis and Crisafi 1982), children's perceptual systems would seem to be especially tuned to identifying basic-level categories that, when identified, are assigned basic-level sortals in the language of thought. The basic-level sortals are all taken as substance sortals. That is what motivates my prediction that children will take any word, other than a proper name, applied to an individual dog as a substance sortal; because I predict that they will make it synonymous with the language-of-thought sortal that they have set up for dogs.

Matters are complicated by an uncertain grasp of the gestalt pattern for dogs. Children may even imagine that cats are dogs; that cats satisfy the gestalt pattern for dogs. But this is corrected when they sort out the gestalt pattern and see that cats do not satisfy it. Throughout such wavering it would seem that children have to hold on to the fundamental form of learning, which anchors a basic-level sortal in the individuals that were used to teach the sortal.

It is possible, as Mervis and Mervis (1982) have suggested, that what is a basic-level kind changes with age. It is possible that cats, tigers, and leopards form a single basic-level kind for some young children and that subsequent experience establishes these as three distinct basic-level kinds. This merely means that children succeed in establishing gestalt patterns for each of the kinds. They can anchor the appropriate sortals in the individuals that were used to teach them the distinct sortals. There is no reason in the theory to expect basic-level kinds or learning associated with them to be immutable.

So, the hypothesis about basic-level sortals is of fundamental importance and enables us to discern how children can find their way through the vast array of kinds, to which any individual belongs, to the appropriate level substance sort that they need. One major problem remains. The foregoing is about discriminating among kinds, but how do children know that sortals and predicates denote kinds? In particular, how do they come to attach the basic-level sortal *dog* to the kind dog? That is the problem I now turn to.

Tying the Sortal to a Kind
Children's perceptual systems identify basic-level pattern types, which interpreters then attach to unique kinds. I do not propose in this section to attempt an explanation of how uninterpreted symbols are converted into interpreted ones, because for one thing I am profoundly skeptical about the possibility of such an explanation. Instead, I would like to give a few broad principles that must constitute part of the relevant

competence. I have already written at some length on the topic in chapter 12 of *Names for Things* (1982), so I can be brief here.

The core of the problem is to account for the assigning of a unique kind to a basic-level sortal, such as *dog*. There are two properties of kinds that are relevant in our discussion of the problem: (1) a kind takes individuals as members; (2) a kind supplies a principle of application for membership.

It is well appreciated today that the principle of application for *dog* is not a set of perceptually given distinctive features, whether in the form of a list or of an image. It is far more promising to look at the principle as an *explanation* for the phenomena that are registered in the basic-level pattern—such as spontaneous movement, breathing, and being sentient. In common speech the explanation is not called the *principle of application* but *nature*. We say dogs grow hair and not feathers because that is their nature. Their nature explains why they must eat, why they squeal when someone steps on their paw, why they have puppies and not calves. Not that people can specify the nature; just that they posit the nature as the explanation of the phenomena. Notice that people do not appeal to nature to explain accidental phenomena, such as the presence of a fly on Spot's nose or his having a sore paw. They do not even appeal to canine nature to explain why Spot is black and not beige. Though they may appeal to his poodle nature to explain his being black.

To individuate the nature or principle of application for dogs, children must assign meaning in conformity with two great metaphysical principles to which Aristotle drew attention: Every phenomenon has an adequate explanation, and differences in phenomena receive different explanations. These principles guarantee both the existence of an explanation for dog phenomena and the uniqueness of that explanation. It is precisely because dogs appear different from floors, rocks, and even cats that the perceptual system is able to set up a pattern type for dogs. Appearing different is presenting different phenomena, hence the uniqueness of dog's nature.

All this assumes that the human mind is essentially an explanation seeker and that it is guided by the two Aristotelean principles just mentioned. It is this that explains how we assign kinds to sortals as their referents. To do so, we do not have to solve the great metaphysical puzzle of what kinds are. They can be whatever they are for all that common sense cares. Neither do we have to know the specifics of the principle of application for a kind, such as dog, in the way that would satisfy a scientist. It is uniquely determined as "the principle of application for the basic-level kind to which Freddie belongs" or in more everyday language "sharing Freddie's nature." The strength of reference from the psychological point of view is that so little knowledge of the referent is required in the user.

Once a principle of application for a kind has been determined, it is clear in principle what the members are. They are all those individuals that satisfy the principle of application. Ordinary language users may have no fully reliable test to decide which individuals those are, especially in hard cases. They may have nothing much better than the basic-level gestalt type with which their perceptual systems started the whole thing off. That our grasp of the principles of application for kinds is less than ironclad is well appreciated by the community of language users. That is why we turn so readily to experts who are in a better position than most to state such principles in a manner that grounds reliable tests of membership in kinds. Errors can lead to being swindled out of one's savings by the purveyors of fool's gold. A cook's errors about the substance sorts to which the dishes that are served belong may lead to poisoning and death. Make no mistake; principles of application are of importance to us all.

8

Hierarchies and Quantifiers

Among kinds there are many relations that ground straightforward inferences. For example, we can make a proper subset of dogs by adding the predicate *black* to dogs to form the set of black dogs. Then, if we learn that Spot is a black dog, we can immediately conclude that he is a dog. We cannot conclude that he is a black because *a black* (unless it means a black person) is not a grammatical expression in English. There are numerous logical puzzles about such subsets. For instance, if we learn that Joe is a former politician, we cannot conclude that he is a politician. We will not, however, be concerned with the logic of predicate-sortal combinations but only with the relations between a basic-level sortal (for example, *dog*) and hierarchically related higher-level sortals (for example, *animal*). The special psychological interest of the higher-level sortals is the fact that the perceptual system does not form anything such as gestalt types for them. Across nearly all breeds of dog it seems to be easy for us to detect the canine resemblances. We cannot perceive the animal resemblances across animals, which include worms, birds, alligators, insects, spiders, lobsters, and centipedes; some with naked skin, some with feathers, some with hair, some with scales, and some with shells for covering. It follows that the story of how children learn a sortal such as *animal* must be rather different from how they learn one such as *dog*.

Because of the hierarchical relations among them, sortals provide a natural context in which to explore the logic and psychology of the quantifiers. The quantifiers are the last constituents of simple sentences that we study. Apart from the numerals, there are many quantifiers in ordinary language: *all, some, many, a few, each, every, any,* and so on. Many of them give rise to special logical problems. To keep things simple, we confine ourselves to *all* and *some*, and yet there is plenty to occupy us. There is extensive psychological literature on *all* and *some* that must be assayed.

In this chapter, then, I study the logical relations between basic-level sortals and sortals superordinate to them and the logic of *all* and *some*.

I then look at the psychology of how children learn them and master the related logic.

The Logic

Sets and Sortals

It is natural to think of the relation between dogs and animals as a relation between a proper subset and a set, and I have been using that language to do so. Each dog is an animal, and there are animals other than dogs. This a useful way to look at things, but before we settle for it, we should satisfy ourselves that it does not lead us astray. So we should briefly compare sets and the kinds named by natural-language sortals.

Although definitions of sets supply principles of application for their members, neither sets nor their definitions supply principles of individuation or identity for their members that are not sets. *Set* is, of course, a sortal, and it supplies all three principles for members that are sets. Thus *set* is similar to a natural-language sortal in relation to members that are sets. A higher-order sortal (such as *animal*) supplies the same principles of individuation and identity as a properly included basic-level sortal (such as *dog*), but it supplies a different principle of application.

Sets that share exactly the same members are identical. It follows that all sets that have no members are identical with the empty set and with one another. If we were to interpret kinds as sets, we might be led to say that *dodo* is synonymous with *dinosaur*. This would be counterintuitive because, although both species are extinct, their members, when there were some, were quite different. The reason that the conclusion that *dodo* and *dinosaur* are synonymous strikes us as odd is that kinds embrace the past, present, and future in a way that sets do not. Sortals, to repeat, are rigid designators that designate the same kind, even if the membership increases, diminishes, or dwindles to nothing. Sets, in contrast, are constructed by pure mathematicians whose purposes have nothing to do with temporal changes. The fact that sortals are rigid designators plays a part in what follows. It means that the relevant membership of the kinds we are dealing with is non-surveyable. It is not, for example, by examining each dog in turn that we prove that dogs are animals, because the truth we seek to establish embraces dogs long since dead and dogs not yet born, not to mention all the dogs that ever might have been born and might be born in the future but will not be.

It is more difficult to understand why we also reject the idea that leprechauns are the same as fairies. Neither kind has ever had or ever will have any members and, being by definition legendary creatures, there can be no possible worlds in which there are any members. The reason that the identification strikes us as wrong seems to have to do with the principles of application for the two kinds. The description of fairies is quite different from that of leprechauns, so even as creatures of the imagination they are different. Considered from the standpoint of membership, however, there is no reason to reject the identity of the kinds. This observation brings out how salient the principle of application is for the kinds of natural language. It also shows that the synonymity of fictitious sortals cannot be handled by the logic given in chapter 7 for nonfictitious ones. I am afraid I have nothing special to say about the logic of fictitious sortals any more than I had about that of vacuous proper names. I do not, then, attempt to account for the learning of fictitious sortals.

The differences noted between sets and kinds do not preclude employing set-theoretic notions; they do mean that we must be aware of possible pitfalls.

Inclusion and Membership

Despite the independently varying memberships (or extensions) of the kinds dog and animal, each dog is by its nature an animal. It follows that being an animal is part of the principle of application for being a dog. To express the relation between dogs (D) and animals (A), we can adapt a symbol from set theory; thus $D \subset A$. I define it for my purposes by the following proposition, in which F and G are arbitrary kinds:

$$F \subset G \equiv (\forall F, x)(x \in G \ \& \ (\exists G, y)(y \notin F)).$$

It is important not to read the (so-called) existential quantifier ($\exists$) as postulating existence. The definition would still imply that the kind dog is properly included in the kind, animal, even if in the actual world there were no animals but dogs. Remember, natural-language sortals, being rigid designators, pick out the kinds in circumstances in which there are no animals other than dogs. We could draw attention to this by placing the modal connective $\square$ immediately before the sentence to the right of $\equiv$.

The relation of proper inclusion ($\subset$) must be distinguished from that of membership ($\in$). Though the kind, dog, is properly included in *animal*, it is not a member of *animal*; unlike an individual dog, the kind, dog, is not an animal. Nonetheless we speak about kinds of kinds as well as about kinds, where a kind of kinds would seem to have kinds as its members.

What about the sortal *animal*? Does it denote a first-level kind or a second-level kind of kinds? Obviously is denotes a first-level kind that properly includes another first-level kind, dog. But is the word ambiguous, denoting in addition a second-level kind of kinds? What might prompt belief in its ambiguity is the common way of speaking of kinds of animals. We might be asked what kind of things animals are and reply that they are dogs and cats and horses and so on. Here, however, it is easy to interpret the response as listing some properly included subkinds, though common speech is none too precise. More supportive of an ambiguity thesis are such expressions as "The dodo is an extinct animal" and "The beaver is an animal that builds dams." Here, the use of the definite article does not normally betoken a definite description; its use is taken as *generic*, inasmuch as such expressions as "the dodo" pick out the kind rather than a particular member. What is more, the kind so picked out is described as an animal. This suggests that *animal* is ambiguous, meaning sometimes a first-level kind and sometimes a second-level one.

I do not propose to settle the matter here, but it will come up again when we consider the learning of sortals such as *animal*. At a certain stage many children say that a particular creature is a pig, for example, but deny emphatically that it is an animal. We have to wonder whether such children do not consider *animal* to be a second-level sortal whose members are kinds. If they did, their denial would be fully intelligible.

Parts, Wholes, and Collections
It helps to bring kinds and the relations among them into sharper focus by contrasting them with other relations that are superficially similar. There is all the more reason to do so because there is extensive psychological literature, which we have to examine, that is flawed by failure to make exact distinctions among these relations.

I begin with the relation between a part and the whole of which it is a part. For example, a leg is part of a body and it is a member of the kind, bodily member. But, although a leg is a bodily member, it is not a body. What this shows is that being a member of a kind is quite different from being part of a whole. We can bring this out more clearly if we take a special symbol, $*$, to refer to the relation "part of." So $x * y$ means x is part of y. To avoid confusion with the sign for inclusion ($\subset$), in this section I use $\rightarrow$ for implication.

Now then, let us consider the three relations $\in$, $\subset$, and $*$. We have

$$\text{Spot} \in \text{dog} \rightarrow \text{Spot is a dog,} \tag{1}$$

but

$$\text{toe} * \text{leg} \nrightarrow \text{a toe is a leg.} \tag{2}$$

This shows that $\in$ and $*$ are quite different in meaning. The difference shows up again when we consider $\subset$:

Spot ∈ dog & dog ⊂ animal → Spot ∈ animal. (3)

leg ∈ bodily part & bodily part ∗ body ↛ leg ∈ body. (4)

toe ∗ leg & leg ⊂ limb ↛ toe ∈ limb. (5)

In some ways the relations are similar. All three are asymmetric: for example, (Spot ∈ dog) → ∼ (dog ∈ Spot). All three are irreflexive: for example, (dog ∉ dog). Yet, although ⊂ and ∗ are transitive, ∈ is not:

Joe ∈ Arts Curriculum Committee & Arts Curriculum Committee ∈ Arts Committees & ∼(Joe ∈ Arts Committees). (6)

poodles ⊂ dog & dog ⊂ animal → poodles ⊂ animal. (7)

toe ∗ leg & leg ∗ body → toe ∗ body. (8)

A collection word or a collective noun, for example, *herd, bunch,* and *forest,* is properly applied only to a plurality of individuals. This marks off collections from sets or kinds because sets or kinds can have just one member or none at all. In some ways the constituent/collection relation resembles the part/whole one we have just been considering. An individual tree is a constituent of a forest, but it is not a forest. The relation is also obviously asymmetric and irreflexive. But it is not the same relation, as statement (9) shows, where the constituent/collection relation, is represented, wrongly, by ∗:

leg ∗ sheep & sheep ∗ flock. (9)

Yet a leg is not a constituent of a flock; to be such a constituent, an individual must be a sheep. Sentence (8) revealed that ∗ is transitive, and now we see that if we treat the constituent/collection relation as synonymous with ∗ things become unstuck. In fact, because collections specify their constituents, we cannot set up transitive relations across constituents and collections. For example, take a beagle named Dolly who has a litter of which Rover is a constituent; imagine that Dolly is a constituent of the Westmount pack. Now represent the constituent/collection relation by #. Although we can write

Rover # Dolly's litter (10)

Dolly # Westmount pack, (11)

this affords no way to obtain a constituent relation between Rover and Westmount pack. Dolly's litter is not Dolly, and Dolly's litter is not a constituent of Westmount pack. This does not deny that Rover may be a constituent of Westmount pack; just that # is a transitive relation. The lack of transitivity for #, then, marks it off from both ∗ and ⊂. It places # closer to ∈, which is also irreflexive, asymmetric, and intransitive. The relations # and ∗ are distinct in that the principle of application for a kind is true of each of the members, whereas the principle of application for a collection is not true of individual constituents. An individual dog is a dog; an individual tree is not a forest.

Note on Mass Nouns

Although I have promised not to make a frontal attack on mass nouns (such as *milk* and *sand*), I am obliged to engage in a brief skirmish with them. In an interesting paper containing several valuable insights and observations about how children learn sortals, Markman (1983) suggested that mass nouns play a special role in children's learning of hierarchically related sortals, such as *dog* and *animal*. The background against which the suggestion was made includes the observation that at a certain stage children who admit that an individual is a pig deny that it is an animal. In addition, Markman has shown that such children often handle certain questions about collections better than they handle similar questions about inclusion—the details need not detain us. Markman's view is that children originally construe sortals such as *animal* as a collection. That would explain their denial that a pig is an animal, and it is supported by their successful handling of questions about collections. She also suggests that children are led to bridge the gap between collections and class inclusion by mass nouns. This suggestion rests on two distinct claims.

The first claim is that natural languages have a strong tendency to denote kinds above the basic level by means of mass nouns. Examples that bear this out are *furniture, food, fuel, equipment*, and *money*; examples that do not bear it out are *animal, plant, fruit, vegetable, instrument*, and *building*. Because Markman does not tell us the proportion or frequency of such words that are mass nouns in any language, the value of the claim is difficult to assess. The corresponding part of this claim is that basic-level kinds and kinds included by them are denoted by count nouns. Examples that bear this out are *dog, cat, cow, sheep, apple*, and *stick*; examples that go the other way are *milk, water, porridge, clay, oats, wheat, sand, rice*, and *meat*. Once again, we are not given the proportion or frequency of such works that are count nouns in any language. All in all, Markman has not succeeded in showing, at least to my satisfaction, a strong correlation between the mass/count distinction and the basic-level/higher-level one.

The second claim is that mass nouns, because of their logic, can mediate between children's supposed construal of a higher-order sortal as a collection and its true status as a sortal that properly includes a number of kinds:

In a sense, mass nouns can be viewed as a compromise between collections and classes which properly include subclasses. Or, to be more precise, as a compromise between "part-whole" and "is a" membership relations. Consider a typical mass such as clay. A piece of clay is part of the whole mass of clay. This is similar to the part-whole organization of collections where each tree, for example, is part of the forest. On the other hand, each piece of clay is itself clay. This is more like the "is a" relation of class inclusion, where each oak is a tree. (Markman 1983)

Markman's language is guarded, and the suggestion is made more for its interest than from the conviction that it is right. A closer look at the logic, however, raises the gravest doubts. A piece of clay is certainly part of a mass of clay, as Markman says, but it is not part of clay. To fit the part/whole relation, Markman had to include some such word as *mass* or *lump*. The relation between a piece of clay and clay is not, paradoxically, a part/whole relation. Neither is it an "is a" or ∈ (membership) relation. To the left of the membership symbol must go a term that picks out an individual member of the kind named to the right. We can say *Rover* ∈ *dog* but not *the litter* ∈ *dog* or any expression that fails to denote an individual dog. It follows that we cannot say, *the lump of clay* ∈ *clay*, because *the lump of clay* does not denote an individual of the kind, clay. I have no idea what an individual of that kind is—which may reflect the reasons for which *clay* is a mass noun. *The lump of clay*, of course, denotes an individual of the kind *lump of clay*, but that is quite a different matter.

The proposed mediation seems rather nebulous, so I do not dwell on it further. The moral I wish to underscore is the leitmotiv of these chapters, the necessity of a thorough analysis of the logic of the cognitive element whose psychology is to be described.

Psychology of Higher-Level Sortals

Model of Learning

The logic of hierarchies of sortals just discussed does not determine the psychology of how higher-order sortals are learned and how the relations among hierarchically related sortals are grasped. The logic determines a competence theory that constrains, without determining, psychological theory. It follows that there is something speculative about the psychology now to be proposed, as there was about each of the psychological theories proposed earlier. The degree of speculation is to be reduced by empirical studies, so in an effort to guide theorizing I will be on the lookout for suitable empirical studies. Unfortunately, the gaps in the psychological literature are broad.

It is natural to begin by seeing whether the theory that explains the learning of basic-level sortals can be modified and pressed into service to explain the learning of higher-level sortals. Recall the basic idea in the theory of how basic-level sortals are learned: (1) children identify basic-level categories by establishing a gestalt type for each; (2) to each gestalt type they assign a sortal in the language of thought; (3) they learn the meaning of English sortals by setting them as synonymous with the sortals in the language of thought. For example, children assign *dog* the same meaning as the basic-level sortal they have assigned to the gestalt for dogs, the link between the two being forged by the demonstration of one or more individuals of the kind. In other words, children assign to *dog* the content that is expressed by "the same basic-level kind as *x* and *y*," where *x* and *y* are to be replaced by expressions that refer to particular dogs known to the children.

Not all of this can apply to the learning of higher-level sortals. There are two problems we have to solve. First, we do not form gestalt types or any perceptual-pattern types for such higher-level sortals as animals. Second, there is not a unique level to which dogs belong; they are quadrupeds and mammals as well as animals.

It seems we can solve the first problem by replacing individuals, as designated by terms (effectively, proper names and demonstratives), with either kinds or individuals, as denoted by basic-level sortals. We assume, with good empirical support (see Wales et al. 1983, Callanan 1985), that children do not learn higher-level sortals, such as *animal*, until after they have learned several basic-level ones, such as *dog*, *horse*, and *sheep*. These can then be used to teach the higher-level sortal. We tell children that *animal* is a word for various kinds of creatures, such as dogs, horses, and sheep. Or we may just tell them that animals are things like sheep, dogs, and horses. Note the use of the plural, which suggests proper inclusion as the relation between the levels. I will come back to empirical evidence about how children construe our explanations, but first a word about the second problem.

The solution to the second problem seems to be that children take a higher-level sortal conservatively, as embracing just those individuals or kinds that share salient properties with the basic-level kinds mentioned in teaching it. They seem to take *animal* initially as *quadruped*, excluding from its embrace humans, birds, worms, fish, insects, spiders, and lobsters. As Carey (1985) has shown, it takes a long time for children to learn that the extension of *animal* is as broad as adults take it to be. She has also shown that it takes a long time for children to learn the properties that are generally known to be essential to animals. The reason they make mistakes at first is ignorance of biology. Their mistakes reveal their conservative learning strategy: Do not embrace in a higher-order sortal more kinds than you have been given grounds for including, where grounds are to be spelled out in terms of salient properties and explicit adult instruction. I do not have any proposals for a theory of psychological salience. Such a theory needs to be worked out, and I assume that it can be on the basis of empirical research.

A conservative strategy would explain the uniqueness of children's guesses as to the meaning of higher-order sortals. It would also explain their errors as to extension. We return now to children's construal of our teaching.

Empirical Studies
One day, Wargny (1976), with whom I worked on the learning of sortals, asked a two-year-old boy what was in a certain box. He said, "Toys." She then took out a toy airplane and asked: "Is that a toy?" With equal assurance he replied, "No, an airplane." On another occasion Wargny asked another two-year-old boy, who had just called the occupant of a fish tank *a fish*, to choose a name for it. The boy chose "Fishy." When asked if Fishy was a fish, he said "No," quite emphatically. It is not that children at that age do not know words such as *toy*, *fish*, and *animal*; it is that there is something odd about their use of them in connection with individuals.

Prompted by these casual observations Wargny and I began to explore systematically children's use of *toy* and *animal*. The details are given in Macnamara (1982, chap. 5). We found that, of twenty-eight two-year-olds whom we examined, only about eight could be relied on to give a correct response when asked if an individual animal (say a pig) was an animal. Many of those children who made mistakes were emphatic that the individual was not an animal. This finding would be explained if they were taking *animal* as a sortal whose members are kinds, not individual animals.

Against this interpretation was a further finding that involved showing two-year-olds plastic bags containing many individual animals. One bag contained ten plastic dogs; the other an assortment of ten different animals, some sheep, horses, cows, etc. Twenty children were asked two questions about each bag: "What are these?" If they did not say "animals," they were asked: "Could you call them *animals*?" All the children said that the first bag contained "dogs"; half of them agreed that they could be called "animals." Half the children said the mixed bag contained "animals," and all but one child said that they could be called "animals." Children who took *animal* as a name for a kind of kinds, if in addition they took the bag of dogs as representing the kind dog, should have been prepared to call the bag of dogs *an animal* (not *animals*). No child did that. This is evidence against the view that the children were construing the higher-level sortal as picking out a kind of kinds—and, incidentally, against the view that they were construing them as a collection (like *forest*).

The main evidence for the collection hypothesis comes in a study by Callanan and Markman (1982). They asked two- and three-year-olds, among other tasks, to place a toy or an animal in a box. In front of the children were four toys or four animals. There was a slight tendency especially among two-year-olds to place more than one object in the box. Some 35% of the responses were of this type. This was taken as evidence in favor of a collection interpretation of *toy* and *animal*. But it is extremely weak evidence. If children take *animal* to mean something such as flock of animals, they ought to put all four in the box when asked to put an animal in it. Callanan and Markman, however, said that there was a collection error if the children put more than one in. On the other hand, the number of errors that the two-year-olds made when asked to place a truck or a cow (basic-level sortal) in the box, though significantly lower than the result just mentioned, is startlingly high (28%). It is not clear in the reporting how many of these errors consisted of placing too many objects in the box. I find the case for the collection hypothesis to be unconvincing.

Three McGill undergraduates—Paul Bloom, Robert di Meco, and Shelly Surkis—and I have made a careful study (reported here for the first time) of the collection hypothesis. We located twelve-year-olds who would not allow that a single pig could be called *an animal*. We showed them a plastic bag containing several pigs and another plastic bag containing an assortment of animals. Of the bag of pigs we asked them two questions: Is there one pig here or a lot of pigs? Is there one animal here or a lot of animals? To both questions they responded that there were a lot. When we showed them the bag of animals, we asked them just "Is there one animal here or a lot of animals?" Again, all responded that there were a lot. Several of the children were given the same test again, and when they responded that there were a lot, they were asked, "A lot of what?" All responded appropriately with either *a lot of pigs* or *a lot of animals*.

All in all there seems to be no reason to believe that children who refuse to allow that a single pig is an animal take the word *animal* either as a kind of kinds or as a collection.

Equally compelling against these two hypotheses is the finding of another test that Wargny and I carried out (Wargny 1976; Macnamara 1982, chap. 5). We held out pairs of objects to sixty-six two-year-olds. One of each pair was either a toy or an animal; the other was something that was neither a toy nor an animal. We asked the children to "take the toy" (when the pair included a toy) or "take the animal" (when it included an animal). Some 90% of their responses were correct. This means that, despite a reluctance to say that an individual toy (or animal) is a toy (or animal), in a forced choice these children could apply those sortals to an individual object. This finding has been replicated in the recent study done with Bloom, di Meco, and Surkis.

All this suggests that two-year-olds have a good grasp on some higher-order sortals. This conclusion is buttressed by an experiment (reported in Macnamara 1982, chap. 5) in which I showed a group of eight toys to each of twelve boys. The objects were four vehicles (a boat, truck, tractor, earthmover) and four animals (dog, pig, cow, horse). All were small plastic toys of roughly the same size. They varied in color. We chose them so as to make it difficult for children to distinguish the animals from the vehicles by irrelevant criteria. All eight toys were shown to a child and, before his eyes, we put the four animals into a box, then poured them out again, mixed them up, and asked the child to do what we had done—the animal condition. Each child was asked to perform another task. Instead of the four animals, we put two animals and two vehicles in the box, poured them out again, mixed them up, and asked the child to do just what we had done—the mixed condition. This tested ability to memorize the particular toys placed by us in the box. The order of conditions was varied across children. No child succeeded in the mixed condition, whereas nine of the twelve succeeded in the animal condition. In fact, one boy placed all the vehicles in the box, so perhaps as many as ten of the twelve succeeded in making the discrimination. We interpreted the result as saying that these two-year-olds have a concept of animal that aided their performance. Failure on the mixed condition indicated that they could not succeed by brute memory. Notice that the experiment did not require the children to apply the word *animal* to an individual animal, though it seems that it required them to apply the concept.

Taking the experiments as a whole, we were led to conclude that the two-year-olds studied have both the word *animal* and a concept of animal that embraces at least quadrupeds. Why, then, did so many of them refuse to allow that a pig is an animal? The best answer we could give was that such children construe *animal* much as we construe *clothes*. My clothes are my pants, shirt, sweater, jacket, and so on. A pair of pants, however, is not a single cloth. I have, of course, a higher-level sortal that applies to each article of clothing, *garment*. The restriction on applying *cloth* to an individual article is an entirely linguistic one, not a conceptual one. The reason the children interpreted *animal* in this way seems to be that that is how parents speak to them (see Anglin 1977 and Shipley et al. 1983). If a single stuffed animal is on the floor, a parent is likely to say, "Pick up your teddy bear." If there are several, the parent tends to say, "Pick up your animals." The findings lend little support to either the kind-of-kinds theory or the collection theory of higher-level sortals.

If this theory of sortal learning is correct, how do children revise their original conservative conception of *animal* as embracing only quadrupeds? They must do so when they are told that birds, fish, insects, and other species that are excluded at first are also animals. The conservative estimate is thus gradually extended until it includes all that adults embrace by the word, but no more.

The theory that links each basic-level sortal with a unique kind serves equally well here. The principle of application for the higher-level kind is posited as the unique explanation for the phenomena that have been isolated as distinguishing the set of basic-level kinds. Nothing new needs to be added here.

I can now express the children's competence at any stage of their learning of *animal* on lines that parallel the expression of their competence in connection with basic-level sortals. In what follows, H means higher-level kind, P is a variable ranging over such kinds, $\Box$ means "at all times," x is a variable over dogs (D), y is a variable over cows (C) . . . , d is an individual constant for an arbitrarily chosen dog, and c is an individual constant for an arbitrarily chosen cow:

$$(\exists H, P)[(D \subset P \,\&\, C \subset P \,\&\, \ldots) \,\&\, (\forall D, x)(x \in P)$$
$$\&\, (\forall C, y)(y \in P) \,\&\, \ldots \,\&\, \{(\exists!Px) \,\Box\, (\text{Exists } d \to d$$
$$= x \,\&\, (\exists!P, y) \,\Box\, (\text{Exists } c \to c = y) \,\&\, \ldots \}]. \tag{12}$$

At the time when children learn *animal*, they need not advert to the third conjunct, though before long they will notice that the identity of an individual dog or cow is also traced under the sortal *animal*. They hear talk of *the same animal*. At the time of learning, if the psychological theory of how higher-level sortals are learned is true, children must advert to most of what is represented in the first two conjuncts. They contain what the children learn and the basis on which they learn it. For reasons quite parallel to those that led us to conclude that children in learning basic-level sortals do not need a symbol (B) for basic-level kinds, they also do not need a symbol (H) for higher-level ones. Indeed, it is questionable whether its use in (12) is logically correct.

The only symbol that we have not encountered in earlier chapters is that for proper inclusion $\subset$. Because children must use this symbol, they must have it available and be able to understand it. Logically, it would be possible for them to learn it if they had the resources necessary to express its definition:

$$A \subset B \equiv (\forall A, x)(x \in B \,\&\, (\exists B, y)(y \notin B)).$$

This includes the symbols $\equiv$, $\rightarrow$, &, $\in$, and the quantifiers A and $\exists$ together with the ability to use and understand them. (Remember that the existential quantifier $\exists$ is not to be read as signifying actual existence.) Alternatively, an equivalent of the symbol $\subset$ together with "interpreters" for using and interpreting it might be available in the language of thought. I have no idea which is correct, nor do I see any easy empirical test that would enable us to choose between them. A small part of the answer emerges in the next section, when I discuss the provenance of the quantifiers.

The Quantifiers All *and* Some

One way of learning whether children grasp the logic of kind inclusion is to see if they appreciate whether all the members of a subkind are also members of the superkind. Do they, for example, realize that all dolls are toys and that all dogs are animals? We have already seen some systematic observations addressed to answering that question, and we have seen that the matter is not settled. We did not, however, put the question to the children in the experiments already described. We did not, for example, attempt to determine if they understand the words *all* and *some*.

Simple Tests of Comprehension
First, we have to ask whether the children understand the words *all* and *some* in simpler contexts. Smith (1979) tested children, aged four or older, and found good grasp of their meaning. But it seems that children understand *all* and *some* at a much earlier age. Bloom (1984) tested twenty-four two-year-olds, asking them to take all or some of four pennies. Twenty-two of the children handled these questions without any difficulty. So it seems that the great majority of (at least middle-class) two-year-olds have little difficulty with the quantifiers *all* and *some*.

Quantifiers and Kind Inclusion: Piaget
A considerable literature has evolved, inspired by Piaget (1952) and Inhelder and Piaget (1964), about children's ability to handle the logic of class inclusion, or what I prefer to call *kind inclusion*. The orthodox position is that until about the age of seven, children do not grasp that all the members of a subkind (dog) are also members of a superkind (animal), which properly includes it and at the same time that there are some members of the superkind that are not members of the subkind. This, Piaget (1963) claimed, shows that children before the age of seven generally do not have a true understanding of any concept or of what

it is to be an individual falling under a concept. I do not dwell on this observation, as it scarcely seems to follow from the evidence. Instead I fix attention on the evidence offered for the conclusion that children do not grasp that the members of a proper subkind are less numerous than those of the superkind.

One experiment will stand for all. Inhelder and Piaget (1964) showed to children aged 5 to 7 pictures that included eight primulas and some other flowers. They then asked the children, "Are there more primulas or flowers?" In various experiments the question was phrased differently. Among the forms used was: "Which is the most, the primulas or all the flowers?" Many children under seven years old answered that there were more primulas. They seemed to construe the question as: Are there more primulas or flowers other than primulas? To that question the answers they gave were generally correct. That, however, was not the question they were asked, so Inhelder and Piaget counted their answers as wrong.

There is little difficulty in replicating the result; it has been done hundreds of times. The problem is with interpretation. Inhelder and Piaget believed that the children answered as they did because they could not coordinate subkinds with superkinds, because they could not understand that the members of the subkind, primulas, are at the same time flowers. Inhelder and Piaget felt confident of their interpretation because they had asked the children, in separate questions, whether the primulas were flowers and whether primulas were primulas. The children had answered correctly. The children's inadequacies were revealed, Inhelder and Piaget concluded, only when they were required to recognize that the primulas were at one and the same time both primulas and flowers. If this were correct, it would, of course, be evidence that young children have little or no understanding of the relation of inclusion and of the partition of classes into subclasses.

The data are, however, susceptible to another and much simpler interpretation. Ford (1976) constructed a series of tests in which both the content and the question form varied. There were three question forms:

1. Give me the Xs or Ys (for example, "Give me the cats or black things"—where some of the cats might be black).
2. Give me Xs or Ys or both (for example, "Give me blue things or dresses, or things that are both"—where some dresses might be blue).
3. Give me Xs or Ys but not both (for example, "Give me blue things or dresses but not things that are both").

The second and third question forms resolve a possible ambiguity in the first. On its own, *or* can be taken inclusively (things that are *X*, things that are *Y*, or things that are both *X* and *Y*) or exclusively (things that are *X*, things that are *Y*, but not things that are both *X* and *Y*).

Ford tested twenty five-year-olds, twenty seven-year-olds, twenty eight-year-olds, and twenty adults. The core of his findings was that all age groups tended equally to interpret *or* exclusively in response to questions of the first form. The only important age differences occurred when the objects formed overlapping groups (such as dogs and animals) and the question was of the second form ("Give me things that are blue or dresses or things that are both"). Questions of the second form explicitly overrule the tendency to take *or* exclusively. In general, older persons overcame that tendency in greater numbers than younger ones.

Back now to the primulas and flowers. Ford's results mean that there is a tendency to take *primulas or flowers* as meaning primulas or flowers other than primulas. They also reveal that when that tendency is countered by an explicit expression, as in *primulas or all the flowers*, more adults than young children heed the countering expression.

But does this mean that young children are incapable of considering primulas as both primulas and flowers? Inhelder and Piaget thought it did. Curiously, they turned their back on one of their own findings. They had included, besides the question forms noted, two others: (1) "If you take all the primulas, will there be any primulas left?" (2) "If you take all the flowers, will there be any primulas left?" (1964, p. 101). They reported (p. 104) that most of the young children who had given a "wrong" answer to the earlier questions gave the "right" answer to these. Notice the absence of *or* in (1) and (2). I venture to say that these results give the lie to Inhelder and Piaget's interpretation.

As a matter of fact, some linguists mark expressions such as "John is an American or a Californian" as ill formed, precisely because Californians are Americans (see Hurford 1974 and Gazdar 1979, p. 81). Just imagine that someone asked, "Are there more children or people in this bus?" You would naturally interpret the questioner as taking *people* to mean adults. You might, then, be indignant with the questioner. It would scarcely occur to you that he meant to include children among the people. Gazdar claims that two predicates can be correctly conjoined by *or* in English only if they are potentially exclusive of one another. Be that as it may, it seems that there is at least a strong tendency (a Gricean implicature, some would call it) to interpret *or* exclusively. It seems that young children have greater difficulty contravening it than adults. When, however, the children were unperturbed by the tendency, because the second form of question did not include *or*, they generally gave the correct answers, thus showing a command of the logic that Inhelder and Piaget thought to deny them. Their conclusion is discussed at greater length in Macnamara (1982, chap. 4).

Further Empirical Evidence
Although Inhelder and Piaget's neglected finding shows that children have a good grasp of the difference in number of members between a subkind and a superkind, the youngest children they tested were five-year-olds. We know that some two-year-olds have trouble answering similar questions because they refuse to allow that a dog, for example, is an animal. But, are young children who have overcome that peculiarly linguistic difficulty able to answer such questions as "Are all dogs animals?" and "Are all animals dogs?"

In a carefully planned study, Smith (1979) found that in favorable circumstances, when children were not fatigued or confused with a plethora of questions, some 80% of four-year-olds responded correctly to both types of question. She pointed out, in keeping with a remark of Inhelder and Piaget's (1964), that some of the errors could have been due to misinterpretation of the questions. For example, some children might have construed "Are all dogs animals?" as "Are all dogs all of the animals?"—a very different question. In fact, Bucci (1978) hypothesized that that is what young children are doing. Bucci suggested that young children impose a "structure neutral" interpretation on a sentence such as "All dogs are animals." The idea is that they read the sentence as being "All; dogs; animals" and simply guess at a relation among the expressions. If they did, the questions "Are all dogs animals?" and "Are all animals dogs?" might well appear synonymous to them. Donaldson and Lloyd (1974) and Donaldson and McGarrigle (1974) made a similar suggestion, but without the appeal to the structure-neutral construction. There is an excellent review of the literature in Braine and Rumain (1983). Notice, however, that the theories referred to all take it that the children know the meaning of *all*; they suggest that what the children are confused about is the semantic import of certain syntactic structures.

Bloom, di Meco, and Surkis in their various investigations put the two types of question that we are discussing to two-year-olds. They found that only one of their seventy-eight subjects, a child almost three years old, answered both questions correctly. They were, however, able to cite evidence that the children interpreted the questions as synonymous. They showed that the children knew and could name animals other than pigs (they asked about pigs and animals). Bloom (1984) cites a conversation with one child aged two years, eight months.

Bloom	Are all pigs animals?
Child:	Yes.
Bloom:	Are all animals pigs?
Child:	Yes.
Bloom:	Are you sure?
Child:	Yes . . . Piggies!
Bloom:	Well, do you know any kind of animals that aren't pigs?
Child:	Uh, doggies and, uh, horsies. Cats, too!
Bloom:	Good. Now listen carefully. Are all animals pigs?
Child:	Yes.

Freeman and Stedmon (unpublished) analyzed the whole range of problems that confront the child psychologist who wishes to test understanding of *all* and *some*. They showed that the children's difficulty is often to determine which set of individuals are intended in such an expression as *all the cars* in the question, "Are all the cars in garages?" Some children may interpret the question as "all the cars in the garages." Freeman and Stedmon argued that there is nothing the matter with children's understanding of *all*, though they may well not grasp the intended domain of a noun phrase in which it occurs. But this, as they aptly pointed out, is a failure in what McCarthy (1980) called "circumscription."

Despite appearances, then, it seems that most two-year-olds know that all dogs are animals and that not all animals are dogs—which means that they can coordinate the force of the quantifiers with simple problems of kind inclusion. Smith (1979) actually showed that most four-year-olds can draw quite difficult inferences of kind inclusion. She found that they can answer correctly such questions as "A yam is a kind of food, but not meat. Is a yam hamburger?" But I do not follow these later developments.

Learning All *and* Some

Surveyable Domains
Children surely learn the meanings of the English words *all* and *some* through their application to easily surveyable domains. A parent says, "All the cookies are gone," meaning the ones in the cookie jar, and the child can see what the parent means by looking inside. Again the parent says, "Pick up all your stuffed animals" and, if the child stops halfway, the parent says emphatically, "I said ALL your stuffed animals." Parents can teach *some* in a similar manner: "I said you could have SOME of the cookies, not ALL of them." (I take it that *some* in

English usually means not all.) The important clue in all this is that the children's perceptual system, working in collaboration with their appraisal of parental reaction to their behavior, guides them to the meaning of the quantifiers.

Nonsurveyable Domains
Clearly, easily surveyable domains are essential to this type of learning. But the quantifiers frequently hold sway over nonsurveyable domains. *All dogs* embraces not only an immense actual domain that is non-surveyable in practice but also all the dogs that ever were, ever will be, ever might have been, and ever might be in the future but actually will not be. Children must come to grasp this in some fashion, for it is precisely this that is in question when we ask them, "Are all dogs animals?" This is because there is a modal element built into sortals. Moreover, *all dogs are animals* means that it is the nature of dogs to be animals, that they are necessarily animals.

Putnam (1975) claimed that the inclusion of dogs in animals is an empirical generalization and not an analytic truth. In other words, he claimed that we cannot know its truth by examining the meaning of *dog* and *animal*. The account that I have worked out of how children learn basic-level and higher-order sortals fits in nicely with his claim. We have children individuate the kind dog through the expression *being in the same basic-level kind as Spot and Towser*. We have them individuate the kind animal through the expression *the smallest kind that includes creatures such as dogs, horses, cows. . . .* These expressions should be taken, not as constituting all or part of the meaning of those sortals, but as fixing their referents. It is clearly a contingent fact that there are dogs, Freddie and Towser; it is equally contingent that there exist dogs, horses, cows. . . . It follows that Freddie and Towser are not essential to the meaning of *dog* and that dogs, horses, cows . . . are not essential to the meaning of *animal*. It is not, then, analytic that dogs are animals, though it is a necessary truth that they are. It is a law that dogs are animals, but it is an empirical one. It is, then, grounded on empirical learning in whatever way the rest of our empirical laws are. I do not understand at all well the logic or the psychology of such conclusions, though it is different from the psychology that accompanies the establishing of nonempirical laws, in logic and mathematics, for example.

Expressing the Meaning of All *and* Some
From their understanding of the meaning of *all* and *some* in surveyable domains, learners have to extrapolate to nonsurveyable domains. How might learners be led to do so? Perhaps we can find a clue by examining

in more detail how they learn the meaning of *all* and *some* through the words' use in surveyable domains.

Let us begin by considering a small girl who is just on the point of learning the meaning of *all*, her first English quantifier. She has been instructed by her mother to put away all her stuffed animals. Let us suppose that she knows a basic-level sortal for each stuffed animal and that she is past the stage of denying that a pig is an animal. She puts away five of her seven stuffed animals, and she finds her mother is not yet satisfied: "I said to put away ALL your stuffed animals." It then dawns on her what *all* means. How can she express what it means?

Wittgenstein has shown that *and* cannot be used to replace *all* without loss, even in surveyable domains. We might be tempted to interpret *all the stuffed animals* to mean the teddy bear and the squirrel and . . . and the rabbit. But that is not enough unless we know that that is all the stuffed animals that are relevant. It follows that children cannot capture the meaning of *all your stuffed animals* solely by a long conjunction. They have to say "the teddy bear and the squirrel and . . . until none are left on the floor" or some such thing. But now *none* is the quantifier they need.

The children we are considering seem to have no English sortal at their command to express the meaning of the English word *all*. Yet it is logically inescapable that, if they are to learn the meaning of *all* through a learning-that event, they need the logical resources to express its meaning. These resources include an expression equivalent in meaning to *all* or expressions through which *all* can be defined, such as *not* and *any*. For the sake of definiteness, I settle arbitrarily for an expression synonymous with *all*. I conjecture that what children have is a quantifier—write it ∀—that combines with sortals to bind variables. A general schema that children could use to learn the meaning of *all* is

$$P(k) \text{ for all the } k \equiv (\forall K, k)P(k),$$

where K is to be replaced by a sortal, k is a variable ranging over individual members of K, and P is to be replaced by a predicate or sortal. Notice that the *all* on the left-hand side is replaced by ∀ on the right-hand side. *Some* can be defined by

$$P(k) \text{ for some of the } k \equiv \sim(\forall K, k) \sim P(k),$$

where, following logical tradition, the definition (on the right-hand side) says that not all the k are not P. This has children learning *some* on the basis of *all*. I could have just as easily had them learning *all* on the basis of *some*. In the absence of empirical data, the choice is arbitrary.

In keeping with lines already worked out, it seems natural to me to suppose that ∀ is an expression in the language of thought. Surveyable domains of this sort are surveyable by the eye, and if children acquire knowledge-that with respect to quantities through perception, as they clearly must, it follows that they must have symbols that carry that knowledge. In particular, they must have a symbol that represents the quantifier *all* or *some*. They need it in any case to represent the meaning of the English word *all* or *some*—whichever is first learned—when they learn its meaning by an act of learning-that. The reason for placing the symbol in the language of thought is that it must combine with other symbols in a single language. And because young children lack the resources to express its meaning in a natural language, I have opted for the language of thought as the appropriate one.

It does not take much probing to see that on this reasoning it follows that children must have and be able to employ with understanding at least one unlearned quantifier.

How does all this help children to extrapolate the force of the quantifiers from surveyable to nonsurveyable domains? My answer is that they do not need to extrapolate at all. They merely learn that *all* is synonymous with $\forall$; and because $\forall$ extends to an at least potentially infinite domain, so does *all*. This is nicely in line with the logic of sortals. Sortals combine with quantifiers, and many sortals place no limits on the number of members they can have. It is to be expected, then, that the quantifier *all* should of itself place no limit to the number of individuals that can fall under a sortal. The interpreter for $\forall$, therefore, should embody no presupposition with respect to limits on cardinality.

The problem that confronts the psychologist now is the complement of the one we began with: How is the range of a quantified expression on a particular occasion restricted to a surveyable number? That is a pragmatic matter, often guided by the presence of a particular expression, such as *your* in "Put away all your clothes" or *the* in "Straighten up all the books." This is a complicated task for children, as the studies of Freeman and Stedmon (unpublished) amply demonstrate. But I do not pursue the matter, as it would lead us far beyond the level at which we have fixed our sights.

9

Settling Accounts

I have been putting off a few issues whose time has now come. I can group them under two headings, learning and competence, the two central themes of this book. There is a sense in which logic can be learned and a sense in which it cannot. Now that we have studied a number of cases of learning, we are in a position to tackle more general questions about learning and logic. One particular issue is the claim that we should revise some of the fundamental principles of logic in view of findings in quantum mechanics. The claim entails the proposition that the true principles of logic include at least some that are empirical. If the claim were justified, it would follow that we have to learn some of the basic principles of logic. The issues here are both technical and delicate; they will demand our utmost attention.

Under the heading of competence are grouped three topics. The first is the consistency of the mind—are the mind's various reasoning capacities mutually consistent? If they were not, the ideal logic, which would be consistent, would not represent a competence theory for the inconsistent mind. The second topic is the well-established fact of systematic error in everyday thought. Its presence constitutes a seemingly plausible argument against the central doctrine of this book—that errorless logic supplies us with a competence theory for part of the psychology of reasoning. We must see if the threat is a real one. The third topic is modal logic. As things stand, there seem to be infinitely many distinct modal logics. They cannot all be realized separately in a finite mind, so their number presents a threat for the theory of logic as psychological competence. We must consider the problem and handle the threat that it incorporates.

General Remarks on Learning and Logic

The Rules of Inference
Lewis Carroll (1895) wrote a splendid fable showing the need in a reasoner for something more than a set of logical propositions. The

something more is obviously a set of devices that perform the operation of drawing an inference, for propositions on their own are inert. Such devices cannot be the immediate result of what I have been calling learning-that because such learning involves a proposition, an interpreted sentence in some language. It might appear at first glance that the devices in question cannot be learned. We will see, but first Lewis Carroll.

The fable takes the form of a discussion between Achilles and the Tortoise about the application of a Euclidean postulate to a particular case. The Euclidean postulate, modified in the interest of clarity, is

A.   Lines that are equal to the same are equal to each other.

The application that Achilles wished the Tortoise to make was in connection with the first proposition of Euclid's, the construction of an equilateral triangle:

B.   The two sides of this triangle are lines that are equal to the same.

On the strength of A and B, which the Tortoise accepted, Achilles urged it to accept the conclusion, which the Tortoise called Z:

Z.   The two sides of this triangle are equal to each other.

When the Tortoise inquired why, Achilles said that Z was implied by A and B. This claim the Tortoise set down as C:

C.   A and B imply Z.

The Tortoise now agreed to C and once again Achilles urged it to accept Z. Once again the Tortoise inquired why and was told that it ought to because it accepted A, B, and C, which together imply Z. This claim the Tortoise set down as D:

D.   A, B, and C imply Z.

The process, of course, can go on indefinitely without the Tortoise ever accepting Z.

The interest of the fable is precisely that the Tortoise does not do what everyone else would do, conclude Z immediately on hearing A and B. Instead of applying the inference rule of instantiation, the Tortoise asked why it should apply it. Achilles' answer is that A and B satisfy the conditions for instantiation. The Tortoise agreed, called that statement C, but still did not apply the rule. Instead the Tortoise asked once more why it should apply it. Notice that each time the Tortoise asks for a reason, the answer is different.

I am not sure what lesson Lewis Carroll wanted to teach; the lesson for us is that principles and rules on their own do not draw inferences. In addition to principles and rules there is a need for what Pylyshyn (1984, chap. 2) called "the functional architecture" of the mind, a set of devices that perform operations. Another way to put it is that the laws of logic are noncausal laws; they do not explain any event. The drawing of a conclusion is an event. It is the type of event that we call an *action*, that is, an event whose rationality can be revealed by an appeal to reasons. It is through reasons that logic enters. Reasons consist of beliefs and desires. In the fable the relevant beliefs are expressed in A and B; the relevant desire would have been to attain a new truth, Z. Those reasons make Z a rational conclusion, but they do not in the strict sense of the word cause the action of concluding Z. For a full discussion of the issues, see Macnamara et al. (unpublished).

So, in addition to the principles and inference rules of logic, we need the functional architecture of the mind or what I earlier called *implicators*. Is it possible to learn an implicator?

The answer is clearly yes, but it needs qualification. Take a woman learning French who is taught the rule that, apart from a few exceptions, in French the adjective comes after the noun. At first, perhaps led astray by her native English, she makes mistakes. Later, however, she does not advert to the rule when speaking French. The words come out in the right order. Her conscious efforts to apply the rule have given rise to an automatic procedure that produces the desired result, seemingly without reference to the rule. She has added to the functional architecture of her mind. Two remarks are in order. The student succeeded only because she understood the French rule including such expressions as *noun, adjective,* and *first.* Second, what justifies the French rule is either the authority of the teacher or the student's own observation of French sentences.

Turn now to logic. Let us suppose that nature does not supply us with the inference rule of modus tollens:

$$\frac{p \supset q, \; \sim q}{\sim p}.$$

An example: *If it is raining, the grass is wet; the grass is not wet. Therefore it is not raining.* We could acquire modus tollens by reflecting on the truth tables for $\sim$ and $\supset$ and then, by practicing inferences that exercise the rule, make it part of the functional architecture of our minds, make it an automatic implicator. Although we know little about *how* we do such things, there can be little doubt *that* we do them. But we cannot learn all logic that way because it involves learning-that. The first act of learning-that presupposes the logical resources to express and understand what we then learn. So there must be what I have been calling a *basic logic* that is unlearned. What that basic logic is is an empirical matter; logic itself does not decide among the possibilities.

To grasp the point more firmly, imagine a little boy who, per impossibile, has available to him the propositional calculus but who lacks the logical resources that must be added to it to yield the first-order predicate calculus. That would mean that he grasps the logical force of the sentential connectives *not, and, or,* etc., but he is blind to any logical structure within simple sentences. He could not, then, *learn* the predicate calculus. The reason is that, lacking the relevant logical resources, he could not formulate hypotheses about the predicate calculus and accept or reject them on the basis of evidence. He could not, for example, hypothesize about the logical roles of sortals (for example, *dog*) and quantifiers (for example, *all*), because to express the relevant hypotheses, he would need the notions of sortal and quantifier, and we have supposed that he lacks them.

If children learned modus tollens along the lines described, how would they know that it is a valid rule of inference, leading necessarily to true conclusions on the asumption that the premises are true? The psychologism debate convinced us that such knowledge is not an empirical generalization. The answer must be that the learners can demonstrate the validity of the rule by appealing to basic logic. But, then, the demonstration presupposes the logical resources to carry through and understand the demonstration. Once again, we are forced to acknowledge an unlearned basic logic.

Though all this means that the human mind is naturally logical, it does not mean that any logic whatever is available at birth. Nature, presumably, selects the stage at which birth occurs without any regard for the neonate's logical capacities. There is, then, no need to claim that logical capacity is innate. All that follows from the arguments just considered is that logic is natural in the sense of being unlearned.

To sum up, there is no reason to deny that substantial learning of logic is possible. The fact that logic's rules are implemented by the functional architecture of the mind does not preclude their being learned and realized in that architecture. What is precluded is the learning of all logic.

Quantum Logic

In what seems on the surface flat opposition to the foregoing remarks on learning, Putnam (1968) has written an important paper to the effect that some of classical logic's fundamental principles have to be revised, not for purely logical reasons but because of empirical findings in quantum physics. The claim touches us in two ways. It implies that the justification for some logical principles is empirical. And because the proposed revisions have surfaced only in the light of recent events in science, Putnam's position seems to entail the claim that some of basic logic has to be learned. The entailment is not perfectly clear. We might argue that we are merely coming to represent logical intuition better as a result of the empirical findings—that classical logic misrepresents basic logical competence. On the other hand, and with more justice, someone who accepts Putnam's position might claim that basic logical competence is flawed and that, almost miraculously, quantum physics is leading us to the true logic. There are other possibilities, too, such as that logic is not, as we always hoped, domain independent, that classical logic holds in the domain of everyday objects but not in the recondite subatomic domain. We, however, are mainly interested in the position that basic competence misrepresents the ideal logic, though what I have to say also has implications for the other positions.

Incidentally, one of Quine's (in 1961) most famous papers, "Two dogmas of empiricism," is in broad sympathy with Putnam's, because it claims that there is no logical or mathematical principle safe from the tribunal of empirical inquiry. Interestingly, Quine (1970) seemed to abandon that position later. Later still, in *Roots of reference* (1973), Quine assumed that the entire set of logical connectives is learned by children but that (if I understand him correctly) the connectives they learn are necessarily those of classical logic. Recently, a position close to Putnam's was proposed by Hughes (1981) in *Scientific American*, so it is widely known.

Quantum logic was developed, originally by Birkhoff and von Neumann (1936), to handle some strange results in quantum mechanics. It differs from classical logic in that it is nondistributive. That is, in quantum logic the following laws of classical logic do not hold:

$$p \mathbin{\&} (q \lor r) \equiv (p \mathbin{\&} q) \lor (p \mathbin{\&} r),$$
$$p \lor (q \mathbin{\&} r) \equiv (p \lor q) \mathbin{\&} (p \lor r).$$

What this means can best be brought out in an example. It is as though we know

John is tall AND he is honest OR he is handsome

but are not entitled to conclude that

John is tall AND he is honest OR he is tall AND he is handsome.

Let us see how this works in quantum physics. The findings that concern us relate to paired properties in the subatomic world. There are several examples, but one suffices. We know of any subatomic particle *a* that it has both position and momentum. Let us, following

Putnam, adopt a simplified model in which all possible positions are represented by statements $p_1, \ldots, p_k$ and all possible momenta by statements $m_1, \ldots, m_n$. We can then say that a particle has both position and momentum by $(p_1 \vee \ldots \vee p_k) \,\&\, (m_1 \vee \ldots \vee m_n)$. Quantum theory, however, denies that any pair consisting of a particular position statement and a particular momentum statement is true. That is, it denies that there is any $p_i \,\&\, m_j$ that is true.

This can be placed in a little better focus. Let us suppose that at time t_1 we measure a's position and find it to be p_i. We would then know that the following proposition is true:

$$p_i \,\&\, (m_1 \vee \ldots \vee m_n).$$

In other words, the particle has the measured position and *some* momentum. Yet we also know that it is false that it has that position and any particular momentum. In short, m_j is false at t_1 for any j, $1 \leqslant j \leqslant n$. This result is impossible in classical logic because, there, $\&$ is distributive over $\vee$. There is, however, no contradiction in this; we do not have both $(p \,\&\, m) \,\&\, \sim(p \,\&\, m)$ for some p and m. The sense of paradox arises because of a habitual tendency to interpret classically the symbols expressing the connectives. For Putnam's connectives, however, distributivity fails. In the jargon, his logic is not Boolean.

But we have a choice, as Bell and Hallett (1982) pointed out, between a strange world and a strange logic. If we situate the strangeness in the world, we can cling to our classical logic; if we situate it in the logic, we can cling to the familiar world. Putnam opted for the second alternative, offering two reasons in support. He claimed that because the modifications of logic that are required are only minor, we should not be uneasy about making them. His second reason is that with those minor modifications "every single anomaly vanishes" (Putnam 1979 [1968], p. 184).

Bell and Hallett have made a thorough study of Putnam's claim about the extent of the modification required in propositional logic. They compare Putnam's quantum logic and classical logic by relating both of them to a common structure, that of general ortholattices. Their study reveals, surprisingly, that the *and* and *or* of classical logic (which is a Boolean structure) can, with the aid of a few general and rather weak notions from set theory, be defined in terms of the ordering relation $\geqslant$ of an ortholattice. This implies that the meanings of *and* and *or* are preserved when they are translated from a Boolean distributive ortholattice to a general ortholattice. This is important because it tells us that we do not need to provide new meanings for *and* and *or* in quantum logic.

The story with *not* is radically different. The *not* of classical logic is definable in a general ortholattice by means of the partial-ordering relation ≤. The closest connective in general ortholattices to classical *not* is an orthocomplement. It is not definable in terms of ≤. It follows that classical *not* does not preserve its meaning when translated into a general ortholattice structure. Intuitively what happens is this: If p is a proposition in a general ortholattice and q is its orthocomplement ($p \perp q$), it follows that both p and q cannot hold. For example, if p means *the surface is red*, q could mean *the surface is green*. Both cannot hold. By contrast, the orthocomplement of *the surface is green* in classical logic is *the surface is not green*. This is a profound change in the meaning of *not*; it is not, as Putnam believed, a relatively trivial one. A change in the meaning of *not* entails a change in the meaning of *true*, and truth is the central notion in logic.

Matters are further complicated. Putnam claimed that we could hold on to classical logic in most domains and confine quantum logic to the subatomic world. But the role of classical logic cannot be so circumscribed, for the logic of the mathematics and of the physics that led to quantum theory is classical. Bell and Hallett pointed to a certain incoherence in this. They cite a mathematical result to the effect that, if the distribution of *and* over *or* is given up, then there can be no subsections of quantum physics that can be consistently interpreted in classical logic. Putnam's move, then, would seem to saw off the branch that he and the whole of quantum mechanics is sitting on. Incidentally, the fact that there is a need to hold on to classical *not* as well as on to the *not* of quantum logic marks this theory development as different from the normal one, in which an old conception is completely replaced by a new one. The replacement of conceptions is illustrated by the change in the conception of electron from Maxwell's day to current quantum physics. In this case there is (pace certain theoreticians) no need to consider that the *meaning* of the word "electron" has changed; it is enough to say that what has changed is how electrons are conceptualized. This move is not possible in the case of quantum logic's *not*, precisely because the old *not* cannot be given up. (This observation came up in a conversation with Bill Demopoulos, though he did not accept it.)

Let us now turn to Putnam's claim that empirical findings have forced a modification of classical logic—that logic is empirical. We now know what the modification in question is. It is the change from a Boolean orthocomplement operation to that of a general ortholattice, a change in the meaning of *not*. This does not, without more ado, entail that classical logic fails in the domain of quantum mechanics. Quantum findings merely show that measurements in a certain area do not satisfy the conditions on Boolean algebras. But classical logic does not require that they should. It is a purely empirical matter what the structure of a set of measurements is. The existence or nonexistence of certain tests has no immediate implications for logic.

What is perhaps more disturbing than the nonexistence of certain physical measurments is the claim that, in principle, not just in practice, there cannot be such measurements. Let us suppose that the claim is true, and let us suppose further that the reason for their nonexistence is not simply that methods of measurement disturb the phenomena they are meant to measure. Then we have to consider the admissibility of physical properties that are, in principle, unobservable. As Dummett (1978, pp. 288–289) pointed out in an intuitionist moment, we are at liberty to regard the notion of such properties as unintelligible. Although the claim that certain properties are, in principle, unobservable is an empirical one, the further claim that the notion of such properties is unintelligible is not empirical.

Dummett is inclined to believe that the case for replacing classical logic in any domain cannot be empirical. Although the decision may be occasioned by empirical findings, it must rest on general philosophical considerations. Dummett drew a parallel with intuitionism in mathematics. In intuitionism the decision to replace classical methods with intuitionistic ones does not rest on any mathematical results but rather on general philosophical views about the nature of mathematical knowledge and specifically about the intelligibility of the notion of a mathematical proposition's being determinedly true or false, independent of mankind's ability to discover which. Thus Dummett's position has the effect of making logic essentially independent of empirical findings. At the same time, Dummett's remark removes the obligation of modifying my thesis that the fundamental principles of logic are unlearned, for if logic need not answer to empirical findings, there is scarcely any room for an argument that basic logical principles are learned.

The parallel with intuitionism in mathematics, although illuminating, is not exact. It is tempting to adapt intuitionistic logic to the purposes of quantum physics by replacing the provability of intuitionistic mathematics with some such notion as testability. Intuitionistic mathematics, however, employs classical logic in the domain of finite mathematics, moving to intuitionistic logic only in the transfinite domain. We have seen that if the distribution of & over ∨ is given up, then there can be no subsections of quantum physics that can be consistently interpreted in classical logic.

I conclude this section with some general remarks about the possibility of revising logic. If Dummett's assessment of the case is right and if we nevertheless decide to replace classical logic altogether, it looks as if the decision would imply that classical logic has been wrong all along. It seems to imply that deeper reflection on the nature of human knowledge and on logical intuition reveals inadequacies in classical logic—that in the interests of logical intuition classical logic has to be replaced.

Suppose, however, that Dummett is wrong; suppose that the sheer pressure of empirical findings on their own is enough to advise the adoption of a nonclassical logic. Let us suppose, further, that classical logic perfectly matches logical intuition. In that case it would seem that logical intuition has been wrong all along. Note, however, that the revision would still be motivated by what is intuitively a greater logical good. It would be in the direction of establishing a larger consistency that embraces both logical intuition (modified) and empirical findings. In other words, the revision would presuppose an ordering of logical intuitions, some being ranked more fundamental than others. The revision would recognize this, sacrificing some logical intuitions in order to protect more fundamental ones. Moreover, any revision presupposes the ability to make the revision. To borrow from the computer world, if we were to revise our logic, we could do so only because we have a program for effecting such a revision on the occasion of a certain experience. If the revision were to satisfy intuition, it would seem highly likely that the ordering of logical intuitions is itself unlearned and that the program for effecting the revision is also unlearned. This observation assumes that the supposed revision would be widely acceptable to minds well enough versed in the science that yields the relevant empirical findings to reach an informed and intelligent judgment. I admit that there is much that is speculative in this. What is not speculative is that any revision of mental structures must call on unlearned structures.

The main point that emerges from the study of Putnam's paper is that the revision of logic that he called for is not necessary; in fact, it would be intellectually disastrous. Besides, there might be grounds for abandoning classical logic, but they would not be empirical. And if we were to abandon classical logic, we would do so in the belief that classical logic has been wrong all along, that it has not faithfully reflected logical intuition. More generally, however, I doubt that quantum mechanics can have any implications at all for logic. Logic seems adapted to a world in which there are distinct individuals. It is just the existence of such individuals that is troublesome in the subatomic world. Because that really has no consequence for the conceptualization of individuals in the ordinary domain of thought, it really has no consequence for the logic that is appropriate to that domain.

Clearing Competence

The Consistency of the Mind as a Whole

The claim that the ideal logic states a competence theory for the psychology of human reasoning makes one large assumption: that the ideal logic is consistent and does not allow valid inferences to any sentence p and its negation, $\sim p$. What if the mind were not a logically consistent system? Then the ideal logic, being consistent, would not supply a competence theory for an inconsistent mind. I have frequently heard psychologists say, airily, that the mind is not consistent, and they point to well-known empirical evidence that the layman's reasoning is frequently fallacious. I deal with the empirical evidence presently, but first I must discuss the theoretical issue.

Perhaps the main reason for taking the mind to be consistent is the age-old observation that an inconsistent system can prove any proposition whatsoever. This strikes people as implausible when they first encounter it, but the reasoning on which it rests is simple, as we saw earlier. Thus, if the mind formed a single logical system and if it were inconsistent, it would be a logical mess.

Recently, some writers have noted that if the mind had subsystems that were isolated from one another, it would not necessarily be a logical mess, even if some subsystems were inconsistent with one another. True, but because such inconsistency has never been demonstrated, the thought of it is merely a mental specter. Why worry about something that might turn out to be the case before it is known to be the case? At the same time, Gödel's (1967 [1931]) famous result shows us that we can never prove the consistency of the mind as a whole. Admittedly, paradox surfaced in set theory from axioms that appeared at their proposal as innocuous as mother's milk. On the other hand, we ought not allow paradox to scare us. Paradox shows that there is something the matter with the formulation of an intuition, not that there is anything the matter with the intuition itself. In fact, the paradoxes of set theory have been removed in a variety of ways, and most mathematicians are now confident that there is nothing seriously amiss with a number of axiomatic foundations.

For all that, the topic deserves brief discussion to see what the implications of inconsistency would be for the overall thesis of this book. The short answer is, not very serious, or at least no more serious than they would be for logic as a whole. At worst, we would be compelled to posit several distinct logical competences, one for each isolated module of logic.

Now the idea of logical modules is distinctly odd. Logic is rather different from geometry. Geometrical intuition requires a number of distinct geometries that give rise to theorems that are mutually inconsistent when viewed across geometries. A famous example is that in Euclidean geometry the internal angles of a triangle sum to 180°, whereas in spherical geometry they sum to more than 180°. The theorems of a geometry depend on the axioms that establish the geometry. Different sets of axioms generate different theorems, hence the inconsistency. The situation in logic seems rather different. We normally see sublogics, such as the propositional logic or the first-order predicate logic, as part of a single vast system. We see the first-order predicate logic as embracing the propositional logic, modal logics as embracing the predicate logic, and so on. The multiplicity of logics is quite unlike the multiplicity of geometries. If that is right, the multiplicity cannot give rise to overall inconsistency.

Rescher (1979, chap. 11) has written about the possibility of inconsistency in science. The sort of example he has in mind is when two branches of science are pursued in isolation from one another. Unknown to the scholars who work in the two areas, inconsistency can arise. Of course, if the inconsistency were discovered, an effort would be made to eradicate it. The effort need not always prove successful, at least in the short run, and even in the fairly long run. This proved to be true as regards the wave and particle descriptions of light. Both descriptions date from Newton's time. The problem, though, is more one of incompatibility than of inconsistency. Even more germane to the topic of this book is the possibility that cognitive and physiological psychology, if they really are describing the same reality from different points of view, should generate mutually inconsistent descriptions. The inconsistency would not be discovered unless it were possible to reduce cognitive to physiological psychology. We can afford to lay that problem aside until the reduction in question is a reality, if it ever is. Even then, the natural reaction would be to eliminate the inconsistency by modifying one or both of the theories related by reduction.

What Rescher has in mind are mutually inconsistent findings of science. That is not my concern here because I am interested in mutually inconsistent logics. In logic, the prospect of inconsistencies seems altogether more remote. And because none has ever been discovered, I dismiss the possibility as unworthy of serious attention. Paradox has never been lacking. But paradox is the springboard for new logical discovery, never a total block.

Empirical Demonstrations of Illogicality
The fact that people make logical errors is hardly at issue. The findings on errors in syllogistic reasoning are well summarized and, indeed, well explained in Johnson-Laird (1983, chaps. 3–6). I have already

commented on Johnson-Laird's rejection of "mental logic" as a result of the findings (see the appendix to chapter 2). Here I would like to make a few remarks about an even better-known set of results collected by a group of researchers on judgments made in uncertainty. Best known in the field are Daniel Kahneman and Amos Tversky.

A typical test in the Kahneman and Tversky work is this. A subject is told to imagine that he is a participant in a TV quiz show and that his answers thus far have won him $100. The quizmaster now offers the participant a choice: (1) take the $100 and quit, or (2) win $500 for a correct answer to the next question but forfeit all, including the $100, if he fails. The participant is told that, of the earlier questions, he has answered one in three correctly. What should the participant choose? Decision theory shows how to estimate the utility of each alternative: that of (1) is $100/1 = \$100$; that of (2) is $500/3 = \$166.67$. Because the utility of the second is greater, decision theory endorses the second choice. Most of Kahneman and Tversky's subjects choose the safe $100. In fact, Kahneman and Tversky have worked out a number of psychological utility functions and have shown their departure from the ideal or mathematical function. It might thus seem plausible that the mathematics of decision do not supply a competence theory for the psychology of decision.

But the mathematics is a simplification and idealization of real situations. The mathematics does not apply, if the participant's life depends on having $100 and if he has no pressing need for an additional $400. It does not apply if the participant is so frightened or bored by being on the quiz show that he would be prepared to pay $67 to be out of it. It applies only within narrowly defined circumstances. Perhaps the tendency of subjects to choose differently from the mathematicians is due in part, though not altogether, to a failure to grasp the mathematical presuppositions or to keep from crowding in considerations that mathematicians studiously block off.

There is, however, much more to be said about the interpretation of Kahneman and Tversky's data. Suppose that instead of testing naive subjects, they tested mathematicians who had studied decision theory. Would not the results be different? Suppose, too, that before taking part in the experiments, subjects were required to read a couple of Kahneman and Tversky's papers. Would the results not be different? Of course they would be, but why? Presumably, because the subjects would then have satisfied themselves that the mathematics of decision theorists reflects intuition better than untutored impulse. But that is precisely to claim that the mathematics is a competence theory, that it does reflect carefully sifted intuition. (For present purposes, I assume that Kahneman and Tversky are applying the appropriate mathematics, though the matter is disputed by Cohen (1981).) Kahneman and Tversky (1982) go some distance toward recognizing all this:

> It is important to emphasize . . . that the [psychological] value function is merely a convenient summary of a common pattern of choices and not a universal law.

Kahneman and Tversky have also gone some distance toward explaining erroneous decisions. Take, for example, the common gambler's fallacy, as manifested by betting on tosses of a coin. A particular case of the fallacy is that it is an advantage to bet heads after a run of tails. Kahneman and Tversky (1973) suggested that the fallacy can be explained if we suppose that the gambler knows that long runs of tails are unlikely but fails to take account of the fact that a coin has no memory. The naive gambler, then, is acting on a belief, in this case a true one, that makes his action intelligible. The irrationality lies in the failure to take account of other relevant facts. Notice, though, that the belief that rationalizes the naive gambler's decision is itself a mathematical one—the probability of a particular outcome is the ratio of the number of event types favorable for an outcome to the number of all relevant event types. Though the gambler may not have quantified things so precisely, the mathematical law does make the intuition precise.

Nevertheless, Tversky and Kahneman (1983) do seem to reject the idea that a mathematical ideal can be a psychologically useful competence theory:

> Indeed, the evidence does not seem to support a "truth plus error" model, which assumes a coherent system of beliefs that is perturbed by various sources of distortion and error. Hence we do not share Dennis Lindley's optimistic opinion that "inside every incoherent person there is a coherent one trying to get out," and we suspect that incoherence is more than skin deep. (p. 313)

This brings us back to the specter discussed in the last section, so I do not repeat here the remarks made there. Instead I would like to comment on what seems to be one of the main grounds for the judgment just cited. It is that "in cognition, as in perception, the same mechanisms produce both valid and invalid judgments" (Tversky and Kahneman 1983, p. 313).

Apart from any scruples we may have about the use of the word "mechanisms" in this connection, there is something unsatisfactory about the last statement. Tversky and Kahneman are drawing a parallel with visual illusions and they observe, correctly, that visual illusions are the product of a perfectly running visual system. But the analogy is in many ways misleading. Just imagine for a moment that what vision delivers in the first instance is a set of uninterpreted, well-formed formulas in a language, a position I am inclined to adopt because of certain findings in visual perception (see Niall (unpublished)). If that position is correct, the parallel Tversky and Kahneman seek to establish cannot be constructed. The reason is that the output of an inference in everyday reasoning is an interpreted sentence. There is nothing wrong with the bent appearance of a straight stick partly submerged in water; it is the interpreted sentence, "The stick is bent," that is unsatisfactory. There is something deeply wrong with the gambler's conclusion that, because runs of tails are rare, the probability of a head increases after such a run.

How does this difference make a difference? Well, it would be odd if the same set of implicators (in my language), properly applied (as Tversky and Kahneman allow), yielded both valid and invalid inferences. Something is needed to explain the variation. To begin, note that the same set of basic implicators must be available to Kahneman and Tversky on the one hand and to their subjects on the other. How, then, could Kahneman and Tversky use such untrustworthy devices to attain such certain results as the mathematics against which they interpret their subjects' responses? Any answer I might offer is going to be far more uncertain than the mathematics in question. But the existence of that mathematics and of Kahneman and Tversky's access to it undermines their rejection of the mathematics as the appropriate competence theory.

In the light of that general stance I can offer one conjecture. In the first place, there are many implicators, and people seem to be able to add to the set that nature has endowed them with. That was the lesson of an earlier discussion in this chapter. It could be that an individual or group of individuals could add a faulty implicator, as the gambler's fallacy suggests. It could be that the implicators involved in decision under uncertainty are remote from the basic ones and require a long train of intermediate inferences in justification of their validity. My conjecture is that the basic set with which we start out comprises only valid implicators and that their operation is infallible in clear cases. It is surely this that enables mathematicians to overcome the impulses they share with the naive gambler—start out from clear and compelling intuitions and build up the system called decision theory. Mathematicians must find sure footing somewhere; I suggest that it is in the basic implicators. This is not to say that the output of the basic implicators is imposed on the mind, that judgment is forced by them. Rather, the idea is that their output is inevitably presented to the mind whenever the conditions for their operation are satisfied. Judgment seems to be another matter.

This all leads to the conclusion that we have seen no good grounds, theoretical or empirical, to reject the thesis that (ideal) logic supplies a competence theory for the psychology of human reasoning.

Modal Logic

Modal logic is the logic of the one-place sentential connectives *necessary* and *possible*, written □ and ◊, respectively. For example: *It is necessary that the whole be greater than the part; It is possible for a person to die by drowning.* Modal logic depends on intuitions that besides the actual there is the possible. Ronald Reagan is the actual president of the United States. Yet in some intuitively appealing sense, it is true that he might not be. Someone else might have been elected president, or Ronald Reagan might have ceased by this time to be president. We also have strong intuitions that the laws of physics place limits on the possible. And we have even stronger intuitions that mathematical truths are necessarily true. It is not possible, for example, that $2 + 2 = 5$ when the symbols have the meaning they bear in arithmetic.

We have already devoted a good deal of attention to necessity. The notion played a central role in the review of the psychologism debate and in building up the thesis about logic as psychological competence. In the discussion of proper names as rigid designators we again encountered it. The idea of a name as rigid designator involves necessity, for a rigid designator is one that cannot fail to pick out the same individual in all *possible* circumstances in which the individual exists. Again, in the chapters on predicate logic we considered the role of sortals in supplying principles of identity for the objects that fall under them. A principle of identity is one that traces an individual through *possible* circumstances and through time. But so far I have not made modal logic the object of focal investigation. Hitherto, modality came in as we were studying something else. Here we must examine it, because on the face of things it presents an embarrassment for the overall position I have been building.

The difficulty is the plethora of distinct modal logics that have been presented. I have spoken throughout of *the* ideal one or ones. Is there any sense of rivalry in the field—any sense that one system should triumph over the others, even if today it is impossible to pick the winner? There does not appear to be that type of tension. It would not embarrass my overall position if it turned out that there is not one ideal logic but two or three. In modal logic, however, the systems are already legion, and there is little reason to believe that we have seen the end of births in the area. Common sense alone rules out the idea that there are as many distinct psychological competences as there are modal logics.

One possible response is, with Quine, to repudiate the lot. Although it might appeal to a number of logicians, it does not appeal to me. Unlike Quine, I believe that modal logic is here to stay, and for good reason. Difficulties in laying its foundations are not grounds for refusing to build at all. The notion of possibility is deeply entrenched in our cognitive life and deserves to have its logic developed. At least so it appears to me, so I cannot take the way out of the problem that Quine offers.

Slightly more sympathetic is the response of several logicians whom I have consulted. They regard modal intuitions as vague and guttering. That is the reason they give for the proliferation of modal logics. This does not preclude the possibility of tidying things up. Certainly, in its modern growth modal logic is younger than the propositional calculus and the predicate calculus. We might reasonably argue that the subject has not settled down yet. We might then hope that the multiplicity would in time be reduced to some manageable and intuitively motivated number. But if we are to adopt that position, we should have some inkling that such an eventuality is desirable and within the bounds of reasonable possibility. We must, then, look more closely at modal logics, see how new ones arise, and ask whether some sense cannot be made of the multiplicity.

Before doing so, however, we should be clear how the opinion just recorded bears on the problem. The opinion is that modal logics are groping to express vague intuitions. If those intuitions are irremediably vague, the multiplicity of systems need not bother us, for my overall position is that the ideal logic expresses the ideal competence theory for human reasoning. It is understood that a logic is ideal when it answers perfectly to intuition working at its best. To say that modal intuitions are vague and cannot be brought into focus means that the logic that attempts to handle those intuitions cannot be ideal. The upshot is, on this account of the matter, that my overall position is not threatened by the actual multiplicity of modal logics, for I do not feel obliged to posit a competence corresponding to each. Rather, I should say that modal logics are all groping to express a single logical structure or some small number of such structures.

The multiplicity arises in the first instance in the choice of axioms that deal with the introduction and elimination of the modal operators. Another source, this time not among systems but among modal logics, is occasioned by the semantics. The semantics of modal logics is expressed in terms of possible worlds. The metaphysical status of such worlds need not detain us. We should regard talk of possible worlds as expressing an ordinary intuition. Among possible worlds is the world we actually inhabit, with all the individuals in it and their actual properties. We all have the intuition that some of the actual individuals might not exist, and there might be individuals other than the actual ones; we have similar intuitions about properties. A possible world, distinct from the actual world, is simply a set of circumstances in which the individuals or their properties (or both together) are different from those of the actual world. The third source of diversity is in the models envisaged for modal logics. The main source of diversity here is in the accessibility relations among worlds.

The idea can best be introduced informally by means of an example. Because there are motorcars in the actual world, it is possible for any actual person to die in a motorcar accident. There are nonactual but possible worlds in which some person actually alive and well dies in a motorcar accident. Intuitively, a possible world in which the person dies is accessible to the actual world, and the actual world is accessible to it. It is not, however, physically possible for the person to die in a motorcar accident in a possible world that has no motorcars. We might, then, want to restrict the set of physically possible worlds that are relevant to the evaluation of the proposition "it is possible for x to die in a motorcar accident" to those in which there are motorcars. We do this by specifying the worlds that are accessible to the actual world for that purpose. Of course, we can allow worlds to be accessible to possible worlds that are not accessible to the actual world. Because we can envisage infinitely many possible worlds and because we are free to specify the accessibility relations among them in any way we please, it follows that there are infinitely many models for modal logics.

In this I am thinking of what are called *standard models*. A standard model is a triple $\langle W, R, P \rangle$, where W is a set of possible worlds, R is a relation (of accessibility) among possible worlds, and P is a set of propositions. Interest attaches mainly to the matter of which modal propositions are true in which possible worlds as a function of the accessibility relations among the worlds.

A final source of diversity, also semantic, is the interpretation of *necessary* and *possible*. We have already distinguished the necessity of logical laws from that of physical laws. Truths that are logically necessary do not have empirical content, whereas those that are physically necessary do, and their truth depends on nature's remaining as it is. Another sort of necessity is closely related to physical necessity; it is the necessity that we normally call *determined*. For example, it is determined that each person now alive will die; for each, death is inevitable. Yet another sort of necessity is moral in its source. For example, it is necessary, in the sense of obligation, for each person not in dire want to avoid theft.

Finally, it is necessary, in the sense of legal obligation, for those who earn incomes above a certain figure to pay income tax.

The only suggestion I have for making sense of the proliferation of modal logics is one I derive from Lemmon (1959), though only in the general idea, not in the details. The idea is that the different axiom schemata and accessibility relations are appropriate for different interpretations of the modal connectives.

In the domains of logic and mathematics, all the axiom schemata are appropriate, though most are otiose. In those domains, too, the accessibility relation among possible worlds is the universal one; that is, any possible world is accessible to any other possible world. For example, $2 + 2 = 4$ is true in all possible worlds. We can therefore say that $\Box(2 + 2 = 4)$ in just that absolute sense. There is no problem either in introducing the $\Box$ connective. If we obtain some result in mathematics we are entitled to introduce the $\Box$ connective, though it does not normally add anything to the result.

Obviously, if the distinction between the necessity of physical and mathematical laws holds, the necessity of physical laws must be circumscribed. The laws must be made relative to some statement, which is difficult to put satisfactorily, to the general effect that the laws hold so long as nature remains the same. For example, it is a law of physics that the speed of light is a constant. This means that, in all the possible worlds that a physicist need consider, the speed of light is the same. The qualification, however, recognizes the intuition that there seems to be something arbitrary about the actual speed of light. It is possible to conceive of the universe's having a different speed of light. We might then want to restrict possible worlds to a set that is accessible to our actual world and within that set say that, if the actual speed of light is c, then it is necessarily c. We might, however, envisage possible worlds not directly accessible to us but accessible to some distant worlds in which the speed of light is still c; in those worlds, which are inaccessible to us directly, the speed of light might be different from c. That is, technically we might wish to reject the axiom schema $\Box A \rightarrow \Box \Box A$.

Even more obviously, we need to circumscribe moral obligation because circumstances make a difference to their applicability. This means placing restrictions on the accessibility relations among worlds, restrictions to those worlds in which circumstances are not relevantly different. A moral interpretation of $\Box$ also makes certain axiom schemata inapplicable. One of the most basic modal intuitions is that what is necessarily true is simply true: $\Box p \supset p$. This fails if $\Box$ is given a moral interpretation. Most people agree to this: "The President is obliged to tell the truth" ($\Box p$). No one, however, would conclude therefrom: "The President tells the truth" (p).

The point of all this is to give a glimpse of how modal logic might be made to serve intuition. I think it is reasonable to hold either that modal intuition is ineradicably vague, in which case we can rule out the possibility of an ideal modal logic, or that modal intuitions can restrain modal logics in some such manner as we have been adumbrating. If the latter holds, then there is nothing even remotely embarrassing about positing a psychological competence theory corresponding to each intuitively motivated modal logic. It follows that modal logic is no obstacle to the general thesis of this book.

10

Laws in Cognitive Science

It would not do to conclude with the settling of accounts that we have just been through in chapter 9. The work there was mainly negative, defending the thesis against attack from a variety of directions. In this last brief chapter we revisit the themes of chapter 2, in which the thesis was developed in a general way. Now that we have worked through a number of particular issues having to do with the logic of certain sentential constituents, we inquire about the sort of science that is possible in the area of cognition. The theme has been that cognition cannot be studied fruitfully without recourse to logic. We have seen what that means for particular questions in cognition. Now, in the light of these particular studies, we can ask more generally: What sort of laws can we reasonably hope to find in cognitive psychology?

Noncausal Laws

In the preceding studies we were led to posit a number of abstract unlearned predicates and sortals (for example, *member, kind, identical,* and *true*) and a number of unlearned sentential connectives (for example, *not, and,* and *or*). If I am right, it follows that it is a natural property of the human mind to have these logical resources available to it. Because logical resources are natural to the mind, there is a law lurking in the background. But it is a noncausal law, in the sense that the consequent of the law is not an event but a property or disposition. To illustrate, containing oxygen is a natural property of water. The fact that a substance is water, though, does not cause it to contain oxygen. Nor is containing oxygen an event. The law is not a causal one. Similarly, the mind's naturally containing certain logical resources is not an event but a property of the mind. And the law that a human mind contains those resources is a noncausal law. Cummins (1983, chap. 1) would call such laws nomic attributions.

I attached the unlearned logical resources to procedurelike devices, interpreters and implicators, that invoke the resources whenever certain

conditions are satisfied. This means that, in the unlearned logical resources together with interpreters and implicators, we are dealing with
natural dispositions of the mind. Such dispositions play an essential
part in science, but the idea can be illustrated with material familiar
in everyday experience and understanding. Glass is brittle. It is a dis-
positional property of glass that it shatters when struck hard with a
large solid object, such as a stone or a hammer. Here again lurks a
law, a noncausal one. Being brittle is not an event, and an object's
being glass does not cause it to be brittle. Similarly, having the dispositions that I labeled interpreters and implicators is not an event;
nor does being a mind cause the possession of these dispositions. It
follows that the laws stating that human minds have these dispositions
are noncausal. More nomic attributions.

My work, then, points to the prospect of a number of fundamental
noncausal laws in cognition—all having to do with unlearned logical
resources and dispositions. It should be noted that it was not necessary
to posit any unlearned beliefs. If none are necessary, then there is no
nomic attribution of beliefs.

There are, of course, noncausal laws relating to logic, such as the
principle of noncontradiction. There is a temptation to include these
noncausal laws among the laws of cognitive psychology. But it should
be resisted, at the peril of lapsing into psychologism. Claiming that
these laws are part of cognitive psychology is, in fact, the essence of
psychologism. In avoiding unlearned beliefs, I have saved us from part
of the temptation, for if we do not posit any unlearned beliefs, we are
not tempted to turn logic's basic principles into psychological properties.

In this connection, the claim that there are unlearned logical resources
should not be construed as psychologistic. I did not say that the notions
of membership and identity, for example, are peculiarly psychological
notions. They are notions that are required equally in all disciplines,
including logic. All that I have claimed is that it is natural to human
minds to have expressions that refer to these concepts. The unlearned
possession of these expressions is an important psychological fact (if
it is a fact); the referents of these expressions are not psychological
objects.

Causal Laws

Davidson (1980, essays 12, 13) has argued that there can be no psychophysical laws. He makes the claim as part of a thesis that there can
be no laws covering actions. Because my thesis implies that there are
psychophysical laws, we should consider Davidson's arguments briefly.

First a clarification about what *psychophysical* means in this discussion. It does not mean what psychology has meant for a hundred years by the word. Psychology has been seeking laws that relate physical stimuli to perceptual states. An example is the Weber-Fechner "law" that relates intensity of lighting to the least increase in intensity that is perceptible. The relata are a physical stimulus and an automatic perceptual response. There is no need for the response to involve interpreted symbols. At a later stage in the process subjects may judge that the light has increased in intensity, and if they do, they will need interpreted symbols to express their judgment. At any rate, Davidson does not seem to be talking about the sort of causal laws that psychology has been talking about. Davidson means laws that connect physical objects or states with intentional objects or states. *Intentional* in this context means essentially involving interpreted symbols. The word is not to be confined to states that involve a purpose.

Because Davidson's claim about the nonexistence of psychophysical laws is made in the context of the claim that there are no laws covering actions, we must first consider his arguments for the latter claim briefly. The reasoning is obscure but, I believe, correct as far as it goes. The sort of law that would cover an action is one that would state a necessary connection between a reason, consisting of a set of beliefs and desires, and an action. As I understand him, Davidson argues that the *only* way to make necessary the connection between a reason and an action is to make the connection analytic. The idea is this: People have many beliefs and many desires, but most of them are never acted on. It follows that the mere possession of a belief and a desire is not enough to necessitate action. To do that, the belief must be held with sufficient conviction and the desire must defeat all competing desires. Imagine a person who desires to see a good movie and has the belief that *1984* is the best movie showing. Suppose that money and transport are no problem. Will the individual go to see the movie? That depends on how firmly the person holds the belief and on whether the desire to see *1984* is stronger than the desire to read, watch TV, oblige friends, while away the time in idleness, and so on. More briefly, going to see the movie depends on holding the belief with *sufficient* conviction and having an *overriding* desire to see the movie. So stated, the claim is no longer empirical but analytic. It is logically impossible for a person to hold a belief with sufficient conviction and to have an overriding desire and yet not act. If no action ensued, we would be forced to say that the person did not have sufficient conviction or that his desire was not overriding or both. There is no more need for empirical studies in the matter than there is for determining whether all bachelors are unmarried. For a fuller discussion, see Macnamara et al. (unpublished).

Davidson, for reasons that need not detain us, rejected the idea that intentional states can be reduced to physiological ones. The important point for us is that, if we were to attempt a reduction of beliefs and desires to physiologically described states, we would succeed in giving the antecedent of the law of action if we somehow reduced the modifiers on the state descriptors as well as the state descriptors themselves. To return to the example, we would have to reduce *sufficient* and *overriding* as well as *belief* and *desire*. But this would rob the new form of the action law of empirical content. It is logically impossible to achieve an adequate reduction of *sufficient belief* and *overriding desire*, which do not issue in action, where the action is possible. Davidson concluded, albeit not so summarily, that there can be no psychophysical causal laws to cover actions.

Notice that in the preceding chapters I never suggested that there are any causal laws to cover actions. The sort of psychophysical laws I envisage relate to the operation of interpreters. Their function is two-fold: a syntactic function, when certain conditions are satisfied, to yield an expression, and a semantic one, to place a person in intentional contact with the interpretation of the expression. It is the semantic part that gives rise to the psychophysical laws.

For example, I assigned to an interpreter the task of bringing into play unlearned logical resources and producing the string

$$That \in dog \; [kind] \; = \; Spot.$$

when the conditions are satisfied for learning the proper name *Spot* for a particular dog. The interpreter must also interpret the string and establish the intentional state of understanding it. Because the interpreter is seen as functioning automatically and because the conditions for its operation are to be described in nonintentional language, we have here a purported psychophysical law.

These causal laws, however, do not cover any action such as a judgment. Undoubtedly, the child who learned Spot's name judged that Spot was the creature in question. He had good reason to make that judgment, namely, his mother uttered *Spot* repeatedly in the presence of the dog and she had not uttered it before the dog's appearance. But such a judgment is not the output of Interpreter-PN.

So far as I can see, nothing in my claims places me in opposition to Davidson's main program.

This holds even with respect to the operation of the implicators. They are intentional in their input and in their output; they take interpreted sentences as input and yield interpreted sentences as output. For example, the implicator that applies modus ponens can be represented schematically as taking p and $p \supset q$ as input and yielding q as output. There is no requirement that p and $p \supset q$ be judged true. In fact, an appreciation that together they imply q might be taken as sufficient grounds for rejecting the truth of both p and $p \supset q$. As I envisage them, the implicators function automatically. If I am right, there are laws connecting intentional states with intentional states. But once again, this is not evidence for laws covering actions.

The laws in question are perhaps slightly peculiar in that the operation of the implicators may well have to be subject to voluntary control. For example, suppose that we have an implicator that applies *and*-introduction. It could be represented schematically as taking p and (separately) q as input and yielding p & q as output. But after operation the conditions are again met for *and*-introduction, yielding p & $(p$ & $q)$, p & $(p$ & $(p$ & $q))$, and so on uselessly ad infinitum. If we follow this line, we seem compelled to subject the functioning of an implicator to voluntary control so as to cut off its idle functioning. In that case the law would state that the implicator would function unless it was blocked from doing so by an act of volition. Alternatively, we might decide that the fact just noted about the output meeting the input conditions rules out the thesis that there is an implicator that applies the rule of *and*-introduction. In that way we would be able to avoid adding unusual ceteris paribus clauses about voluntary control. Notice that the rule of modus ponens does not yield an output that can serve as input to itself. Perhaps this consideration should weigh on the side of there being an implicator to apply modus ponens.

It is not, however, my purpose to lay out a set of criteria by which the existence or nonexistence of any proposed implicator can be decided. It is, rather, to draw attention to a type of law that can be hoped for in cognitive psychology, if the thesis of this book turns out to be right. All in all it appears that the thesis permits plenty of laws, both causal and noncausal.

Concluding Remarks

I have now completed the presentation of the thesis that logic supplies a competence theory for the psychology of human reasoning. The theory did not lead us to propose any foundations for logic. I am not sure that logic needs such foundations. Instead, the theory led to a psychological theory that casts some light, I hope, on how we *grasp* logical truths, not on how we know them to be *true*. I argued that the logical aspect of psychological competence resides in certain procedurelike devices, interpreters and implicators, that among other things invoke unlearned expressions in perceptual languages. I should note that we were not compelled to endow the child's mind with any unlearned beliefs or knowledge, only with unlearned logical resources.

I see this work as distinctly optimistic. Cognitive psychologists are often depressed when they consider the complexity of the human mind, and they feel that they have made but little progress in unraveling its secrets. I do not for a moment underestimate the difficulty of the task, but I do think that progress is greater than many psychologists realize. One of the intellectual glories of the past hundred years has been the rebirth and vigorous growth of logic. This means that we have available to us extensive and enriching studies in the competence whose psychology most concerns us. Wilhelm Wundt, who was so interested in logic, could not have said that when he founded the first psychological laboratory at Leipzig in 1879. That was the year from which many would date the rebirth of logic with the publication of Frege's *Begriffsschrift*. Admittedly, the development of the competence theory has not been the work of psychologists, but it is none the worse for that. Admittedly, too, cognitive psychologists do not seem to have realized the treasure that was being prepared for them by their academic colleagues. But it has grown strong and is even more inviting today than it was ten years ago. I consider my labor in writing this book well worthwhile if it helps some cognitive psychologists to appreciate the relevance of logic to their work.

A fonder hope is that logic will one day form part of the professional equipment of cognitive psychologists. Today statistics enjoys such a place, and it is a useful tool, enabling psychologists to test hypotheses. Only rarely do probability values enter psychological theory. If what I have been arguing is correct, logic forms an essential ingredient in the core of what has traditionally been known as psychology, that is, in cognition.

Glossary of Logical Expressions

p, q	Schematic symbols for propositions.
$\sim p$	Not p.
p & q	p and q.
$p \lor q$	p or q.
$p \supset q$	p implies q; if p, then q.
$p \not\supset q$	p does not imply q.
$p \equiv q$	p if and only if q; p and q are logically equivalent.
$\Box p$	Necessarily p.
$\Diamond p$	Possibly p.
K	Schematic symbol for sortal.
P	Schematic symbol for predicate.
x, y	Variables over individuals in a kind.
$(\exists K, x)Px$	Some members of K are P; at least one K is P.
$(\forall K, x)Px$	All Ks are P.
$(\exists !K, x)Px$	Just one K is P.
$\imath(K, x)Px$	The unique x that is K is P.
$x \in K$	x is a member of kind K.
$x \notin K$	x is not a member of kind K.
$K \subset K'$	Kind K is properly included in kind K'; every member of kind K is also a member of kind K' and there is at least one member of kind K' that is not a member of kind K.
$K \not\subset K'$	Kind K is not properly included in kind K'.
$\langle x, y \rangle$	The ordered pair consisting of x and y in that order.
$\langle x_1, x_2, x_3, \ldots, x_n \rangle$	The ordered n-tuple consisting of $x_1, x_2, x_3, \ldots, x_n$ in that order.

Analytic proposition. A proposition whose truth is guaranteed by the meanings of the words in which it is expressed.

A priori truth. A truth whose justification does not require perceptual judgments.

Axiom. A proposition whose truth requires no proof in a logical system.

Axiomatic presentation. A presentation of a logic that uses axioms as well as rules of inference.

Bivalent. Recognizing only two truth values.

Classical logic. First-order predicate logic, which is a bivalent logic that embraces the predicate calculus and is the central system of logic.

Complete. Having the property that every proposition that is logically true can be proved in a logic.

Connective, one-place. A logical symbol that can be added to a single sentence to form a more complex sentence, for example, $\sim$, $\square$.

Connective, two-place. A logical symbol that can be used to form a single larger sentence from two sentences, for example, &, $\vee$.

Consistent/inconsistent. A system is inconsistent if some proposition p and also its negation $\sim p$ can be proved in the system; otherwise the system is consistent.

Decidability. A logic is decidable if there is a mechanical procedure that can determine whether or not any sentence expressible in a logic is provable in the logic.

Empirical truth. A truth whose justification requires the use of perceptual judgment.

Extension. The individuals of which a predicate or sortal is true; the individuals that are members of the kind referred to by the predicate or sortal.

First-order predicate calculus. A predicate calculus in which quantification (generalization) is confined to the individuals in a domain.

Interpretation. A function that assigns (1) individuals in a domain D to singular terms in a language (for example, proper names and definite descriptions); (2) extensions from D to sortals and predicates); (3) n-tuples from D to n-place predicates; and (4) for function expressions, interpretation assigns functions from n-tuples of D to individuals in D.

Intuition/intuitively known truth. A proposition that is seen to be true without being deduced from premises.

Intuitionism. (Not to be confused with *intuition* or *intuitively known truth*.) A theory of logic, due to Brouwer, that rejects the principle of excluded middle.

Knowledge-how. A skill that does not essentially involve interpreted symbols.

Knowledge-that. A form of knowledge that essentially involves interpreted symbols.

Learning-how. A form of learning that does not essentially involve interpreted symbols.

Learning-that. A form of learning that essentially involved interpreted symbols.

Many-valued logic. A logic that recognizes more than two truth values.

Mass noun. A common noun that refers to a kind whose membership is a stuff or material, for example, *water, milk*.

Modal logic. A logic of the connectives *necessary* and *possible*.

Model. An interpretation of a sentence is a model of the sentence if the sentence is true in the interpretation.

Model theory. The theory that studies properties of models.

Modus ponens. A rule of inference that warrants the drawing of the conclusion q, given the premises p and $p \supset q$.

Modus tollens. A rule of inference that warrants the drawing of the conclusion $\sim p$, given the premises $p \supset q$ and $\sim q$.

Natural deduction system. A system of logic that does not employ axioms, only rules of inference.

Paradox. A contradiction derivable in an interpreted language. The most famous is the liar paradox: *This sentence is false*, which seems to be true if false and false if true. In some contexts *paradox* means an intuitively alarming result.

Platonism. The doctrine that there exists outside space and time a realm of objects that comprises the numbers, universals, and other abstract entities.

Pragmatics. The science that studies the interpretation of linguistic expressions as a function of their nonlinguistic context of use.

Predicate. A verb or adjective in its semantic rather than syntactic role. It refers to a property and supplies a principle of application but not principles of individuation or identity, for members of the kind.

Predicate calculus. A logic that considers the internal structure of simple sentences including the quantifiers $\forall$ and $\exists$.

Propositional calculus. The logic that ignores the internal structure of simple sentences and attends to the logic of the truth-functional connectives.

Psychologism. The doctrine that logic is a subbranch of psychology, drawing its fundamental principles and inference rules from psychology.

Quantum logic. The logic that has been developed to handle the results of quantum physics.

Reductio ad absurdum. A form of inference that allows the conclusion $\sim p$ once a contradiction has been deduced from p.

Relevance logic. A logic that restricts the class of valid inferences to those in which the premises are relevant to the conclusion.

Rule of inference. A rule that warrants the drawing of a class of conclusions from a class of premises.

Schema. An expression containing a symbol for which expressions of a certain sort are to be substituted. For example, $p \supset (q \supset p)$ is a schema in which any sentences can be substituted for p and q.

Second-order predicate calculus. A predicate calculus in which quantification is permitted over predicates and sortals.

Semantics. The rules that specify the interpretations of linguistic expressions.

Sortal. A common noun in its semantic rather than syntactic role. *Sortal* refers to a kind and supplies principles of application, identity, and (if not a mass noun) individuation for members of the kind.

Syntax. That part of grammar that specifies the rules for combining words as a function of their grammatical category.

Theorem. A proposition that can be proved in a logical system.

Truth conditions for a proposition. The set of circumstances that must obtain for the proposition to be true.

Truth value. The value of a proposition on the truth dimension: true, false, or something else in a many-valued logic.

Truth-functional connective. A connective whose effect on the truth value of a proposition in which it occurs is entirely a function of the truth values of the propositions to which it is added.

References

Anderson, A. R., and Belnap, N. D. 1968. Entailment. In *Logic and Philosophy*, G. Isemonger (ed.). New York: Appleton-Century-Crofts, 76–110.

Anderson, A. R., and Belnap, N. D. 1975. *Entailment*, vol. 1. Princeton, N.J.: Princeton University Press.

Anderson, R. C., and Ausubel, D. P. (eds.). 1965. *Readings in the Psychology of Cognition*. New York: Holt, Rinehart and Winston.

Anglin, J. M. 1977. *Word, Object and Conceptual Development*. New York: Norton.

Anscombe, G. E. M. 1975. The first person. In *Mind and Language*, S. Guttenplan (ed.). Oxford: Clarendon, 45–66.

Armstrong, D. M. 1978. *Nominalism and Realism*, 2 volumes. Cambridge: Cambridge University Press.

Armstrong, S. L., Gleitman, L. R., and Gleitman, H. 1983. What some concepts might not be. *Cognition* 13:263–308.

Barwise, J., and Perry, J. 1983. *Situations and Attitudes*. Cambridge, Mass.: MIT Press, A Bradford Book.

Bell, J., and Hallett, M. 1982. Logic, quantum logic and empiricism. *Philosophy of Science* 49:355–379.

Berlyne, D. E. 1965. *Structure and Direction in Thinking*. New York: Wiley.

Birkhoff, G., and von Neumann, J. 1936. The logic of quantum mechanics. *Annals of Mathematics* 37:823–843.

Bloom, P. 1984. Young children's representation of natural language hierarchies. Unpublished paper, Psychology Department, McGill University.

Boring, E. G. 1957. *A History of Experimental Psychology*, second edition. New York: Appleton-Century-Crofts.

Bowerman, M. (to be published). First steps in acquiring conditionals. In *On Conditionals*, E. Traugott, C. A. Ferguson, J. Snitzer, and A. ter Meulen (eds.). Cambridge: Cambridge University Press.

Braine, M. D. S. 1978. On the relation between the natural logic of reasoning and standard logic. *Psychological Review* 85:1–21.

Braine, M. D. S., and Rumain, B. 1983. Logical reasoning. In *Handbook of Child Psychology*, fourth edition, P. H. Mussen (ed.). vol. 3, 263–340.

Bransford, J. D. 1979. *Learning, Understanding and Remembering*. Belmont, Calif.: Wadsworth.

Brentano, F. [1874] 1973. *Psychology from an Empirical Standpoint*. London: Routledge and Kegan Paul.

Bruner, J. S., Goodnow, J. J., and Austin, G. A. 1956. *A Study of Thinking*. New York: Wiley.

Bucci, W. 1978. The interpretation of universal affirmative propositions. *Cognition* 6:55–77.

Callanan, M. A. 1985. The role of input in the acquisition of category hierarchies. *Child Development* 56:508–523.

Callanan, M. A., and Markman, E. M. 1982. Principles of organization in young children's natural language hierarchies. *Child Development* 53:1093–1101.

Carey, S. 1985. *Conceptual Change in Childhood*. Cambridge, Mass.: MIT Press, A Bradford Book.

Carnap, R. [1928] 1976. *Der logische Aufbau der Welt*. Berlin: Weltkreis-Verlag. Translated as *The Logical Structure of the World and Pseudoproblems in Philosophy*, R. A. George (trans.). Berkeley: University of California Press.

Carroll, L. 1895. What the tortoise said to Achilles. *Mind*, new series, 4:278–280.

Chomsky, N. 1965. *Aspects of the Theory of Syntax*. Cambridge, Mass.: MIT Press.

Chomsky, N. 1980. *Rules and Representations*. New York: Columbia University Press.

Chomsky, N. 1984. Changing perspectives on knowledge and use of language. Paper presented at a Sloan Conference, MIT, May 1984.

Chomsky, N. (to be published). Aspects of a theory of mind. *New Ideas in Psychology*.

Churchland, P. M. 1984. *Matter and Consciousness*. Cambridge, Mass.: MIT Press, A Bradford Book.

Cohen, L. B., and Younger, B. A. 1983. Perceptual categorization in the infant. In *New Trends in Conceptual Representation*, E. K. Scholnick (ed.). Hillsdale, N.J.: Erlbaum, 197–200.

Cohen, L. J. 1981. Can human irrationality be experimentally demonstrated? *Behavioral and Brain Sciences* 4:317–370.

Cummins, R. 1983. *The Nature of Psychological Explanation*. Cambridge, Mass.: MIT Press, A Bradford Book.

Davidson, D. 1970. Mental events. In *Experience and Theory*, L. Foster and J. W. Swanson (eds.). Amherst: University of Massachusetts Press.

Davidson, D. 1980. *Essays on Actions and Events*. Oxford: Clarendon.

Dennett, D. 1978. *Brainstorms*. Montgomery, Vt.: Bradford Books. Reprinted by The MIT Press, 1980.

Donaldson, M., and Lloyd, P. 1974. Sentences and situations. In *Problèmes actuels en psycholinguistique*, F. Bresson (ed.). Paris: Centre National de la Recherche Scientifique.

Donaldson, M., and McGarrigle, J. 1974. Some clues to the nature of semantic development. *Journal of Child Language* 1:185–194.

Dretske, F. I. 1981. *Knowledge and the Flow of Information*. Cambridge, Mass.: MIT Press, A Bradford Book.

Dummett, M. 1978. Is logic empirical? In *Truth and Other Enigmas*, M. Dummett. London: Duckworth.

Dummett, M. 1981. *Frege: Philosophy of Language*, second edition. London: Duckworth.

Ennis, R. H. 1977. Conceptualization of children's logical competence: Piaget's propositional logic and alternative proposals. In *Alternatives to Piaget*, L. S. Siegal and C. J. Brainerd (eds.). New York: Academic.

Fodor, J. A. 1975. *The Language of Thought*. New York: Crowell.

Fodor, J. A. 1980. On the impossibility of acquiring "more powerful" structures. In *Language and Learning*, M. Piattelli-Palmarini (ed.). Cambridge, Mass.: Harvard University Press, 142–162.

Fodor, J. A. 1981. *Representations*. Cambridge, Mass.: MIT Press, A Bradford Book.

Fodor, J. A. 1983. *The Modularity of Mind*. Cambridge, Mass.: MIT Press, A Bradford Book.

Ford, W. G. 1976. The language of disjunction. Unpublished Ph.D. thesis, University of Toronto.

Freeman, N. H., and Stedmon, J. A. (unpublished). What children understand about natural-language quantification. Department of Psychology, University of Bristol.

Frege, G. [1884] 1959. *The Foundations of Arithmetic.* Oxford: Basil Blackwell.

Frege, G. [1891] 1952. Function and concept. In *Translations from the Philosophical Writings of Gottlob Frege*, P. Geach and M. Black. Oxford: Basil Blackwell.

Frege, G. [1892a] 1952. On sense and reference. In *Translations from the Philosophical Writings of Gottlob Frege*, P. Geach and M. Black. Oxford: Basil Blackwell.

Frege, G. [1892b] 1952. On concept and object. In *Translations from the Philosophical Writings of Gottlob Frege*, P. Geach and M. Black. Oxford: Basil Blackwell.

Frege, G. [1893–1903] 1952. *Grundgesetze der Arithmetik.* Partial translation in *Translations from the Philosophical Writings of Gottlob Frege*, P. Geach and M. Black. Oxford: Basil Blackwell.

Frege, G. [1893, 1903] 1964. *Grundgesetze der Arithmetik*, M. Furth (trans.). Vol. 1, 1893; vol. 2, 1903. Berkeley: University of California Press.

Frege, G. [1894] 1952. Review of E. Husserl, *Philosophie der Arithmetik*. In P. Geach and M. Black. *Translations from the Philosophical Writings of Gottlob Frege.* Oxford: Basil Blackwell. 79–85.

Frege, G. [1918] 1968. Der Gedanke. *Beitrage zur Philosophie des Deutschen Idealismus* 1:58–77. Translated, in *Essays on Frege*, E. D. Klemke (ed.). Urbana: University of Illinois Press.

Frege, G. 1979. *Posthumous Writings*, P. Long and R. White (trans.). Oxford: Basil Blackwell.

Gazdar, G. 1979. *Pragmatics: Implicature, Presupposition, and Logical Form.* New York: Academic.

Geach, P. T. 1957. *Mental Acts.* London: Routledge and Kegan Paul.

Geach, P. T. 1962. *Reference and Generality.* New York: Cornell University Press.

Geach, P. T. 1972. *Logic Matters.* Berkeley: University of California Press.

Gelman, S., and Taylor, M. 1984. How 2-year-old children interpret proper and common names for unfamiliar objects. *Child Development* 55:1535–1540.

Gentner, D. 1982. Why nouns are learned before verbs. In *Language Development*, S. Kuczaj (ed.). Hillsdale, N.J.: Erlbaum, vol. 2.

Gibbard, A. 1975. Contingent identity. *Journal of Philosophical Logic* 4:187–221.

Gillis, S., and de Schutter, G. (unpublished). Transitional phenomena revisited: Insights into the nominal insight. Department of Psychology, University of Antwerp.

Gleitman, H. 1981. *Psychology.* New York: Norton.

Gödel, K. [1931] 1967. On formally undecidable propositions of *Principia Mathematica* and related systems 1. In *From Frege to Gödel: A Source Book in Mathematical Logic, 1879–1931*, J. van Heijenoort (ed.). Cambridge, Mass.: Harvard University Press, 596–616.

Goldin-Meadow, S., Seligman, M., and Gelman, R. 1976. Language in the two-year-old. *Cognition* 4:189–202.

Greenfield, P. M. 1973. Who is "Dada"? Some aspects of the semantic and phonological development of a child's first words. *Language and Speech* 16:34–43.

Grice, P. 1975. Logic and conversation. In *Syntax and Speech Acts 3: Speech Acts*, P. Cole and J. L. Morgan (eds.). New York: Academic.

Gupta, A. K. 1980. *The Logic of Common Nouns.* New Haven: Yale University Press.

Gupta, A. 1982. Truth and paradox. *Journal of Philosophical Logic* 11:1–60.

Hakuta, K., deVilliers, J., and Tager-Flusberg, H. B. 1982. Sentence coordination in Japanese and English. *Journal of Child Language* 9:193–207.

Harper, R. J. C., Anderson, C. C., Christensen, C. M., and Hunka, S. M. 1964. *The Cognitive Processes.* Englewood Cliffs, N.J.: Prentice-Hall.

Hebb, D. O. 1958. *A Textbook of Psychology.* Philadelphia: Saunders.

Henle, M. 1962. The relation between logic and thinking. *Psychological Review* 69:366–378.

Henle, M. 1978. Foreword to *Human Reasoning*, R. Revlin and R. E. Mayer (eds.). Washington, D.C.: Winston.

Heyting, A. 1956. *Intuitionism: An Introduction.* Amsterdam: North Holland.

Hughes, R. I. G. 1981. Quantum logic. *Scientific American* 245(4):146–157.

Humphrey, G. 1951. *Thinking.* New York: Wiley.

Hurford, J. R. 1974. Exclusive or inclusive disjunction. *Foundations of Language* 11:409–411.

Husserl, E. 1894. *Philosophie der Arithmetik.* Leipzig: Pfeffer.

Husserl, E. [1900] 1970. *Logical Investigations,* second edition, 1913. London: Routledge and Kegan Paul.

Inhelder, B., and Piaget, J. 1958. *The Growth of Logical Thinking from Childhood to Adolescence.* New York: Basic Books.

Inhelder, B., and Piaget, J. 1964. *The Early Growth of Logic in the Child.* London: Routledge and Kegan Paul.

Jackendoff, R. 1983. *Semantics and Cognition.* Cambridge, Mass.: MIT Press.

Jackendoff, R. (unpublished). *Cognition and Consciousness.*

Johnson, D. M. 1955. *The Psychology of Thought and Judgment.* New York: Harper and Row.

Johnson-Laird, P. N. 1983. *Mental Models.* Cambridge, Mass.: Harvard University Press.

Kahneman, D., and Tversky, A. 1973. On the psychology of prediction. *Psychological Review* 80:237–251.

Kahneman, D., and Tversky, A. 1982. The psychology of preferences. *Scientific American* 246(1):160–173.

Kant, I. [1781] 1929. *Critique of Pure Reason,* N. K. Smith (trans.). London: Macmillan.

Kant, I. [1800] 1974. *Logic,* R. S. Hartman and W. Schwarz (trans.). New York: Bobbs-Merrill.

Kaplan, D. 1977. Demonstratives: An essay on the semantics, logic, metaphysics and epistemology of demonstratives and other indexicals. Department of Philosophy, UCLA.

Katz, J. J. 1981. *Language and Other Abstract Objects.* Totowa, N.J.: Rowman and Littlefield.

Katz, N., Baker, E., and Macnamara, J. 1974. What's in a name? A study of how children learn common and proper names. *Child Development* 45:469–473.

Kellaghan, T., and Macnamara, J. 1967. Reading in a second language. In *Reading Instruction: An International Forum,* M. D. Jenkinson (ed.). Newark, Del.: International Reading Association.

Kintsch, W. 1977. *Memory and Cognition,* second ecition. New York: Wiley.

Kripke, S. 1979. A puzzle about belief. In *Meaning and Use,* A. Margalit (ed.). Dordrecht: Reidel, 239–283.

Kripke, S. 1982. *Naming and Necessity.* First published in 1972. Oxford: Basil Blackwell.

Lemmon, E. J. 1959. Is there one correct system of modal logic? *Proceedings of the Aristotelean Society,* supp. 23.

Leopold, W. F. 1948. Semantic learning in infant language. *Word* 4:173–180. Reprinted in *Child Language,* A. Bar-Adon and W. F. Leopold (eds.). Englewood Cliffs, N.J.: Prentice-Hall, 1971, 96–102.

Lindsay, P. H., and Norman, D. A. 1972. *Human Information Processing.* New York: Academic.

Lust, B., and Mervis, C. A. 1982. Development of coordination in the natural speech of young children. *Journal of Child Language* 7:279–304.

Macnamara, J. 1970. Comparative studies of reading in two languages. *Tesol Quarterly* 4:107–116.

Macnamara, J. 1972. The cognitive basis of language learning in children. *Psychological Review* 79:1–13.

Macnamara, J. 1976. Stomachs assimilate and accommodate, don't they? *Canadian Psychological Review* 17:167–173.

Macnamara, J. 1977a. From sign to language. In *Language Learning and Thought*, J. Macnamara (ed.). New York: Academic, 11–35.

Macnamara, J. 1977b. Children's command of the logic of conversation. In *Language Learning and Thought*, J. Macnamara (ed.). New York: Academic, 261–288.

Macnamara, J. 1982. *Names for Things: A Study of Human Learning*. Cambridge, Mass.: MIT Press, A Bradford Book.

Macnamara, J., Govitrikar, V., and Doan, B. (unpublished). Free will and scientific psychology.

Malcolm, N. 1984. Consciousness and Causality. In *Consciousness and causality*, D. M. Armstrong and N. Malcolm. Oxford: Basil Blackwell.

Mandler, J. M., and Mandler, G. 1964. *Thinking: From Association to Gestalt*. New York: Wiley.

Markman, E. M. 1983. The acquisition and hierarchical organization of categories by children. Unpublished paper read at the 18th Annual Carnegie Symposium on Cognition.

Markman, E. M., and Hutchinson, J. E. 1984. Children's sensitivity to constraints on word meaning: Taxonomic vs. thematic relations. *Cognitive Psychology* 16:1–27.

McCarthy, J. 1980. Circumscription—A form of non-monotonic reasoning. *Artificial Intelligence* 13:27–39.

McCawley, J. D. 1980. *Everything That Linguists Have Always Wanted to Know about Logic But Were Ashamed to Ask*. Chicago: Chicago University Press.

McDermott, D., and Doyle, J. 1978. Non-monotonic logic 1. MIT AI Memo 486 (August).

Mervis, C. B., and Crisafi, M. A. 1982. Order of acquisition of subordinate-, basic-, and superordinate-level categories. *Child Development* 53:258–266.

Mervis, C. B., and Mervis, C. A. 1982. Leopards are kitty-cats: Object labeling by mothers for their thirteen-month-olds. *Child Development* 53:267–273.

Mill, J. S. 1843. *System of Logic*. London: Longman's.

Mill, J. S. 1874. *Examination of Sir William Hamilton's Philosophy*, 2 volumes. New York: Henry Holt.

Miller, G. A. 1951. Speech and language. In *Handbook of Experimental Psychology*, S. S. Stevens (ed.). New York: Wiley, 789–810.

Mitchell, J. 1984. Common and proper noun acquisition in four-year-old children. Unpublished thesis, Scotland.

Montague, R. 1970. Universal grammar. *Theoria* 36:373–398. Also in *Formal Philosophy: Selected papers of Richard Montague*, R. H. Thomason (ed.). New Haven: Yale University Press, 1974.

Neisser, U. 1976. *Cognition and Reality*. San Francisco: W. H. Freeman.

Niall, K. (unpublished). Projective invariance and visual perception. Ph.D. thesis, McGill University.

Noonan, H. W. 1980. *Objects and Identity*. The Hague: Martinus Nijhoff.

Notturno, M. A. 1982. Frege and the psychological reality thesis. *Journal of the Theory of Social Behavior* 12:329–344.

Osgood, C. E. 1953. *Method and Theory in Experimental Psychology*. New York: Oxford University Press.

Osherson, D. N., and Smith, E. E. 1981. On the adequacy of prototype theory as a theory of concepts. *Cognition* 9:35–38.

Oshima-Takane, Y. 1985. The learning of pronouns. Unpublished Ph.D. thesis, McGill University.

Perry, J. 1970. The same F. *Philosophical Review* 79:181–200.

Perry, J. 1979. The problem of the essential indexical. *Nôus* 13:3–21.

Petitto, L. 1983. From gesture to symbol. Unpublished Ph.D. thesis, Harvard University.

Piaget, J. 1952. *The Child's Conception of Number*. New York: Humanities Press.

Piaget, J. 1953. *Logic and Psychology*. Manchester, England: Manchester University Press.

Piaget, J. 1963. Le language et les operations intellectuelles. In *Problèmes de psycho-linguistique*, J. de Ajuriaguerra, F. Bresson, B. Fraisse, B. Inhelder, P. Oléron, and J. Piaget (eds.). Paris: Presses Universitaires de France, 51–61.

Piaget, J. 1964. *La formation du symbole chez l'enfant*. Neuchâtel: Delachaux et Niestle.

Putnam, H. 1968. The logic of quantum mechanics. In *Mathematics, Matters, and Method* H. Putnam. Cambridge University Press, second edition, 1979.

Putnam, H. 1975. The meaning of "meaning." in *Language, Mind, and Knowledge*, K. Gunderson (ed.). Minnesota Studies in the Philosophy of Science. Minneapolis: University of Minnesota Press.

Pylyshyn, Z. 1972. Competence and psychological reality. *American Psychologist* 27:546–552.

Pylyshyn, Z. 1984. *Computation and Cognition*. Cambridge, Mass.: MIT Press, A Bradford Book.

Quine, W. V. 1960. *Word and Object*. New York: Wiley.

Quine, W. V. 1961. *From a Logical Point of View*, revised edition. Cambridge, Mass.: Harvard University Press.

Quine, W. V. 1970. *Philosophy of Logic*. Englewood Cliffs, N.J.: Prentice-Hall.

Quine, W. V. 1973. *The Roots of Reference*. La Sake, Ill.: Open Court.

Reeves, J. W. 1965. *Thinking about Thinking*. London: Secker and Warburg.

Reiter, R. 1980. A logic for default reasoning. *Artificial Intelligence* 13:81–132.

Reitman, W. R. 1965. *Cognition and Thought*. New York: Wiley.

Rescher, N. 1979. *Cognitive Systematization: A Systems-Theoretic Approach to a Coherentist Theory of Knowlege*. Oxford: Basil Blackwell.

Rips, L. J. 1983. Reasoning as a central intellective ability. In *Advances in the Study of Human Intelligence*, R. J. Sternberg (ed.). Hillsdale: N.J.Erlbaum.

Rosch, E. 1973. On the internal structure of perceptual and semantic categories. In *Cognitive Development and the Acquisition of Language*, T. E. Moore (ed.). New York: Academic, 112–144.

Rosch, E. 1975. Universals and cultural specifics in human categorization. In *Cross-Cultural Perspectives on Learning*, R. Breslin, S. Bochner, and W. Lonner (eds.) New York: Sage/Halsted.

Rosch, E. H. 1977. Human categorization. In *Advances in Cross-Cultural Psychology*, N. Warren (ed.). London: Academic.

Rosch, E. H. and Mervis, C. B. 1978.

Rosch, E., Mervis, C. B., Gray, W. D., Johnson, D. M., and Boyes-Braem, P. 1976. Basic objects in natural categories. *Cognitive Psychology* 8:382–439.

Ryle, G. 1949. *The Concept of Mind*. London: Hutchinson.

Seidenberg, M. S., Tanenhaus, M. K., Leiman, J. M., and Bienkowski, M. 1982. Automatic access of the meanings of ambiguous words in context. *Cognitive Psychology* 14:489–537.

Shipley, E. F., Kuhn, I. F., and Madden, E. C. 1983. Mother's use of superordinate category terms. *Journal of Child Language* 10:571–588.

Smith, C. L. 1979. Children's understanding of natural language hierarchies. *Journal of Experimental Child Psychology* 27:437–458.

Sober, E. 1978. Psychologism. *Journal for the Theory of Social Behavior* 8:165–192.

Stalnaker, R. C. 1984. *Inquiry*. Cambridge, Mass.: MIT Press, A Bradford Book.

Strawson, P. F. 1952. *Introduction to Logical Theory*. London: Methuen.

Swinney, D. 1979. Lexical access during sentence comprehension: (Re)consideration of context effects. *Journal of Verbal Learning and Verbal Behavior* 18:645–660.

Tanenhaus, M., Leiman, J., and Seidenberg, M. 1979. Evidence for multiple stages in the processing of ambiguous words in syntactic contexts. *Journal of Verbal Language and Verbal Behavior* 18:427–441.

Tarski, A. 1956. The concept of truth in formalised languages. In *Logic, Semantics and Metamathematics*, A. Tarski. Oxford University Press.

Thomason, R. H. 1970. *Symbolic Logic: An Introduction*. London: Collier Macmillan.

Tversky, A., and Kahneman, D. 1983. Extensional versus intuitive reasoning. *Psychological Review* 90:293–315.

Tyler, L. K., and Marslen-Wilson, W. D. 1977. The on-line effects of semantic context on syntactic processing. *Journal of Verbal Learning and Verbal Behavior* 16:683–692.

Wales, R., Colman, M., and Pattison, P. 1983. How a thing is called: A study of mother's and children's naming. *Journal of Experimental Child Psychology* 36:1–17.

Wargny, N. 1976. Cognitive aspects of language learning in infants: What two-year-olds understand of proper, common, and superordinate nouns. Unpublished Ph.D. thesis, McGill University.

Wason, P. C., and Johnson-Laird, P. N. 1972. *Psychology of Reasoning: Structure and Content*. Cambridge, Mass.: Harvard University Press.

Wertheimer, M. 1945. *Productive Thinking*. New York: Harper.

Wiggins, D. 1967. *Identity and Spatio-Temporal Continuity*. Oxford: Basil Blackwell.

Wiggins, D. 1980. *Sameness and Substance*. Oxford: Basil Blackwell.

Wittgenstein, L. 1953. *Philosophical Investigations*. Oxford: Basil Blackwell.

Woodworth, R. S., and Schlosberg, H. 1954. *Experimental Psychology*. London: Methuen.

Index

⊣⊢ Bradford Books